WITHDRAWN
UTSA Libraries

Innovations in Financing Public Services

Also by Stephen J. Bailey

STRATEGIC PUBLIC FINANCE

PUBLIC SECTOR ECONOMICS: Theory, Policy and Practice 2nd Edition

LOCAL GOVERNMENT ECONOMICS: Principles and Practice

LOCAL GOVERNMENT CHARGES: Policy and Practice (*with P. Falconer and S. McChlery*)

THE REFORM OF LOCAL GOVERNMENT FINANCE IN BRITAIN (*co-edited with R. Paddison*)

LOCAL GOVERNMENT FINANCE: International Perspectives (*co-edited with R. Paddison*)

Also by Ari-Veikko Anttiroiko

ELECTRONIC GOVERNMENT: Concepts, Methodologies, Tools, and Applications Volumes I-VI

ENCYCLOPEDIA OF DIGITAL GOVERNMENT: Volumes I-III (*co-edited with M. Mälkiä*)

E-CITY: Analysing Efforts to Generate Local Dynamism in the City of Tampere (*co-edited with A-V. Kasvio*)

Innovations in Financing Public Services

Country Case Studies

Edited by

Stephen J. Bailey
Professor of Public Sector Economics,
Glasgow Caledonian University, UK

Pekka Valkama
Head of Research at the University of Tampere, Finland and
Adjunct Professor at the University of Turku, Finland

and

Ari-Veikko Anttiroiko
Adjunct Professor, Department of Regional Studies,
University of Tampere, Finland

First published 2010 by
PALGRAVE MACMILLAN

Palgrave Macmillan in the UK is an imprint of Macmillan Publishers Limited, registered in England, company number 785998, of Houndmills, Basingstoke, Hampshire RG21 6XS.

Palgrave Macmillan in the US is a division of St Martin's Press LLC, 175 Fifth Avenue, New York, NY 10010.

Palgrave Macmillan is the global academic imprint of the above companies and has companies and representatives throughout the world.

Palgrave® and Macmillan® are registered trademarks in the United States, the United Kingdom, Europe and other countries.

ISBN: 978–0–230–24159–6 hardback

This book is printed on paper suitable for recycling and made from fully managed and sustained forest sources. Logging, pulping and manufacturing processes are expected to conform to the environmental regulations of the country of origin.

A catalogue record for this book is available from the British Library.

A catalog record for this book is available from the Library of Congress.

10 9 8 7 6 5 4 3 2 1
19 18 17 16 15 14 13 12 11 10

Printed and bound in Great Britain by
CPI Antony Rowe, Chippenham and Eastbourne

Contents

v

Figures

Tables

Acknowledgements

Chapter 4: This study was carried out with the financial support of the Spanish National R&D Plan – Research Project SEJ2007–62215 ECON-FEDER.

Chapter 7: The basis of part of this chapter is a paper which appeared in *The Geneva Papers on Risk and Insurance: Issues and Practice*, 34 (2). The authors wish to thank the Geneva Association for their kind permission to reproduce parts of that article.

Chapter 10 is a much reduced and amended version of a paper published in *Public Policy and Administration* in 2001 (see Valkama and Bailey 2001 in the list of references). The authors wish to thank the journal for its kind permission to reproduce parts of the original article.

Notes on Contributors

Basilio Acerete is a Senior Lecturer in the Department of Accounting and Finance at the University of Zaragoza. He is a member of the research group GESPUBLICA, which deals with public sector accounting and management and participates in national and international research projects. His research interests include Public-Private Partnerships, performance measurement systems and e-government, and his work has been published in refereed journals.

Pinar Akkoyunlu is Associate Professor in the Department of Public Finance at Istanbul University, Turkey. Her area of interest is government budgeting and privatisation and she has published several articles on public economic enterprises and on their divestiture procedures. She has recently published a book on the means of financing institutions of education.

Nicholas Anderson is Senior Vice-President at the Swedish Export Credit Corporation (SEK). His career in finance spans 39 years and, prior to joining the SEK in 2002, he was Chief Executive Officer of Finland's Municipality Finance Ltd. He is author of four books on finance, capital markets and investment matters, a regular columnist for several national newspapers and a regular speaker on finance and investments.

Ari-Veikko Anttiroiko is an Adjunct Professor in the Department of Regional Studies, at the University of Tampere, Finland. He is an expert in local development policy, high-tech centre studies and e-government. He has published several articles and books on new trends in public governance, including comprehensive reference books on e-government.

Darinka Asenova is a Reader in the Department of Accounting, Finance and Risk at Glasgow Caledonian University. Her research interests are in the areas of risk management in new methods for financing capital projects, public/private sector risk management and accountability, as well as various aspects of contemporary public policy.

Stephen J. Bailey is Professor of Public Sector Economics in the Department of Economic Studies and International Business at Glasgow Caledonian University. He has published many books and articles dealing with public finance and has presented many papers in the UK and overseas. He has undertaken work for UK government departments and international organisations and is currently researching local government charges for the Chartered Institute of Public Finance and Accountancy.

Miroslav Beblavý is Associate Professor of Public Policy at the Comenius University in Bratislava, Chairman of the Slovak Governance Institute and Senior Research Fellow at the Centre for European Policy Studies in Brussels. His research interests include social and education policy, public administration and political economy. He has also served as consultant to numerous international organisations including the OECD, the World Bank, the European Commission, USAID and DFID.

Matthias Beck is Professor of Public Sector Management and Research Director at the University of York Management School. He has published extensively in the areas of risk management and risk regulation with a particular focus on the public sector, Public-Private Partnerships and state-business relationships. He is editor of the *Journal of Risk and Governance*.

Ian C. Elliott is a Lecturer and Programme Leader of the Executive Masters in Public Services Management at Queen Margaret University. His research interests include public service innovation, sport services management and workplace health policy. Previous research clients include NHS Health Scotland, Careers Scotland and the Scottish government.

John Hood is a Senior Lecturer in the Department of Accounting, Finance and Risk at Glasgow Caledonian University. He has published widely in academic and professional journals and books on a range of risk-related topics, including risk management in public organisations, insurance and risk financing and Public-Private Partnerships. He has also undertaken consultancy projects for a number of public and private organisations.

Nevenka Hrovatin is Professor of Economics in the Faculty of Economics, University of Ljubljana. She is also a member of the Council for Public-Private Partnerships at the Slovenian Ministry of Finance, a member of the Council of the Slovenian Government for Energy and Head of the Public Sector Institute at the University of Ljubljana.

Surk-Tae Kim is a Professor in the Department of Public Administration at Kyungpook National University, Daegu, South Korea. He has published many articles dealing with local government, management and public finance. He has undertaken research on the optimal size of local government and is currently researching the political economy of the reorganisation of local jurisdictions in Korea.

Hulya Kirmanoglu is a Professor in the Department of Public Finance of the Faculty of Economics at Istanbul University. She lectures in the fields of public sector economics, cost-benefit analysis and development. She has undertaken research in migration and its effects on development, and has published several articles, reports and a book on public sector economics, local governments, public finance balances in Turkey and global public goods.

Peter Mederly is an Associate Professor at Comenius University in Bratislava, Slovakia, and works as an independent consultant in Slovakia and abroad. From 1999 to 2006, he worked in the top management of the Ministry of Education and was responsible for several fundamental reform projects in the Slovak education system. He has published in mathematics, applied computing and administration and financing of higher education in journals and conferences in Slovakia and abroad.

Hartwig Pautz is a Lecturer in the Department of Economic Studies and International Business at Glasgow Caledonian University. He has researched and published on the role of think-tanks in the UK and Germany. He has also published on Scottish think-tanks, the modernisation of Germany's Social Democratic Party and on aspects of German national identity.

Emília Sičáková-Beblavá is Associate Professor of Public Policy at the Comenius University in Bratislava, Slovakia, and a former President of Transparency International Slovakia. In 2003, she was World Fellow at Yale University. Her research interests include corruption, public service provision and multi-level governance.

Bill Stein is a Senior Lecturer in the Department of Accounting, Finance and Risk at Glasgow Caledonian University. His career has been divided between the commercial insurance industry and academic research and teaching. He is a Fellow of the Chartered Insurance Institute and a Fellow of the UK Institute of Risk Management.

Pekka Valkama is Head of Research at the University of Tampere, Finland and Adjunct Professor at the University of Turku, Finland. He is also an expert member of the Finnish Market Court. He has published articles on the models and effects of alternative ways of organising public services.

1
Innovative Public Finance: Definition, Practice and Context

Pekka Valkama, Ari-Veikko Anttiroiko and Stephen J. Bailey

Classic public finance versus the new public finance

Taking a narrow view, public finance means the provision of money for public expenditures by taxation, charges and borrowing (Bannock and Manser 1999). Public finance can also be conceptualised in a more functional way to include drafting and implementing relevant tax laws, safeguarding public money, managing public budgets, selling government bonds and assessing financial aspects of public policy programmes.

Classic public finance has been concerned with the economic effects of taxes and public expenditures on private sector activities. It is a relatively theoretical field of economics, and classic questions have been concerned with, for example, how to optimally tax individuals and enterprises without causing too much of a drag on the growth of an economy, how much public sector borrowing may crowd out (i.e. deter) private investments, how to allocate public expenditures to the different service sectors and what are the effects of public subsidies on output (Buchanan 1987; Reed and Swain 1990; Rosen 2005).

By focusing especially on optimal taxation and tax types as the key problems of public funding, classic public finance has neglected other ways of financing public services. This book addresses that deficiency by focusing on alternative and innovative sources of public finance and highlighting new solutions. It is intended to provide an enriched, contextualised view using case studies of innovations in public finance.

Defining and evaluating innovation in public finance

Generally speaking, innovation refers to implementation of a new idea or to novelty in the action and application of a new product, service

1

or method fostering economic growth. (Altshuler and Zegans 1997, 73; Ammer and Ammer 1984; Betz 1998, 4; Mote 2000, 981–982). However, innovative public finance is not a strictly defined concept and depends on context and evaluation criteria used to distinguish minor policy changes from policy innovations. This is made evident by the case studies in the following chapters.

According to classic criteria, a change or reform is innovative if it is both new and successful, perhaps leading to 'creative destruction', in the Schumpeterian sense. Taking this perspective, innovation in public finance should destroy old methods and solutions or, at least, supplement them in a value-adding way.

Innovativeness can be evaluated on the basis of how soon a financial innovation has been adopted by a local government, how many municipalities have adopted it and how effective it is (Gianakis and McCue 1997). Chapter 2 illustrates how specific criteria can be used to evaluate innovativeness when external (private sector) funding has been used in public infrastructure projects. Broadly following Price (2002), these include:

- new sources of repayment that have not before been applied to secure external financing;
- new methods of service delivery that offer operative service or efficiency improvements;
- new sources of investment capital that represent funding methods not used previously;
- new ways of paying financial returns to investors that either lessen the financing cost for the project sponsor or transfer risks to external investors.

Searching for innovation in public finance

Study of public sector innovations in general has been a relatively neglected topic in the recent literature on innovation, which has focused on the private sector and the enormous potential of creating added value through innovation. Discussion has generally revolved around such topics as innovation policy and innovation processes, the role of innovation in economic growth and the development and functioning of innovation systems. In comparison, innovation in the public sector gained surprisingly little attention until recently. When it has been considered, the most widely discussed aspects have been innovation relating to public policy-making, regulation, public governance, public management, public service delivery and e-government. However, innovation in public finance remains underdeveloped.

Past discussion of public finance did not recognise the contextual aspects of finance and focused on a few traditional topics relating to taxes, income generation and public spending. In this sense a new approach to public finance is needed in order to conceptualise government's multifaceted role in a complex environment and to reflect the diversity of institutions and tools of financial management. It is necessary to challenge conventional conceptualisations and theorisations and to open new horizons to innovation in public finance.

Innovative public finance can be based on new external (i.e. private and third sectors) or internal (i.e. public sector) funding solutions or new combinations of both. It raises questions concerning how to pool resources from different sources in order to fund public services, how to encourage stakeholders of public services to participate in funding activities, and how to utilise private sector capacity for purposes of public finance. The following case-study chapters provide examples of all these issues.

Innovative internal public finance also includes tax innovations (including environmental taxes, emissions taxes and a Tobin tax) but these are not within the scope of this book. Instead, the following chapters will reveal and analyse the kind of public sector financial packages and models that are not directly related to taxation.

These packages and models include, among others, private funding initiatives, service vouchers, co-funding, co-payments, risk-funding methods and debt-funding institutions of the local government sector. This book addresses each of these non-tax methods and highlights their use through country case studies, pointing out differences in the institutional frameworks and capacities of public authorities to adopt and generate innovations.

The connectivity of innovations in public finance

Funding innovations represent a very promising field of public sector innovation because, in multi-service governments, hardly any single policy innovation would promote economic efficiency in different service sectors as effectively as funding solutions (Gianakis and McCue 1997).

Innovative public finance also has direct or indirect connections with other public policy developments. The mobilisation of alternative service delivery systems (including service vouchers, joint ventures and concessions) makes possible private funding for public purposes. For example, public service delivery by vouchers (see Chapters 11 and 12) was originally introduced as an instrument of citizen choice but also interfaces with public finance. Modern approaches to zoning and urban planning policy may also open up fresh perspectives on financing land use using new instruments including lease-back contracts, impact fees, infrastructure charges and demand management techniques (Chapman 2008 and Chapter 10).

To create and implement successful financial innovations in public services is a huge challenge, not only for policy-makers but also for administrators. Some of the following chapters demonstrate that cooperation of different public authorities and engagement of stakeholders may be necessary in order to overcome institutional limitations in innovation processes.

It can be expected that innovative public finance will produce more professional, sophisticated and project-based funding models and methods in the future. For example, the number and type of international public funding mechanisms have increased substantially and new financiers in international cooperation have appeared since the 1960s (Conceição 2006).

These developments raise questions about how to ensure the transparency and accountability of more complex public finance systems and how to evaluate the effects of public sector financial engineering on income distribution among citizens and regions. As different kinds of stakeholder-funding models increase alongside more or less traditional public funding, the concept of public finance will become more diffuse and the boundary between private and public finance will become increasingly blurred. Research is required into the implications of innovative public finance for public ownership, for management of public authorities and for maintenance of competitive pressures on joint-funding arrangements.

The public sector emphasis has traditionally been on incremental (rather than radical) innovations, minimising risks associated with change rather than rewarding those who are the most innovative. At the risk of over-generalisation, innovations in public finance seem to occur despite, rather than because of, the way incentives for innovations are formulated or organised. In general, the innovative potential of public finance is high and, if utilised optimally, will improve the performance of public sector service organisations. Furthermore, through transactions and wider inclusion of stakeholders, it will generate growth in one or more of three ways: *direct* (e.g. new co-funded services), *indirect* (e.g. risk-management solutions in capital projects), or *induced* (e.g. consumption of better services using vouchers topped up by fees).

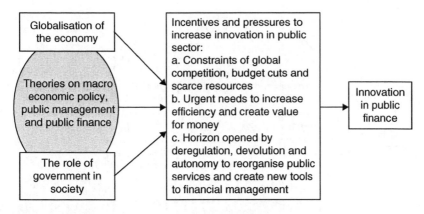

Figure 1.1 A contextual view of innovation in public finance

Contextualising innovation in public finance

Interest in public sector innovation has increased in recent decades due to various pressures posed by globalisation, other contextual challenges and emerging opportunities created by deregulation, increased autonomy and new managerialism in public sectors. These changes have diverse sources and similarly diverse and context-specific impacts, and so the overall picture of innovation in public finance is unavoidably complex.

To understand the current situation, especially in Western developed countries, we have to recognise the influence of globalisation, related macroeconomic policies of international organisations and influential countries and the emerging neo-liberal and other conceptions of the state and of the role of public sectors. In addition, widely adopted theories and doctrines, ranging from monetarism to public choice and New Public Management (NPM), form an essential part of this picture. All these and other such contextual factors have affected public policies, reforms and directions for innovation in public sectors. Figure 1.1 illustrates how they drive innovation in public finance.

Global challenges for public finance

The megatrends that continue to condition the development of public sectors include globalisation, the information society, new forms of social organisation and postmodern cultural trends. Such contextual

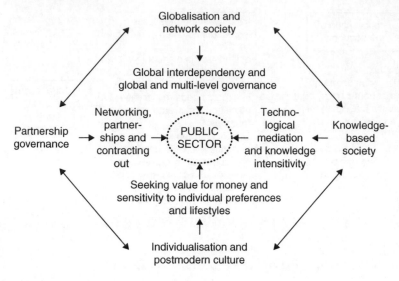

Figure 1.2   Contextual factors shaping the public sector

trends change both the political and administrative dimensions of government, as illustrated by Figure 1.2.

Globalisation refers to a gradual 'macrostructuration' of world order, implying development towards a world-scale systemic interdependency (Anttiroiko 2009). It reflects such changes as an erosion of institutional boundaries, a new consciousness of the world as a whole, increased regional and global interdependencies and accelerated growth of economic activity that spans national and regional boundaries. In economic life, the essence of this profound transformation is free-market policy bringing with it a competitive global economy and consequently a challenge to both national and sub-national governments (Barnet and Cavanagh 1995; Brecher and Costello 1994; Graham and Richardson 1997).

Such developments have a direct impact on national strategies (Kaul and Conceição 2006; Weiss 1999). Similarly, as the regulatory framework of the state loosens, flows of capital and other assets have more direct connections to local communities irrespective of their origins (Anttiroiko 2009; Douglass 2002; Huggins 1997; Maskell et al. 1998). Such a techno-economic paradigm makes itself visible in the ways public sector organisations work and interact with their stakeholders and customers (Deighton-Smith 2001; Steinert 2003).

The global economic landscape began to change dramatically during the post-1945 Cold War era. One of the main actors in international politics and global governance has been the USA which, as the most influential country in the world, imposed the neo-liberal doctrine, both in direct interactions with other countries and through its influence in international organisations such as the World Trade Organization (WTO), World Bank and International Monetary Fund (IMF). This policy has been supported by more or less like-minded member states of the Organisation for Economic Co-operation and Development (OECD).

The USA's ideological influence was particularly strong during the Reagan presidency in the 1980s. Simultaneously, Prime Minister Margaret Thatcher's hardline neo-liberalism paved the way for dramatic changes in the UK. In general the UK was the most active innovator on the European scene with its Financial Management Initiative (FMI), the development of performance indicators (PIs), Compulsory Competitive Tendering (CCT) in the 1980s, Best Value programme from the late 1990s, Private Finance Initiatives (PFIs) and Public-Private Partnerships (PPPs). Subsequent chapters refer to many of these initiatives. New Zealand and Australia were early adopters of such neo-liberal policies, the former becoming renowned as a pioneer of NPM-oriented reforms based on economic policies promoted by Finance Minister Roger Douglas.

The 1980s and 1990s can be regarded as the era of increased influence of free-market policy, deregulation and privatisation, even if such changes took place slowly and resulted in only fairly moderate reforms in many countries. The autonomous ability of governments to control monetary and fiscal policies became increasingly constrained by economic and financial globalisation.

In order to realise material gains from this process they have tended to assume new roles as proactive business promoters and financial market players. Governments apply increasingly private sector methodologies to promote the public interest and they are both suppliers and consumers of financial innovation. This dual role results from their position in the global competition of territorial communities and renewed engagement with global capital.

The financial sector (banking, insurance, non-depository financial institutions and financial and commodity brokers) is perhaps the most globalised sector in developed economies, and the gradual integration of public policy and market interests led to market orientation, generative interaction and hybrid organisations that are an important source of innovation in public finance. Consequently, the scope for innovation in public finance increased progressively and considerably.

Paradigmatic examples of public sector organisations as financial market players are:

- debt management offices (DMOs), acting in a fairly autonomous manner in linking public policies to private methodologies;
- sovereign wealth funds (SWFs), government investment vehicles funded by foreign exchange reserve assets that are managed separately from the official reserves of the central bank and reserve-related functions of the finance ministry.

This neo-liberal view of government as an owner of companies, an investor in securities and a hybrid authority challenges the classical liberal (libertarian) view of the minimalist state. The current trend is said to reflect the reality of embedded neo-liberalism (Cerny 2008), which, in essence, is a product of network-based public-private symbiosis (Datz 2008). Another example of this trend is the large number of publicly owned or PPP-based development corporations in different parts of the world creating high-quality business environments, attracting high-tech industries and providing business services in a business-like manner.

In spite of globalisation, many OECD countries have kept their levels of public expenditure and taxation fairly high both in real expenditure terms and as a share of total national expenditure and income (Alm et al. 2002; Bailey 2004). Moreover, even if globalisation through global agreements, macro-regional arrangements and globally organised market forces is assumed to decrease the financial autonomy of nations and their governments, persistent attempts to control or reduce public expenditure are constrained by the perceived need to compensate through redistributive policies disadvantaged groups for some of the side-effects of globalisation (Dreher et al. 2008). Additionally, diverse responses to economic challenges must be kept in mind (Weiss 1999).

The diminishing latitude of public finance

Use and consumption of public welfare services are relatively stable, requiring the public sector to provide a sustainable financial base for production and delivery of public services. However, governments face difficulties in maintaining their financial capacity and responding to service demands. Recurrent deep economic recessions dramatically erode public revenues, at least temporarily. In the long term, structural problems adversely affect the public finances and create 'structural gaps' between incomes and expenditures (Bailey 2004).

A comprehensive system of public services has become so expensive for taxpayers that governments encounter many objections from citizens to increasing tax rates further. It is believed widely that high taxes may reduce incentives to work (Bailey 2002), and the increased globalisation of markets and internationalisation of some tax bases may force governments to harmonise taxation systems and tax rates (Musgrave 2006; PM 1999). Governments' ability to borrow money is an important institutional capacity constraint, not just because of cautious financial investors but also because of the European Union's Stability and Growth Pact. The pact requires EU member states to maintain fiscal discipline by limiting public sector borrowing to no more than 3 per cent of GDP and public debt to no more than 60 per cent of GDP.

At the same time, there are growing consumption needs for public services. Demographic restructuring (e.g. ageing demography), immigration, urbanisation and development of the knowledge economy generally require improvement and expansion of public services. In this scenario, the most critical challenge for public services concerns the sustainability of public finance required to fund them. The development of sufficient financial capacity for public services is crucial for nations competing internationally for private investments, research and development (R&D) activities and a highly skilled labour force.

The combination of rising expenditure needs and heavily constrained (even diminishing) tax revenues causes fiscal stress in the public finances. In the past, fiscal stress has been more binding at the regional and local government levels because sub-national governments' ability to borrow and to tax has been more limited that than of national governments (Bailey 1999). At all three levels of government, however, there are particularly severe problems relating to the funding needs of public infrastructure investments. In growth areas, there are many requirements for new public utilities and facilities, especially for transportation investments (Price 2002; Pagano 2008). In some regions, existing public infrastructure is ageing rapidly due to maintenance being neglected.

The construction and renovation costs of infrastructure have usually been funded through capital budgets, while maintenance and operating costs have been funded though revenue budgets. This has meant that public infrastructure policy may have not been well coordinated because decisions relating to infrastructure provision and maintenance have been made in separate accounting 'silos', leading to a 'bunker mentality'.

However, two insights have revolutionised the traditional way of thinking about the funding of public sector capital projects. First, a variety of organisational and contractual forms can be used to advance and manage infrastructure projects. Second, the funding of upfront acquisition costs of the new infrastructure is now seen as only one part of a financial solution. A life-cycle perspective requires operating, maintenance, renovation and terminal costs also to be taken into account in the financial planning of public infrastructure projects.

Private sector financial institutions and financial intermediaries are highly developed and offer a wide set of modern financial services that can be used to finance public sector infrastructure. There are also new market players such as pension, investment, mutual and risk funds looking for new ways to diversify their investment portfolios and interested in positioning their capital for public facilities.

Financial innovations in the financial services sector include subordinated debentures, eurodollars, credit cards, insurances and mortgage-backed securities (Moles and Terry 1997; Silber 1975). Some of these innovations and new financial services (e.g. securitisation of public sector mortgages and interest rate swaps of public sector debt) may also help public finance and financial risk management in the public sector.

However, the credit crunch, which started in 2007 and gradually escalated and caused the dramatic collapses of some retail and investment banks in several countries, is a painful example of a combination of too innovative financial engineering and too loose monetary policy. Many governments had to bail out and nationalise banks in order to maintain the confidence of the monetary system in them. This rescue operation became expensive for central governments and some public authorities lost their investments in a wave of bankruptcies (Boakes 2008, 135–136).

Hence, traditional sources of funding using general taxation, intergovernmental grants and loans from banks may not now be as freely available to governments as they used to be, and this may force them to look for alternative funding solutions. Additionally, more relaxed regulation of public services and administration, together with changed political, economic and financial environments, have created more favourable circumstances than before for creativity and diversity in public finance.

At the same time, there are higher demands in the public sector to do more with less and bring extra value for public money. The case studies of financial innovation in the following chapters reflect all the issues considered above, which should be borne in mind when seeking to understand and draw lessons from them.

References

Alm, J., Holman, J. A. and Neumann, R. M. (2002) Globalization and State/ Local Government Finances, July, http://aysps.gsu.edu/publications/2002/ globalization.pdf (accessed 22 April 2009).

Altshuler, A. A. and Zegans, M. D. (1997) Innovation and the Public Management: Notes from the State House and City Hall. In A. A. Altshuler and R. D. Behn (eds), *Innovation in American Government: Challenges, Opportunities, and Dilemmas*. Washington, DC: Brookings Institution Press, 68–80.

Ammer, C. and Ammer, D. S. (1984) *Dictionary of Business and Economics*. Revised and Expanded Edition. New York: The Free Press.

Anttiroiko, A-V. (2009) Urban Responses to Global Intercity Competition. In J. Kultalahti, I. Karppi, O. Kultalahti and E. Todisco (eds) *Globalisation: Challenges to Research and Governance*. Helsinki: East-West Books, 257–279.

Bailey, S. J. (1999) *Local Government Economics: Principles and Practice*. Basingstoke: Palgrave Macmillan.

Bailey, S. J. (2002) *Public Sector Economics: Theory, Policy and Practice*. (2nd edition) Basingstoke: Palgrave Macmillan.

Bailey, S. J. (2004) *Strategic Public Finance*. Basingstoke: Palgrave Macmillan.

Bannock, Graham and Manser, William (1999) *International Dictionary of Finance*. London: Profile Books.

Barnet, R. J. and Cavanagh, J. (1995) *Global Dreams, Imperial Corporations and the New World Order*. New York: Simon & Schuster, 1994. First Touchstone Edition 1995. A Touchstone Book.

Betz, F. (1998) *Managing Technological Innovation: Competitive Advantage from Change*. New York: John Wiley.

Boakes, Kevin (2008) *Reading and Understanding the Financial Times*. Harlow: Pearson Financial Times Prentice Hall.

Brecher, J. and Costello, T. (1994) *Global Village or Global Pillage: Economic Reconstruction from the Bottom Up*. Boston, MA: South End Press.

Buchanan, James M. (1987) *Public Finance in Democratic Process: Fiscal Institutions and Individual Choice*. Chapel Hill, NC: The University of North Carolina Press.

Cerny, P. G. (2008) Embedding Neoliberalism: The Evolution of a Hegemonic Paradigm, *Journal of International Trade and Diplomacy*, 2 (1): 1–46.

Chapman, Jeffrey I. (2008) Fiscalization of Land Use. The Increasing Role of Innovative Revenue Raising Instruments to Finance Public Infrastructure, *Public Works Management & Policy*, 12 (4), April: 551–567.

Conceição, Pedro (2006) Accommodating New Actors and New Purposes in International Cooperation. In I. Kaul and P. Conceição (eds) *The New Public Finance: Responding to Global Challenges*. New York: Oxford University Press, 269–280.

Datz, G. (2008) Governments as Market Players: State Innovation in the Global Economy, *Journal of International Affairs*, 62 (1), Fall/Winter: 35–49.

Deighton-Smith, R. (2001) National Competition Policy: Key Lessons for Policymaking from its Implementation, *Australian Journal of Public Administration*, 60 (3), September: 29–41.

Douglass, M. (2002) From Global Intercity Competition to Cooperation for Livable Cities and Economic Resilience in Pacific Asia, *Environment & Urbanization*, 14 (1): 53–68.

Dreher, A., Sturm, J.-E. and Ursprung, H. W. (2008) The Impact of Globalization on the Composition of Government Expenditures: Evidence from Panel Data, *Public Choice*, 134: 263–292.

Gianakis, Gerasimos A. and McCue, Clifford P. (1997) Administrative Innovation Among Ohio Local Government Finance Officers, *American Review of Public Administration*, 27 (3), September: 270–286.

Graham, E. M. and Richardson J. D. (1997) Competition Policies for the Global Economy. Policy Analyses in International Economics 51. Washington, DC: Institute for International Economics.

Huggins, R. (1997) Competitiveness and the Global Region. The Role of Networking. In James Simmie (ed.) *Innovation, Networks and Learning Regions?*, 101–123; *Regional Policy and Development*, 18. London and Bristol, Pennsylvania, PA: Jessica Kingsley; London: Regional Studies Association.

Kaul, I. and Conceição, P. (eds) (2006) *The New Public Finance: Responding to Global Challenges*. New York and Oxford: Oxford University Press.

Maskell, P., Eskelinen, H., Hannibalsson, I., Malmberg, A. and Vatne, E. (1998) *Competitiveness, Localised Learning and Regional Development: Specialisation and Prosperity in Small Open Economics*. London: Routledge.

Moles, Peter and Terry, Nicholas (1997) *The Handbook of International Financial Terms*. Oxford: Oxford University Press.

Mote, Dave (2000) Innovation. Updated by Karl Heil. In Jane A. Malonis (ed.) *Encyclopedia of Business*. I-Z, volume 2. (Second Edition). Detroit, MI: Gale Group.

Musgrave, P. B. (2006) Combining Fiscal Sovereignty and Coordination: National Taxation in a Globalizing World. In Inge Kaul and Pedro Conceição (eds) *The New Public Finance: Responding to Global Challenges*. New York and Oxford: Oxford University Press, 167–193.

Pagano, Michael A. (2008) Financing Infrastructure in the 21st Century City, *Public Works Management & Policy*, 13 (1), July: 22–38.

PM (1999) Public Finances in the Twenty-First Century: Limitations, Challenges and Direction of Reforms. Working Group Report. Prime Minister's Office Publication Series 1999/1. Helsinki: Prime Minister's Office.

Price, Willard (2002) Innovation in Public Finance: Implications for the Nation's Infrastructure, *Public Works Management & Policy*, 7 (1), July: 63–78.

Reed, B. J. and Swain, John W. (1990) *Public Finance Administration*. Englewood Cliffs, NJ: Prentice Hall.

Rosen, Harvey S. (2005) *Public Finance*. (Seventh Edition) New York: McGraw-Hill.

Silber, W. L. (1975) Towards a Theory of Financial Innovation. In W. L. Silber (ed.) *Financial Innovation*. Lexington, MA: Lexington Books, 53–86.

Steinert, H. (2003) Participation and Social Exclusion: A Conceptual Framework. In Heinz Steinert and Arno Pilgram (eds) *Welfare Policy from Below: Struggles Against Social Exclusion in Europe*. Aldershot: Ashgate.

Weiss, L. (1999) *The Myth of the Powerless State: Governing the Economy in a Global Era*. First published in 1998. Reprinted in 1999. Cambridge, UK: Polity Press.

2
Beyond PFI: Procurement of Public Sector Infrastructure and the Evolving Plurality of Methods in the UK

Darinka Asenova, Matthias Beck and Stephen J. Bailey

Introduction

The 'credit binge' of the 1990s and early 2000s facilitated the use of private finance for public services. However, this 'easy money' debt-fuelled period of economic growth was followed by the 'credit crunch' beginning in 2007. Combined with the 2009 economic recession, the UK government faced a pronounced dilemma because its plans for increased spending on public service infrastructures were increasingly undermined by difficulties faced by Private Finance Initiatives (PFIs) and similar ventures in obtaining commercial bank loans. Many private companies involved in the construction and management of Public-Private Partnerships (PPPs) facilities also experienced severe financial problems. In the changing macroeconomic and microeconomic conditions, it therefore became essential for public sector departments to identify the most effective and efficient methods for the financing and delivery of public services and related physical infrastructure.

This chapter therefore considers the advantages and disadvantages of the standard PFI/PPP model and investigates the evolving plurality of procurement approaches with a view towards identifying evidence of policy learning and policy transformation within changing financial, political and institutional contexts in both the public and private sectors. Analysis is based on discussion of non-profit models and the related Hub initiative, followed by an analysis of area-specific procurement

14

models, such as Building Schools for the Future (Education), LIFT and Express LIFT (Health).

The following analysis will make clear that there is no 'magic wand' public procurement model for service infrastructures and programmes. The standard PFI model was well suited to the economic and political conditions of the 1990s and early 2000s, but has had to be adapted to meet changing circumstances during the later 2000s.

The Private Finance Initiative

UK PFI has been intended to improve the delivery of public services by involving private sector companies in the design, construction, financing and operation of the related facilities. It was introduced in the early 1990s when investment in public services was at a record low level. The utilisation of private finance was expected to increase the volume and quality of public services, while allowing government agencies to conform to budgetary constraints and direct limited resources to other areas (Glaister 1999). The efficient distribution of project and service risk between the public and private sector partners for the duration of the contract was a key requirement and justification for the selection of the PFI option.

The standard (i.e. original) PFI model (outlined below) has been well researched and a large body of academic and non-academic literature exists (e.g. Asenova and Hood 2006; Bovaird 2004; Hellowell and Pollock 2009; Hodge and Greve 2007). The literature deals with a variety of issues, such as perceived benefits and problems, efficiency of risk transfer, quality of the services provided and the achievement of value for money (VFM). The literature has been generally very critical of the PFI model, especially in terms of poor VFM (see below).

In an attempt to avoid the negative connotations associated with PFI, the New Labour government attempted to rebrand these schemes as PPPs, a label which covers a range of institutional arrangements designed to combine the expertise of the public and private sectors in new capital investment and procurement projects. In reality, however, PFI has become the de facto acronym for any PPP and until recently has frequently been alluded to as being 'the only game in town'. This changed only very recently when a number of project and financing arrangements developed that resemble to various degrees the standard PFI model, but differ in terms of a number of contractual and financial aspects. This chapter provides an overview and evaluation of the main models.

Despite continuous support from the UK government for PFI, these schemes have become subject to considerable criticism both at a technical level and in terms of their political implications. For UK policymakers, the weaknesses of the standard PFI model have presented an impetus for potentially innovative spin-off procurement mechanisms such as Local Improvement Finance Trusts (LIFT), Express LIFT and ProCure 21 programmes in health; Building Schools for the Future (BSF) in Education and, specifically in Scotland, various forms of non-profit PFI.

The key feature of these innovative variants of PFI is that they attempt to address various perceived weaknesses of the standard PFI model by modifying some aspects while preserving its key characteristics. For example, the non-profit variant aims to address primarily the concerns associated with the excessive profits made by some private sector companies. While some of these new procurement approaches have already found widespread use, others are currently being developed or implemented.

The devolution of powers to Scotland in 1999 added an additional dimension to these developments when the minority Scottish National Party (SNP) government came to power in 2007 and imposed an effective moratorium on standard PFIs. This created a momentum for local governments and health authorities to find alternatives. The SNP government disassociated itself from PFIs by introducing the Scottish Futures Trust (SFT), described as a version of non-profit PFI (see Chapter 6).

Central to the PFI contract is the concession agreement between a government agency (client) and a vehicle company created by the sponsors to build and operate the facility (Beenhakker 1997). In order to participate in the project, the private companies set up a legal entity called the special purpose vehicle (SPV) or consortium. The SPV members are also known as sponsors because they usually provide the 'seed equity capital' and thus 'own' the project during the concessional period (Merna and Smith 1999). The SPV usually consists of a construction company, a facilities management company and an additional equity provider. The principal financier, generally a bank, provides the project finance, often made up of approximately 90 per cent debt and 10 per cent equity stake injected by the consortium members (Spackman 2002).

The SPV is a legal entity (i.e. company) in its own right, distinct from the mother organisations of its members. Unlike conventional firms, the SPV is a purpose-built organisation for one project that has a limited lifespan corresponding to the length of the concessional agreement. It is legally responsible to the client for the project's management and one of its key functions is to distribute the project's cash flows directly to the project lenders and equity investors (Finnerty 1996). Because in a PFI the client (usually a public sector department) contracts for service delivery, payment to the private sector partners does not commence until service delivery has begun, and its continuation is conditional on the satisfactory quality of the service provided (Tiffin and Hall 1998).

In Scotland, as elsewhere in the UK, PFI has enabled significant investments in the school estate that have improved the teaching and learning experience of staff and students. Specifically, a total of £5 billion had been invested in building more than 200 schools and refurbishing others by 2008 (Anon 2008). However, this investment flow has been adversely affected by the 2007–2009 credit crunch, which led to the collapse of bank lending as the cost of (both retail and wholesale inter-bank) credit became prohibitively expensive or completely unavailable.

The credit crunch, which owes its origins to lax regulatory regimes for banks and weak central bank safety nets (Bailey et al. 2009), had immediate wider ramifications, sparkling a global financial crisis and recession. Its impact on the UK public finances is profound because of the subsequent recession and because the government bailed out the banks to prevent their bankruptcy.

In 2009/10, the UK government is expected to have to borrow £175 billion, equivalent to 12.5 per cent of GDP, to deal with these problems (Chote 2009). Public sector borrowing had previously been below 3 per cent of GDP and the projected figure for 2009/10 is a record level in peacetime. As a consequence, net public sector debt is forecast to increase from below 40 per cent of GDP in 2008–2009 to nearly 80 per cent of GDP by 2013–2014.

Debt repayment, the welfare payment costs of recession, the reluctance to raise tax rates and revenues, the UK government's promise to protect spending on the National Health Service (NHS) and schools and achieve the United Nations' target (0.7 per cent of GDP) for aid to developing countries will, in combination, require significant cuts in spending (of 20–40 per cent) on individual service programmes.

In order to rebalance the public finances, cuts needed in total public spending of 0.1 per cent per year in real terms over the three-year Spending Review period beginning in 2010 have been estimated by the Institute of Fiscal Studies (Chote 2009). Between 2011 and 2014, the real reduction in investment spending could amount to 17.3 per cent per year.

By limiting the availability of private sector financing, by changing the overall economic environment and by adversely affecting the public finances, the credit crunch has potentially profound implications for the delivery of public services in the UK and specifically for PFI.

A major attraction for government was that PFI spending was 'off balance sheet' prior to the introduction of the International Financial Report Standard (IFRS) in April 2009. This separated PFI transactions from government accounts and so removed them from centrally controlled budgetary allocations and cash limits on public sector expenditure (Bovis 1999). Therefore it was perhaps not surprising that the UK Treasury's (2000) announcement with regard to the future of PPP envisaged a continuation of this type of procurement while suggesting that a wider range of PFI-type options with alternative financial and contractual arrangements should be explored. Similarly, in Scotland:

> The Scottish Executive [i.e. Government] should therefore consider the benefits of promoting real choice between procurement options for schools projects. Creating a framework that allows councils to choose between a mixture of procurement options (ie both PFI and non-PFI should help secure best value from PFI. (Audit Scotland (2002: 9))

The Non-Profit Distributing (NPD) model

Some Scottish local authorities have recently initiated, negotiated and signed privately financed projects using the NPD (rather than standard PFI) model. For example, Argyll and Bute Council, North Ayrshire Council, Aberdeen City Council, Falkirk Council and Angus Council have used NPD for the renovation and modernisation of their school buildings and educational facilities (Scottish Executive 2003). Some of these authorities already had experience with PFI and, being aware of its benefits and problems, opted for a modified version.

The NPD model is not an entirely new approach to procurement. Similar structural arrangements have been used since the 1990s by some local authorities in England for the provision of leisure and other cultural services. The Scottish National Party government considers NPD to be better and more politically viable, as its focus is on improving rather than radically changing the PFI/PPP approach to public procurement: 'The introduction of the NPD model was designed to improve the traditional PPP model whilst maintaining an efficient risk transfer.' (SFT 2008, 8).

The main drivers for utilisation of the NPD are capping 'excessive' private sector profits and reducing business rates and tax liabilities. However, there are also other important considerations related to wider participation of community stakeholders in the decision-making process, as well as incentives related to possible cost–efficiencies and productivity gains (ODPM 2003). The NPD is defined by three broad principles (SFT 2008, 4):

- Enhanced stakeholder involvement in the management of projects;
- No dividend-bearing equity;
- Capped private sector returns.

In addition to maintaining an optimum allocation of risk between the public and private sectors, the model envisages that other key benefits of the traditional equity-based PFI should be retained, for example whole-life costing, life-cycle maintenance and facilities management, performance-based payments to the private sector and improved overall service provision.

The standard PFI model places no restrictions on private sector profits whereas the NPD approach is intended to eliminate excessive rates of returns to private partners. Using NPD, private sector contractors and lenders invest loans rather than equity and are expected to make only a 'normal' market rate of return. However, government documents do not clarify what constitutes this 'normal rate'.

The SPV shareholders' returns are capped at the point of signing the NPD contract. Any surpluses made by the SPV are then passed to a charitable company and so distributed back to the community, rather than being paid as dividends to the SPV members as in the standard PFI model (Hellowell and Pollock 2009). This is illustrated by the Outline Business Case of Angus Council, which states that any profits/surpluses generated by the SPV will be distributed in four main directions corresponding to the agreed priorities (Angus Council 2002, 63):

- To provide incentives for the management of the SPV such as bonuses;
- To create some limited contingency reserves for the SPV;
- To improve/expand the scope of the service;
- To allocate funds to an agreed charitable organisation, which should have no explicit or implicit links with the council.

While the procuring authority still has to fulfil the statutory VFM requirement, the case is tested against a set of criteria for suitability, which includes (SFT 2008, 5–6):

- Investment in a major capital program which necessitates effective risk allocation;
- Availability of private sector expertise;
- Clearly defined service outputs;
- Possibility for whole-life costing of assets and services;
- Reliance on relatively stable technologies;
- Assets have a long-term life span;
- Robust incentives for the private sector.

As in standard PFI schemes, in the NPD model the SPV relies entirely on senior and subordinated debt provided by banks and other financial institutions.[1] As far as concerns the financial structure, there are no other restrictions apart from 'zero dividend bearing equity' (SFT 2008, 9). The performance of the SPV companies is promoted through performance/penalty incentives rather than through distributed profits. As a consequence, the subcontractors have to take on an even larger proportion of the project risk as they have a responsibility to provide services to a specified standard. In order to achieve off-balance-sheet treatment, councils are required not to be directly involved in the running of the SPV.

As noted earlier, risk transfer remains a central pillar of NPD. Despite the lack of equity capital in these schemes, the client should, in principle, aim for a level of risk transfer (to the private sector) similar to the level achieved via standard PFI; the negotiated risk transfer determines the contractual rate of return. Achievement of VFM for the duration of the contract means that the contractual risk distribution should be maintained and evaluated against the cash flows. This also means that all risks should be managed in the absence of an equity cushion: dividends can be reduced or not paid at all if profits are insufficient, whereas debt interest cannot be waived. The procuring authorities, meanwhile, should also pay special attention to the long-term sustainability of contractual risk-allocation arrangements, as this is crucial to the viability of the project.

As noted above, the introduction of the IFRS in 2009 encourages local authorities to explore alternative commercial and financial structures for provision of public service infrastructures. PFI projects now being 'on balance sheet', the client can be flexible in terms of selecting the most appropriate level of risk transfer, but this should be evaluated against VFM criteria. For example, if the client wants to reduce the financing costs, it can offer an explicit guarantee for a part of the senior debt, known as 'supported debt structure'.

The procuring authority may also be willing to make capital injections in the form of direct payments, loans, land contributions, credit facilities, etc. Government guidance warns against such payments being made before successful completion of the construction phase and stresses that, when considering this option, the guiding principle is once again based on achievement of VFM.

The NPD model is at a relatively early stage of development and has not yet been subjected to detailed academic analysis. However, preliminary analysis indicates that NPD does not resolve the long-standing problems of standard PFI, such as high transaction costs, questionable risk transfer, insufficient market competition and prolonged and expensive negotiations (Hellowell and Pollock 2009). Contrary to expectations, senior debt and shareholders' loans were again provided at a relatively high price (Cuthbert and Cuthbert 2008).

Perhaps, the NPD model remains too similar to its PFI predecessor to be able to resolve the latter's shortcomings. Moreover, the recent financial crisis has affected the NPD model and the standard PFI in a similar way. While the main impact of the crisis can be traced to the availability and cost of finance, at the same time there are additional adverse implications in terms of reduced competition and risk avoidance by the private sector as well as a tougher market environment and spending cuts.

Schools procurement options

When the UK's New Labour government came to power in 1997, it declared education to be its main priority. Education was seen as a means of regenerating the economy, creating national competitiveness and simultaneously promoting social justice by extending individual opportunity for self-advancement. This entailed various initiatives from cutting class sizes to providing choice and diversity of supply of foundation secondary schools (Commission on 2020 Public Services 2009). One of the ways of improving educational outcomes was seen to be through the reorganisation of schools' infrastructure in line with local demographic changes. This reorganisation emphasised the need for a radical transformation of existing school facilities, including the building of new schools, the elimination of surplus school places and/ or reduction in the number of schools, improvements in school environments and the provision of state-of the-art computer technology equipment.

In 2003 the Department of Children, Schools and Families (DCSF) decided to increase capital investment in England and Wales through a programme known as BSF. BSF is a programme that utilises the PFI model but is not entirely privately funded (see below). Subject to ongoing public spending decisions, it is envisaged that it will involve the renewal of 3500 secondary schools (pupils aged 11 to 18) between 2005 and 2020. The overall value of this 15-year programme was estimated at £55 billion. Together with provision of modern information and communication technology (ICT) facilities, it entails the rebuilding of over half of the school estate, 35 per cent being structurally remodelled, the rest being refurbished (NAO 2009). The DCSF delegated overall responsibility for commissioning and maintaining the facilities to individual local authorities. A specialised body, Partnership for Schools (PfS), was created to improve local authorities' procurement activities and provide central programme management. It also scrutinises the business cases before the departmental approval.

Via the BSF, the government aims to adopt a more radical and holistic view towards educational needs aimed at modernising facilities and technological infrastructures: 'Over time this investment will see the entire secondary school building stock upgraded and refurbished in the greatest school renewal programme in British history' (Prime Minister's Office 2004, 3).

Although BSF is not simply a capital finance method, its inclusion in this analysis is justified as follows:

- It involves long-term partnership arrangements between public and private sector organisations;
- It relies heavily on private finance which, by 2011, is intended to account for 41 per cent of the total BSF capital value (NAO 2009);
- It is used for capital-intensive projects;
- There is a strong political will to utilise private sector skills and management expertise as well as significant service element which make it akin to PFI.

Within BSF, the PFI option is used only for building *new* schools. Similarly to other PFI contracts, the private sector companies are expected to undertake the design, construction, financing and maintenance of the facilities over a period of 25–30 years. During the operational phase, local authorities pay unitary charges to the private sector companies, which are funded through PFI credits from the central government. Local authorities take a leading role as project planners, procurers and clients. Private finance is used in several ways (NAO 2009):

- PfS is co-funded by central government and its quango, Partnership UK, with a view to supporting BSF;
- Local authorities are encouraged to use PFI for new-build schools;
- Local education partnerships (LEP) are usually created as a joint venture between the local authority, consortia, financiers and Building Schools for Future Investments (BSFI);
- BSFI is a joint-venture organisation between the department and PUK that invests equity in the projects.

Conventional funding (provided by central government) is used mainly in refurbishment projects and for the provision of ICT facilities within BSF. In this particular case, conventional funding is provided mainly through a capital grant from the DCSF. By 2011 the capital grant allocation is expected to reach £5.8 billion, or 52 per cent of planned funding. Local authorities can also use supported borrowing for the BSF, with the DCSF providing the Revenue Support Grant (RSG) to cover the loan payments. While supported borrowing is expected to account for 7 per cent of planned funding, it has not been used since 2007–2008 because caps on the RSG have effectively made it inoperable.

Regardless of the source, and following the selection of the private sector partner, the provision of funding for BSF projects is channelled through subsequent 'waves', which last from three to five years. Smaller projects can be renewed through one funding wave but bigger projects may require several waves. By mid-2009, local authorities had received between £80 million and £410 million of capital funding for each individual wave.

A National Audit Office report identified a range of potential problems related to BSF, such as overly optimistic assumptions and expectations regarding time scales and cost estimates (NAO 2009). At the time, the NAO noted that there was a delay of 21 months and possible cost overruns in the range of £10 billion. A subsequent report by the House of Commons Public Accounts Committee (PAC) confirmed that the BSF 'created expectations it could not meet' (BBC 2009, 1). According to the report, of the 200 schools originally planned to be completed by December 2008, only 42 actually had been. Furthermore, the overall completion of the programme was more likely to be 18 years rather than the initially planned 15. The PAC chairman noted that the centralised management of the programme had brought certain benefits, but suggested that:

> BSF has been beset from the beginning by poor planning and persistent over-optimism. This has led to widespread disappointment in the rate at which schools are being completed, inevitably damaging confidence in the department's [DCSF] ability to complete the programme even by the revised date of 2023 ... It's going to be a tall order to double the number of schools being procured and constructed. (BBC 2009, 1)

In response, the Schools Minister claimed that the vast majority of local authorities will complete their programmes by the initial completion date of 2020 and that BSF has full support from the private sector companies. However, the reduction of the availability of funding due to the credit crunch has adversely affected the BSF programme because of its impact on PFIs. Kent County Council agreed one BSF PFI deal in October 2008, but over the following five months there were no other agreements. Nevertheless, the UK Treasury, government and PfS believe that BSF remains attractive for private sector bidders, but at the same time they are looking for alternative sources of private finance, including the European Investment Bank (NAO 2009).

Similar to the BSF programme for England and Wales, in 2003 the Scottish government and the Convention of Scottish Local Authorities (COSLA) published a joint strategy called the 21st Century School, Building our Future: Scotland's School Estate. It reiterated that education is a key priority for the government and states that every young person should have:

> ... the chance to meet their full potential and that the gap for those not sharing the general level of attainment and well-being is closed. Local authorities – who, through COSLA, have jointly developed this strategy with the Scottish Executive, parents, teachers and others with an interest in education – share the view that every young person should have the best possible start in life. (Scottish Executive/COSLA 2003, 1)

The vision for the twenty-first-century school estate refers to well-designed and well-built schools that will be effectively managed and maintained over the long term. They should be provided over the following 15 years. As regards funding, the document is not very specific and fails to indicate particular funding options. Instead, it outlines the process for ensuring the funding requirements are met:

- Local authorities develop school estate management plans, which set out realistic and prioritised options for improvement. These will provide a basis for future decisions at a local level, and information and insights across the school estate at a national level.
- The Scottish government takes national decisions, taking account of wider priorities and available resources, and informed by the picture of the school estate identified in local authorities' plans.
- Both local authorities and the Scottish government give due weight to committing resources and to the stability and sustainability of funding to implement the strategy.

In reality, most of the school renovation projects in Scotland prior to 2007 were conducted through PFI and some through NPD, the latter including the Hub initiative.

The Hub initiative

As noted above, the SNP government came to power in Scotland in 2007 and effectively imposed an immediate moratorium on new PFIs. As a result, its schools building programme came to a virtual halt, with no new schools being commissioned by the SNP government during its first two years in office. Hence, there has been significant slowing down of Scottish public infrastructure projects.

In order to counter these developments, the SNP government created a new procurement initiative under the title 'Hub'. It announced the first pilot Hub initiative worth £64 million in August 2009, which is to be used for building and renovating health centres, schools and other public facilities in south-east Scotland (PPP Bulletin 2009a). The Hub project will be run by the SFT, which had been created as an alternative to standard PFI procurement almost two years previously. Following the first Hub scheme, the SFT plans to implement a wave of five Hub schemes across Scotland with a total value of £300 million. The trust will be in charge of all projects in a purely advisory capacity, and will not be involved in their financing as had been initially envisaged (see Chapter 6).

The long delay of the first Hub scheme attracted widespread criticism over whether the SFT would be able to meet public expectations. Nevertheless, the announcement of the Hub pilot project was met with significant interest by the Scottish construction industry, which had been disappointed with the lack of new building projects. More than 100 companies were reported to have expressed interest (PPP Bulletin 2009b).

Similar to the standard PFI, the Hub will involve private sector partners in the co-management of projects over a period of 20 years (Dinwoodie 2009). Contractors will enter a partnership agreement comprising the SFT, local councils and other public sector bodies located in the Hub area.

The Hub scheme was presented by the SNP government as a substantial innovation in public service delivery. On closer examination, however, it resembles other 'PFI-lite' schemes, such as LIFT and BSF, which were already in operation in England and Wales. Indeed, a key document published by the Scottish government makes clear that private sector participation lies at the heart of the new proposal (Scottish Executive 2006, 1): 'The hub is an initiative...designed to enhance the delivery of local services and improve procurement through public-private sector partnering.' The guidance document explicitly recognises that the Hub is virtually identical to some existing arrangements (Scottish Executive 2006, 23): 'While the commercial arrangements are along the same lines of the LIFT and BSF programmes we will want the focus of our consultation effort to be on tailoring the hub approach to the Scottish context.'

The similarities with the other PFI-lites are hardly surprising considering that the above document was drafted jointly with Partnership UK, a body originally tasked with the promotion and acceleration of partnerships and which had helped with the development of LIFT for the UK's NHS (see below). The Labour Shadow Finance Minister in Scotland criticised the delay, noting that the SNP spent two years dithering over the SFT and eventually created a scheme no different from PFI (Dinwoodie 2009).

According to the Scottish government (Scottish Executive 2006, 2), the key objectives of the Hub initiative are to:

- Provide enhanced local services by increasing the scale of joint service working and interaction between Community Planning Partners across Scotland;
- Deliver a sustainable programme of investment into community-based infrastructure and development so that more and more services are provided locally in communities through multi-disciplinary teams working from single sites;

- Establish a more efficient and sustainable procurement methodology for public sector bodies including NHS Boards and local authorities;
- Share learning and improve the procurement process for both public sector procurement teams and their private sector partners.

These key objectives indicate that, despite the obvious similarities, the Hub initiative can be considered a step further than LIFT and BSF in terms of:

- Increased devolution of decision-making powers at a local level rather than departmental level;
- Amalgamation of different types of public service projects aiming to meet local service needs in a more holistic 'joined-up' way.

Scottish government guidance gives special attention to the enhanced opportunities for joint working, service integration and for meeting the premises-development needs of a range of community partners. Specifically, the Hub approach intends to create oppor-tunities for local stakeholders to have real stake in long-term service development. Other perceived benefits from the initiative are rather similar to the potential benefits of a standard PFI, such as the possibility for efficient procure-ment, VFM, property ownership and central support.

At a local level, joint ventures or Hub (rather than SPV) companies will be established between the local sponsors such as health boards, local authorities, police authorities, voluntary agencies, the SFT and private sector partners (PSP). The initial plans envisaged that the share-holding structure of a Hub company would include a 60 per cent con-tribution from the PSP, 20 per cent from the SFT and 20 per cent from local sponsors, thus allowing profits to be split between the public and private sector partners.

According to Scottish government guidance, Hub companies will act as a bridge between public and private sector participants, performing a number of key functions including:

- Establishing the development needs with local public sector partners and planning for local premises, contributing asset management and property development expertise;
- Acting as a single point of contact for all participants, aggregating demand and procuring efficiently, bringing in private finance when and where required;

- Working with the local public sponsors to develop suitable new projects in response to evolving service requirements;
- Assisting the public sector partners in complying with existing governance arrangements for project approval; and
- Delivering projects more quickly and effectively.

Hub companies will aim to invest in commercially viable projects, raising debt and equity from banks or private equity markets, utilising a range of funding options from conventional (central government) funding to private finance, depending on the specific project requirements. The projects have to be selected in such a way that they can deliver a portfolio of flexible, fit-for-purpose, VFM facilities while generating a commercial-level rate of return for investors.

Hub companies will manage the construction, building and operational side of the projects up to the letting of the completed facilities. During the operational phase, they will receive regular lease rentals from the public sector clients and, where possible, from third parties. Rental income from leased facilities and/or payments for design-and-build projects will provide income streams to cover the local Hub companies' ongoing management costs and to provide a return on project investment. Procurement costs are expected to be lower compared to third-party providers and all associated whole life-cycle risks will be taken by the local Hub company.

Local Hub companies will have an important role in safeguarding the public interest in terms of VFM, accountability and governance by:

- Providing representation of the public sector joint-venture partners on the Board of the Hub company;
- Working with public sector authorities to develop, agree and maintain an ongoing programme of future improvements to local services.

All community planning partners as well as individual user groups will have access to the services provided by local Hub companies.

The Scottish government will provide initial financial support by making available limited amount of funding towards the establishment of the local Hub companies. This support will be used towards set-up costs and land acquisitions, as well as some local development and support costs, including revenue and capital. There is an option for other requirements to be considered in the context of the spending reviews. Local authorities and health boards are entitled to use capital and revenue funds identified in future plans to support planned premises and to fund their delivery through the Hub.

As noted earlier, the SFT and the Hub companies will not rely on a single funding option. Speaking at a recent Scottish Finance Committee meeting, the first SFT chairman confirmed that all funding models would be considered: 'We completely understand the political territory that the decisions will be made in, but we will make recommendations based on best advice. Our approach will be ecumenical' (PPP Bulletin 2009c, 1).

This reflects the understanding that, through the Hub initiative, the SFT will try to adopt a flexible and pragmatic approach to the funding of capital projects, which is essential particularly in the current economic environment.

LIFT and Express LIFT

The Local Improvement Finance Trust (LIFT) initiative was launched in England in 2000 as part of the NHS Plan's 'World-Class Commissioning' initiative, with planned spending of £1 billion. Its main goal was to address long-term under-investment in primary and community care facilities. These include family doctor/general practitioner (GP) services, pharmacists, dentists, opticians and minor surgery care facilities, lack of which had affected poor inner city areas in particular. These types of investments are relatively small in scale by PFI standards. Hence, there was a concern that standard PFI would not be able to attract sufficient private sector interest for the planned improvements.

One of the principal technical innovations of LIFT, therefore, was to allow Primary Care Trusts (PCTs), as clients, to contract with private sector partners on a long-term, rather than project, basis to build new premises in new locations, providing a variety of health services under one roof. This PFI-lite public procurement model was intended to be attractive to the private sector, because a private sector partner, once selected via a tendering process, would be able to access a stream of deals and/or projects over time, without facing the costs of bidding for these projects on an individual project-by-project basis.

Although in December 2005 government sources announced that there had been a broad interest and quick uptake of LIFT with potential investment of £771 million and 51 participating companies, it soon became clear that private sector participation was not as easy to obtain as initially envisaged. This led the Department of Health (DoH) to broaden the remit of LIFT beyond the initial targeting of deprived areas. This broader remit sees LIFT as a means of addressing long-standing under-investment in primary care facilities, which meant that less than 40 per cent of facilities were purpose-built. Additionally there was an expectation that LIFT would help in the creation of multipurpose 'super-surgeries', as well as contribute to the reinvigoration of local economies.

Also known as 'polyclinics', these super-surgeries are GP-led health centres meant to be 'one-stop shops' for patients. Costing around £20 million each, and with a government-backed tenant on a long-lease, polyclinics are expected by the government to attract sufficient interest on the part of private sector developers. The government thinks that this will be the case even though rents are determined by the district valuer, because developers should still be able to make sufficient profits to make contracts commercially viable. Overall, this extended remit allowed LIFT quickly to become a qualified success to the extent that, by 2008, 48 LIFT partnerships delivering an estimated £1.4 billion of investment had been formed and will continue to operate under the existing LIFT scheme.

However, in 2008 the existing LIFT scheme was replaced by its successor, Express LIFT, and new partnerships are now being created. Interestingly, in technical terms, Express LIFT differs very little from LIFT except that for Express LIFT public sector clients choose their private sector partners from a limited range of seven pre-selected/approved companies that participated in a national bidding round in early 2009. In essence, LIFT and Express LIFT represent an attempt to simplify the contracting procedures associated with PFIs and, in so doing, to reduce overheads and upfront bidding costs of the public procurement process.

LIFTs and Express LIFTs are local initiatives based on health authority boundaries, and current legislation allows any Primary Care Trust in England that has a health service strategy for its area to form a LIFT trust and create a LIFT company (LIFTCo). Similar to SPVs, LIFTCos are private sector companies limited by share capital. However, for LIFTCos there is an explicit requirement that the DoH and local NHS interests become shareholders with seats on the board and an entitlement to share in the profits, which can then be reinvested. The relative shareholding of local LIFTCos is as follows:

- A local health economy stakeholder: 20 per cent;
- A private sector partner: 60 per cent;
- The national joint-venture Partnerships for Health (PfH): 20 per cent.

The PfH is owned jointly by the DoH and Partnership UK, the latter being 51 per cent privately owned. Hence, in combination, there is a very large private sector shareholding in LIFTCos of in the region of 70 per cent.

In order to create a LIFTCo, a local health care provider runs a competitive procurement process in order to identify a private sector partner to join in the LIFT as a long-term partner and supplier of services and infrastructure. The future plans of this partnership are then assessed by a Strategic Partnering Board in order to agree a Strategic Service Development Plan (SSDP). Operating in line with this SSDP, the LIFTCo invests over a defined period in a rolling programme of premises modernisation. This includes:

- Planning future estates service requirements;
- Implementing agreed investments;
- Delivering agreed services;
- Receiving payment for delivering investments and services to agreed standards.

While the basic set-up of a LIFTCo essentially mirrors that of an SPV with a 20–35-year PFI contract, there are some crucial differences. These include the following:

- LIFTCos have exclusive rights to develop new primary care premises in their areas over 25 years, using a standardised procurement process and subject to VFM tests;
- Although the partners in the LIFTCo contribute equity, some 90 per cent of the capital for developing LIFT properties is provided through debt;
- The properties are owned by the LIFTCo and income is earned through rental payments from tenants such as PCTs, general practitioners (GPs), pharmacists and local authorities;
- PCTs usually reimburse GPs' rents in full, but do not necessarily reimburse contractors such as pharmacists;
- Tenants occupy space in LIFT buildings under Lease-Plus Agreements (LPAs), with rents covering the life-cycle costs of the building (and increased in line with the retail price index, RPI).

Although LIFT has been described above as a qualified success, a number of analyses have noted that the scheme is not without problems. LIFT is still perceived by many public and private sector organisations as being overly bureaucratic and cumbersome. This issue has been partially addressed by the introduction of Express LIFT, which envisages a reduction in the time required for negotiations from one–two years to three–six months. Additionally, some researchers have highlighted concerns over the poor quality of some LIFT buildings, together with an increased risk exposure for public sector organisations because of local rent variations and other complex property market issues. Perhaps most importantly, recent research on the financial structure and performance of LIFTCos has indicated that these schemes may have allowed private sector partners to continue to reap excessive profits, which, in turn, may have resulted in affordability gaps for PCTs.

Conclusions

PFIs are clearly well embedded in the renewal of the UK's public sector infrastructure and have delivered many positive achievements in terms of service provision. However, there has been ongoing concern about excessive costs and profits. Excessive costs are seen to be associated with unnecessarily high interest rates payable on private sector borrowing (via corporate bonds) compared with the lower interest rates on public sector borrowing. Also, rates of return (profits) have often been greater than those originally envisaged by both public sector clients and, indeed, by members of SPVs. Excessive profits have often been associated with debt restructuring (to take advantage of lower interest rates on offer subsequent to initial borrowing) and with subcontracting of service provision in order to take advantage of cheaper contract prices subsequent to those written into PFI contracts.

Such excessive profits led to new PFI/PPP contracts making provisions for profit sharing between SPVs and public sector clients. However, existing contracts could not be rewritten and new contracts were still seen as too inflexible, being binding for 25 years or more, and so lacking the flexibility to deal with inevitable changes in service requirements over the long term. PFIs were also seen as contrary to the public service ethos, seeking to promote profits rather than the welfares of service users. Although there have been many successes (at least as far as can be judged before 25–30-year contracts are completed), critics of PFIs have highlighted contractual and service failures and the lack of significant risk transfer as public sector organisations have sometimes had to bail out failed projects.

As noted above, attempts have been made to develop PFI-lite contracts in the devolved decision-making of the post-1999 UK territories of England, Scotland and Wales. Forms of PFI-lite contracts now vary by

UK territory and by public service within any one territory. In England, the form of PFI-lite varies quite markedly between local government and the NHS.

Whatever their structural differences, these new models have all attempted to:

- Reduce transaction costs (i.e. the costs of writing 'water-tight' contracts);
- Reduce (or eliminate completely) dividends paid to shareholders;
- Increase debt financing (i.e. debt/equity leverage);
- Share revenue surpluses (whether foreseen or not at the time of signing contracts);
- Allow service structures to be adapted to changing service conditions over time (without the need for costly renegotiation of original contracts);
- Allow more attention to be paid to the public service ethos (notwithstanding the continued involvement of private sector profit-seeking partners).

Nevertheless, the experiences of NPD models, LIFT and the SFT make abundantly clear the considerable difficulties faced by the public sector in trying to develop new, highly innovative, models of public service financing and delivery that avoid the worst manifestations of the standard PFI model while retaining its significant advantages for service procurement.

The most significant advantage seems to have been the off-balance-sheet nature of PFIs. However, introduction of the IFRS in April 2009 seems to have significantly reduced scope for this creative accounting of the public finances. Additionally, private sector funding was very severely reduced by the 2007–2009 credit crunch, the collapse (or near collapse) of major PFI-funding banks and their consequent greatly increased reluctance to take on risk exposure over such extended periods of time.

At the same time, the very high public finance costs of world-wide economic recession and of bank bailouts by governments has also severely restricted the availability of public finance to replace the much-diminished private finance. A return to traditional procurement directly by the public sector itself is therefore not feasible.

This simultaneous occurrence of capital rationing in both the private and public sectors has stimulated the search for new, ever more innovative, models for the financing of public service infrastructure. While the various PFI-lite models seem to have achieved a greater emphasis on the public service ethos and coordination, there is considerable risk of a return to the capital rationing of the pre-PFI era as the hugely increased net public sector debt associated with bank bailouts and recession has to be repaid.

The expected significant cuts in spending on many UK public services mean that more innovative public procurement models will have to focus increasingly on higher service quality at lower financial costs by reducing the costs of duplication and bureaucracy. To this end, 13 'Total Service' pilot studies were being tested in England during late 2009 for final analysis in spring 2010 (Wintour 2009). Their aim is to identify and account for all public spending in each of their geographic areas and to determine if that spending can be better managed, for example, if various public sector bodies could form partnerships with each other so as to avoid duplication of services and replication of buildings.

The UK government envisages that billions of pounds can be saved in this way, with these savings forming a key element in the UK New Labour government's strategy to halve the public sector deficit by 2014. For this to be the case, public procurements would have to become increasingly multifunctional and multi-agency. This will require a change in the culture and behaviour of public bodies so as to facilitate adoption of radically different ways of working together in a particular neighbourhood. For example a municipality could work closely with a health authority to provide services to elderly people. More generally, local authorities could be given powers to scrutinise all spending on public services within their jurisdictions, irrespective of whether it is their own spending or not. However, their geographical boundaries may not coincide with those of other government bodies and departments, which is particularly problematic for joint working in respect of roads, public transport and other public services that extend beyond existing political borders. Some joint working will have to be at a regional rather than local level and so involve more than one municipality.

In summary, innovations in public service infrastructure financing models can only be analysed and understood in the context of:

- The overall state of health of the public finances and of the wider economy;
- The increasingly neo-liberal political philosophy of governments seeking to involve the private sector in the provision of public services;

- The ever-rising expectations of citizens in general and users of public services in particular.

It is clear that there is not, never has been and never will be a 'magic wand' procurement model that can solve all the problems faced by public service infrastructures and programmes. The standard PFI model was a creation of its time and will no doubt continue to evolve in various PFI-lite incarnations. There is little or no likelihood of a return to traditional procurement with the public sector bearing all financial risks beyond the construction of physical infrastructures.

However procured, the financing of infrastructure also needs to be considered. The 2007 Lyons Report supported greater use of a plurality of infrastructure charges in England, including not just planning obligations but also the proposed planning gain supplement, business improvement districts (BIDs) and the so-called 'roof tax' (actually a standard fee or charge per house built). These financing options are considered in detail elsewhere (Bailey 2009).

Note

1. Senior debt is provided by commercial banks and its repayment takes priority over repayment of other forms of debt.

References

Angus Council (2002) *Outline Business Case: Angus Schools PPP*, http://www.scotland.gov.uk/Resource/Doc/923/0059169.pdf (accessed 14 July 2009).

Anon (2008) Making the Grade: All our Schools Should be Fit for Purpose, *The Herald*, 20 March, 16.

Asenova, D. and Hood, J. (2006) PFI and the Implications of Introducing New Long-Term Actors into Public Service Delivery, *Public Policy and Administration*, 21 (4): 23–41.

Audit Scotland (2002) *Audit Review, Taking the Initiative: Using PFI Contracts to Renew Council Schools*. London: Accounts Commission.

Bailey, S. J. (2009) *Local Government Charges*, CIPFA Technical Information Services. London: Chartered Institute of Public Finance and Accountancy, www.tisonline.net.

Bailey S. J., Asenova D. and Beck M. (2009) UK Public Private Partnerships and the Credit Crunch: A Case Of Risk Contagion? *Journal of Risk and Governance* (forthcoming).

BBC (2009) *School Rebuilds 'Over-Optimistic'*, http://news.bbc.co.uk/1/hi/education/8093839.stm (accessed 15 June 2009).

Beenhakker, H. L. (1997) *Risk Management in Project Finance and Implementation*. London: Quorum Books.

Bovaird, T. (2004) Public-Private Partnerships: From Contested concepts to Prevalent Practice, *International Review of Administrative Sciences*, 70 (2), 199–215.

Bovis, C. (1999) Who's Afraid of the Private Finance Initiative? *The Private Finance Initiative Journal*, 3 (6): 20–23.

Chote, R. (2009) *Two Parliaments of Pain*, Institute of Fiscal Studies, http://www.ifs.org.uk/publications/4509 (accessed 15 July 2009).

Commission on 2020 Public Services (2009) *A Brief History of Public Services Reform*, London: 2020 Public Services Trust.

Cuthbert, J. and Cuthbert, M. (2008) *Analysis of the Financial Projections for Two Non-Profit Distributing PFI Schemes and Implications*, Memorandum to the Scottish Parliament Finance Committee. In Hellowell, M. and Pollock, A. (eds) (2009).

Dinwoodie, R. (2009) South-East Set to Pilot New Approach to Public Buildings, *The Herald*, 4 July, 6.

Finnerty, J. D. (1996) *Project Financing, Asset-Based Financial Engineering*. USA: John Wiley & Sons Inc.

Glaister, S. (1999) Past Abuses and Future Uses of Private Finance and Public Private Partnerships in Transport, *Public Money & Management*, 19 (3): 29–36.

Hellowell, M. and Pollock, A. (2009) Non-Profit Distribution: The Scottish Approach to Private Finance in Public Services, *Social Policy and Society*, 8 (3): 405–418.

Hodge, G. A. and Greve, C. (2007) Public-Private Partnerships: An International Performance Review, *Public Administration Review*, 67 (3), 545–558.

Lyons, M (2007) *Lyons Inquiry into Local Government: Place-Shaping: A Shared Ambition for the Future of Local Government*, http://www.communities.gov.uk/index.asp?id=1165334 (accessed 6 October 2009). London: HMSO.

Merna, A. and Smith, N. (1999) Privately Financed Infrastructure in the 21st Century, *Proceedings, Institution of Civil Engineers*, 132, November, 166–173.

NAO (2009) The Building Schools for the Future Programme: Renewing the Secondary School Estate. London: National Audit Office.

ODPM (2003) The Role of Not-for-Profit Organisations in Strategic Service Delivery Partnering: A Discussion Paper, Wetherby (West Yorkshire): Office of the Deputy Prime Minister.

PPP Bulletin (2009a) Scotland's Hub Project up and Running, On-line publication, http://www.pppbulletin.com/news/view/14792 (accessed 6 July 2009).

PPP Bulletin (2009b) Firms Jump at Prospect of Scottish Projects, On-line publication, http://www.pppbulletin.com/news/view/14850 (accessed 11 August 2009).

PPP Bulletin (2009c) PFI Could Still be in Use in Scotland, On-line publication, http://www.pppbulletin.com/news/view/14846 (accessed 6 August 2009).

Prime Minister's Office (2004) *Building Schools for Future Factsheet*, http://www.number10.gov.uk/Page5801 (accessed 15 July 2009).

Scottish Executive/COSLA (2003) *The 21st Century School, Building Our Future: Scotland's School Estate*, http://www.scotland.gov.uk/library5/education/bofs-00.asp (accessed 15 July 2009).

Scottish Executive (2006) Building Better Local Services Together: Your Guide to the Hub Initiative, On-line publication, http://www.scotland.gov.uk/Resource/Doc/924/0041326.pdf (accessed 10 August 2009).

SFT (2008) *NPD Explanatory Note, November 2008.* Edinburgh: The Scottish Futures Trust.

Spackman, M. (2002) Public-Private Partnerships: Lessons from the British Approach, *Economic Systems,* 26: 283–301.

Tiffin, M. and Hall, P. (1998) PFI – the Last Chance Saloon, *Proceedings, Institution of Civil Engineers,* 126, February: 12–18.

Wintour, P. (2009) Labour Drive to Make Services More Efficient, *The Guardian,* 21 October. On-line publication, http://www.guardian.co.uk/society/2009/oct/20/john-denham-public-finances-services (accessed 23 October 2009).

3
Innovations in Private Sector Provision of Infrastructure in South Korea

Surk-Tae Kim

Introduction

The growth of the Korean economy has necessitated a continuous investment in infrastructure facilities. However, limited resources in the pubic sector have led the Korean government to utilise private capital investment in infrastructure facilities. Since the introduction of Public-Private Partnerships (PPPs) in 1994, private participation in infrastructure (PPI) projects has been growing rapidly to meet current infrastructure demands.

PPP is a concept which involves the public and the private sectors working in cooperation and partnership to provide public services. PPI is a variant of PPP whose focus is on investment in infrastructure. Korean PPPs and PPIs took the UK's PFI as a model (see Chapter 2).

Besides meeting financial necessities, PPI is used for realising efficiency in infrastructure delivery and for transferring part of the risk to the private sector. Thus the Korean government has endeavoured to develop PPI as an innovative financing method. As a result, in 2008, PPI projects amounted to 15.3 per cent of the total infrastructure investment. According to the McKinsey Quarterly (April 2007), Korea is classified as a 'hot spot' of PPP in transportation, after the UK and Australia.

As is the case in other countries, PPI is not a panacea for solving public sector financial and efficiency problems. Rather, it is often accused of transferring the fiscal burden to the next generation and also of being an expensive method for delivering public services. Thus, new challenges, problems and opportunities in the way governments implement

PPI projects are causing government leaders at all levels to rethink strategic plans for future economic and social infrastructure provision.

This chapter analyses the current issues and challenges for the Korean PPI system as an innovative financing method, as well as its shortfalls. The following section begins with the rationale for the Korean PPI system. Subsequent sections outline the Korean PPI system focused on institutional settings, describe private investment trends and analyse innovative adaptation process of PPI projects in Korea and the final section draws together concludes.

The rationale for the South Korean PPI system

PPI is a concept which involves the public and the private sectors working in partnership to provide various physical and social infrastructures (Grimsey and Lewis 2004). The rationale for PPI may be different between countries, but the Korean government claims PPI can be rationalised as follows (MOSF and KDI 2008a).

First, PPI is a new option for the effective provision of infrastructure delivery. The role of private investment in infrastructure facilities is expected to grow as government revenue is limited and expenditure in sectors such as welfare is increasing. A PPI programme enables the public sector to break the short-term constraints on infrastructure investment imposed by insufficient tax revenues and limited public sector borrowing (Yescombe 2007). As a complement to public investment, PPI may provide economic infrastructure such as roads and railways, as well as social infrastructure such as schools and cultural facilities.

Timely provision of various social infrastructure facilities is becoming a social issue in Korea. Delays in the initiation of public facilities projects will ultimately raise construction and land acquisition costs. Relying on the government budget alone may not provide public services in a timely fashion. For instance, it would take at least 20 years to renovate old elementary and middle school buildings across the nation that are more than 30 years old. However, introducing the build-transfer-lease (BTL) scheme, could allow renovation of about 70 per cent of them within two to three years. By expanding public facilities earlier, BTL projects narrow the gap in educational, cultural and welfare services among different regions across the country (MOSF and KDI 2008b).

Second, PPI is an efficient and effective method for the delivery of public services. By combining such responsibilities as design, building, financing and operating (DBFO) in a single contract and transferring part of the risks and responsibilities to the private sector, PPI projects may realise value for money (VFM) with lower project costs and improved service quality compared to conventional public procurement. PPI also encourages the private sector to utilise its professional skills, creativity and ability to innovate, which can be extended to the public sector.

It is often claimed that PPI projects have a lower likelihood of construction delays or cost overruns since the contract terms and conditions are fixed before work begins and the private company in the project bears most of the risks of construction delays and additional costs. The private company maintains and operates the newly constructed facilities for 10–30 years. Therefore, it undertakes construction with a long-term perspective, starting with the design stage.

Finally, PPI provides a stable and long-term investment opportunity for the private sector. The PPI system can mobilise more capital than the government can do alone by eliciting extra capital to invest in PPI projects from pension funds as well as the private sector. PPI will not only help the circular flow of money in the economy by inviting private capital which is looking for investment opportun-ities into public projects, but will also enhance economic growth and competitiveness.

The above rationale can be a reality when PPIs are properly formulated and managed. Thus the Korean government has endeavoured to establish a well functioning PPI system.

An outline of the South Korean PPI system

Legal frameworks

To engage in a PPI process requires governments to define a clear legal and policy framework and to ensure that the appropriate capacity exists within the government to initiate and manage such projects.

Before August 1994, private participation in infrastructure projects was brought about with individual laws such as a road act or port act. In order to remove the impediments to private participation in infrastructure, the Korean government enacted 'The Act on Promotion of Private Capital into Social Overhead Capital Investment' in August 1994.

The limited success of the initial effort and the effect of the Asian financial crisis of 1997 led the government to revise the act in 1998 as 'The Act on Private Participation in Infrastructure'. The goal of the new PPI Act was to provide more incentives for the private sector to participate in PPI projects. It introduced an unsolicited project- and risk-sharing scheme that was missing from the 1994 act.

The amendment to the 1998 PPI Act of January 2005 introduced the BTL scheme and diversified the types of facility available for development from 35 to 44. Also, the PPI organisations were consolidated as the Public and Private Infrastructure Investment Management Center (PIMAC) of the Korea Development Institute (KDI), which is a leading think-tank in Korea.

The hierarchy of the legal and administrative framework of PPI system is as follows: PPI Act – PPI Act Enforcement Decrees – Basic PPI Plan – PPI Guideline. The PPI Act and the PPI Act Enforcement Decrees are the principal components of the legal framework of PPI. The act is a special act that takes precedence over other acts, in which PPI projects are exempt from strict regulations in national property management and a special purpose company (SPC) is allowed to play the role of a competent authority.

The PPI Act directs the Ministry of Strategy and Finance (MOSF) and PIMAC to issue an annual PPI plan that provides detailed and practical guidelines for implementing PPI projects. They are:

- The yearly focus of PPI policy;
- Details of PPI project implementation procedure;
- Financing and refinancing guidelines;
- Risk allocation and minimum revenue guarantee;
- Payment of government subsidy;
- Directions for documentation.

As the legal framework is very important for the success of the PPI system, the Korean government tried to set a solid one for both adherence to international standards and a clear and consistent implementation procedure regulated by the PPI Act and implementation guidelines. The legal framework was designed to provide for the fair and equal treatment of both domestic and foreign investors.

Organisations

Building proper institutional capacity to create, manage and evaluate PPI projects is a critical element in supporting an efficient PPI scheme. A dedicated PPI unit should be established to create a knowledge centre that can provide individual departments with technical assistance. As in most other countries, Korea has located the PPI unit within its finance ministry.

The MOSF is responsible for managing the PPI Act, the enforcement decree and the basic PPI plan, and for preparing the draft budget for

PPI projects. Under the PPI Act, the PPI Review Committee (PRC) is organised and managed by the MOSF. The Committee members are composed of the Minister of Strategy and Finance (chairperson), vice ministers of the ministries in charge of implementing PPI projects and private experts.

The main responsibilities of the PRC are deliberations on the following:

- Establishment of major PPI projects;
- Designation and cancellation of large PPI projects (total project cost with KRW 200 billion or above);
- Formulation and modification of the Request of Proposals for a large PPI projects;
- Designation of a concessionaire for large projects;
- Other matters which the Minister of Strategy and Finance proposes for the active promotion of PPI projects.

In order to provide comprehensive and professional support for the implementation of PPI projects, PIMAC was established under the PPI Act. An affiliated body of the KDI, PIMAC was established in January 2005 as a merger of the Public Investment Management Center (also PIMAC) at KDI and the Private Infrastructure Investment Center of Korea (PICKO) at the Korea Research Institute for Human Settlement (KRIHS). As a result of the merger PIMAC can establish its position as a competent institution. The purpose of the move seems to have been to isolate PIMAC more clearly from political influence, in order to enable it to take a more objective approach (Yescombe 2007).

The main functions of the PIMAC include the execution of Pre-Feasibility Studies (PFS) and Reassessment Studies of Feasibility (RFS) on large-scale publicly financed projects, for which comprehensive research is conducted on the basis of economic and policy analyses. As a think-tank, PIMAC produces various reports and policy recommendations on improving the public investment system in Korea.

On the other hand, PIMAC supports the government in developing policies and plans on PPPs and in implementing PPIs. PIMAC conducts VFM tests and lends assistance in the designation of concessionaires. This is done through support in formulating requests for proposals, evaluation of project proposals and negotiations with potential concessionaires. PIMAC is also in charge of the capacity-building of public officials and provides support for foreign investors through investment consultation.

When PIMAC was established, the number of staff was around 30 but this had risen to around 80 by late 2009. The staff includes economists, financial specialists, accountant, lawyers and engineers.

The role of PIMAC is vital to the success of any PPI scheme. In sum, the duties of PIMAC in the PPI system can be classified as research, development and market promotion. As a researcher, PIMAC formulates the annual PPI plan, studies theoretical and policy problems of the PPI system and advises government agencies on project management. As a developer, PIMAC reviews and executes feasibility studies for PPI projects, supports VFM testing and the formulation of request for proposals (RFPs), assists in tendering and negotiating and reviews the calculation of refinancing gains. As a market promoter, PIMAC consults foreign investors, provides support for inducing foreign capital to be invested in the Korean PPI market, develops education programmes on the PPI system, promotes international cooperation and undertakes database management.

Implementation Schemes

Various types of contractual schemes including build-own-operate (BOO), build-operate-transfer (BOT), build-transfer-operate (BTO) and build-transfer-lease (BTL) can be applied to PPIs. Among these, BTO and BTL are the two most common methods that the Korean government has adopted, since it prefers ownership of infrastructures built by the private sector to be transferred to government. Through the two methods, private builders are granted contracts to construct roads, railways, ports, schools and social welfare facilities at their own expense and to operate them to earn income, with ownership transferred to the government after a given period. The basic structure of the two schemes can be shown in Figure 3.1.

The differences between BTO and BTL schemes are as follows:

- For BTOs, the concessionaire collects user fees to recover project costs and an agreed internal rate of return (IRR);
- For BTLs, the government pays the unitary charge covering the construction costs inclusive of profit and operating costs;
- BTOs are used for highways, ports, railways and environmental facilities;
- BTLs comprise schools and welfare and cultural facilities;
- BTOs are subject to high risks and high returns;
- BTL are subject to low risks and low returns.

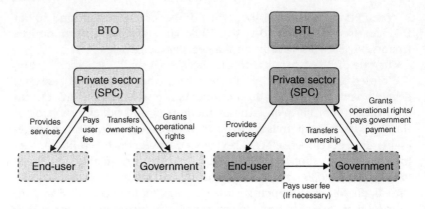

Figure 3.1   Basic structures of BTO and BTL schemes

Note: A special purpose company (SPC) is a legal entity which is to be designated as a con-cessionaire upon the award of a PPP contract.

Source: Data taken from pimac.kdi.re.kr/eng/policy/private.jsp

Eligible infrastructure types

The PPI Act defines 47 types of eligible infrastructure facilities in 15 categories, which fall under any of the following sectors: road, rail-way, port, communications facilities, water resources facilities, energy facilities, environment facilities, logistics, airport, culture and tourism, military housing, education facilities, forest, public rental housing and welfare facilities. Eligible infrastructure types are shown in Table 3.1.

Incentives

Various incentives are offered to induce private investment in the Korean PPI system. Incentives include tax benefits, land expropriation, infrastruc-ture credit guarantees and compensation on termination and for bidding.

Tax benefits

Various preferential tax rates are applied to PPI projects including the following:

- 0 per cent tax rate is applied on value added tax for construction services for BTO and BTL projects;
- 5 per cent of the amount invested is recognised as investment reserve and thus considered as expenses when imposing corporate taxes;
- The acquisition tax and registration tax for BOT projects are exempt;

- A separate tax rate of 14 per cent is applied to the interest income generated from the infrastructure bonds with 15 years of maturity or longer;
- A separate tax rate is applied to dividends from infrastructure fund investment: 5 per cent on invested amounts below 300 million won and 14 per cent above 300 million won.[1]

Table 3.1 Eligible infrastructure types

Sector	Infrastructure type
Road (3)	Road and ancillary facilities, off-road parking facilities, intelligent transportation systems
Rail (3)	Railways, railway facilities, urban railways
Port (3)	Port facilities, fishing port facilities, eligible facilities for new port construction
Airport (1)	Airport facilities
Water resources (3)	Multi-purpose dam, river-affiliated ancillary structures, waterworks
Communications (5)	Telecommunication facilities, information communication systems, information super-highway, map information systems, general city infrastructure
Energy (3)	Electricity supply facilities, gas supply facilities, collective energy facilities
Environmental (5)	Sewage treatment facilities and public livestock waste-water treatment facilities, waste disposal facilities, waste-water treatment facilities, recycling facilities, public waste-water treatment facilities
Logistics (2)	Distribution complexes and cargo terminals, passenger terminals
Culture and Tourism (10)	Tourist site or complex, youth training facilities, public sports facilities, libraries, museum and art galleries, international conference facilities, culture centres, science museums, urban parks, professional training facilities
Education (1)	School facilities
National defence (1)	Military housing facilities
Housing (1)	Public rental housing
Welfare (4)	Senior homes and welfare medical facilities, public health and medical facilities, childcare facilities, welfare facilities for the disabled
Forestry (2)	Natural recreational resorts, arboretums

Note: The figure in parenthesis is the number of types in each category.

Source: Data taken from pimac.kdi.re.kr/eng/policy/private.jsp

Land expropriation

Private investors are granted the right to expropriate land and use national and public land without charge. In most BTL projects, the government acquires and secures project sites in advance.

Infrastructure Credit Guarantee Fund

The Infrastructure Credit Guarantee Fund issues credit guarantees for PPI project finance to ensure timely of debt servicing.

Compensation on termination

When a contract is terminated during the construction or operation period due to unavoidable circumstances, the government compensates upon request from the concessionaire in exchange for the operational rights of the facility, as stipulated in the PPP Act.

Compensation for bidding costs

To encourage the private sector to participate actively in BTL project bidding, the government partly reimburses the project proposal costs of unsuccessful bidders.

Procurement procedure and steps

Value for money test (VFM)

The VFM test was introduced in Korea in 2005. The PPI Act stipulates the implementation of the VFM test. The aim of the test is that a PPI option should be pursued only when it delivers value for money. VFM is the optimum combination of the whole life cost and sufficient quality to meet the user's requirements and investment objectives.

Conducting a feasibility study and assessing VFM are done by comparing PPI against a public sector comparator (PSC) to test if PPI procurement improves the value for taxpayers' money. The competent authority uses VFM reports as basic material to make a judgement on whether to move forward with the PPI project proposed by the private proponent.

The VFM test has been tightly controlled by PIMAC since 2005. The test is carried out according to the following phases:

- Phase 1: feasibility study for the decision to invest in a project (i.e. whether a project is worth the social benefit);
- Phase 2: VFM assessment for decision to implement through PPI;
- Phase 3: formulation of a PPI alternative to present a best implementation practice.

Pre-feasibility study (PFS)

PFS is a short and brief evaluation of a project to produce information for a budgetary decision as stipulated by the National Finance Act. It was introduced in 1999 and is conducted by PIMAC. The aim of PFS is to enhance fiscal productivity through launching large-scale public investment projects based on transparent and objective ex-ante project evaluations.

All new large-scale projects with total costs amounting to 50 billion won or more are subject to PFS. Before the National Finance Act, PFS was centred on infrastructure projects, but it has since expanded to non-infrastructure (e.g. R&D) projects. PPI projects which are proposed by local governments are also subject to PFS if the central government subsidy exceeds 30 billion won. Typically, building projects and legally required facilities are exempted from PFS.

The PSC test is carried out according to the following stages. The first stage is a benefit-cost analysis (B/C). If B/C > 1, then the proposal moves to the next stage – the VFM test. If VFM > 0, this means that the PPI project is more cost effective than traditional procurement in terms of the fiscal burden, so the proposal is moved to the next stage. In the third stage, a PSC test identifies the optimal cost, toll level, fiscal support, etc.

Procurement steps

The procurement steps are quite complicated. Detailed procurement steps can be seen in Figures 3.2 and 3.3. BTO projects can be divided into solicited and unsolicited projects. For solicited projects, the competent authority identifies a project for private investment and announces an RFP. In response to the request, a private company submits a project proposal, and the competent authority examines and designates it as a PPP project. For unsolicited projects, RFP are submitted by a private company, and the competent authority examines and designates it as a PPP project.

Private investment trends

The amount of money invested in PPIs to complement public investment has increased rapidly. In 1998, the amount was only 0.5 trillion won. But this figure had increased to 3.7 trillion won in 2008. The share of PPI to public investment increased from 3.9 per cent in 1998 to 18.0 per cent in 2008 as shown in Table 3.2. The overall scale of the PPI programme is very large, comparable to that of the UK.

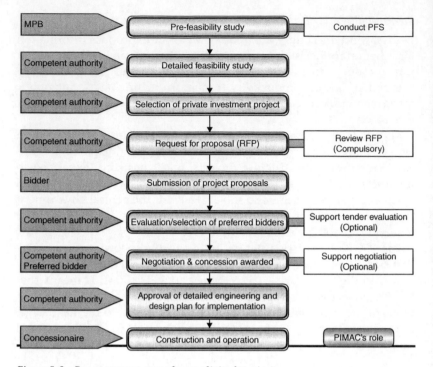

Figure 3.2   Procurement steps for a solicited project
Source: Data taken from Kim (2007).

PPI investment comprises primarily BTO and BTL. The total project costs of signed BTO projects as of April 2009 amount to 48.7 trillion won. Roads, railways and ports are major parts of the programme. Meanwhile, the total project costs of signed BTL projects which had been announced as RFPs as of the same month amounted to 19.4 trillion won. Among 345 projects, 263 had been signed, amounting to 13.3 trillion won. The figures for various sectors are shown in Table 3.3.

The distribution of solicited and unsolicited projects in various BTO sectors is shown in Table 3.4. A notable feature in the table is the high number of environmental projects. Of the 170 projects, 77 are unsolicited comprising 45 per cent of the total.

The high number of unsolicited projects is often interpreted as evidence of poor capacity on the part of the PPI authority, especially in economically disadvantaged regions. It illustrates the capacity of the private

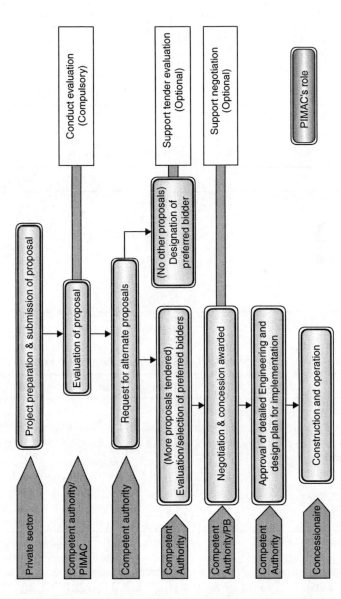

Figure 3.3 Procurement steps for an unsolicited project

Source: Data taken from Kim (2007).

Table 3.2   PPI investment trends (trillion won)

	1998	2000	2002	2004	2006	2007	2008
Public Investment in Infrastructure (A)	12.7	15.2	16.0	17.4	18.4	18.4	20.5
PPI Investment (B)	0.5	1.0	1.2	1.7	2.9	3.3	3.7
B/A (%)	3.9	6.6	7.5	9.8	15.8	17.9	18.0
B/(A+B) (%)	3.8	6.2	7.0	8.9	13.6	15.2	15.3

Source: Data taken from Lee (2009).

Table 3.3   BTO and BTL projects by facility type (trillion won)

	BTO	BTL
Road	28.9 (59%)	
Rail (Railway)	10.0 (21%)	2.4 (12%)
Port	6.1 (12%)	
Educational		7.2 (37%)
Environmental		5.4 (28%)
Military		3.1 (16%)
Cultural, welfare, etc		1.3 (7%)
Other	3.7 (8%)	

Source: Data taken from Lee (2009).

Table 3.4   Distribution of BTO projects as of December 2007 (trillion won)

Phase	Road	Rail	Port	Environment	Others	Total
National projects						
Solicited	10	7	12	1	10	40 (27.8)
Unsolicited	21	3	7	6	2	39 (27.5)
Competent authority projects						
Solicited	9	–	–	17	27	53 (2.0)
Unsolicited	4	–	–	28	6	38 (2.6)
Total	44	10	19	52	45	170 (59.9)

Source: Data taken from Lee (2009).

sector to opportunistically abuse the procurement guidelines (UM and Dinghem 2005).

The distribution of the various BTL sectors is shown in Table 3.5. Social infrastructure such as educational facilities and sewage systems comprises the major BTL projects.

Table 3.5   Distribution of BTL projects

	Number	Amount (trillion won)
Schools	136	5.3
University dormitories	14	0.9
Vocational colleges	3	0.1
Sewage systems	61	4.3
Military quarters	37	2.9
Cultural facilities	24	0.6
Medicare and welfare	9	0.1
Railways	1	2.3
Science museums	3	0.07
Total	288	16.5

Source: Data taken from Lee (2009).

Innovations: Upgrading procurement schemes

Incentives for more investment

The legal, institutional, procedural and regulatory frameworks are critical for the success of PPI projects. Government support or incentives to private companies are seen as necessary to induce private investment.

Government support or incentives can be divided into two types: financial and legal. The most general forms of financial supports are tax incentives and subsidies. As noted above, tax incentives for BOT projects include:

- Acquisition and registration taxes on real estate are exempted;
- No value added tax is imposed for construction services;
- Tax reductions are applied for infrastructure.

The government may also grant a construction subsidy to the concessionaire, if it is required to maintain the user fee at a reasonable level. The land compensation cost is usually borne by the government. The maximum construction subsidy, as rule of thumb, is 30 per cent for roads and 40 per cent for metro rails.

Legal support is largely related to land acquisition by the concessionaire. As noted above, the concessionaires are granted land expropriation rights for construction. National and public property in the designated area may be sold to the concessionaire. Concessionaires are allowed to use national or public property without charge or at a reduced price.

The Korean government's fiscal commitment to construction subsidies and land acquisition payments amounts to 18.0 trillion won (more than 38 per cent of the total cost) for the 145 BTO projects awarded. Total public financing steadily increased since the early stage of PPI to a peak in 2007.

However, these incentives may not be sufficient to attract enough private investment, especially foreign investment. The worldwide economic recession in recent years may weaken the incentives even more. To cope with the changing PPI market situation, the Korean government continuously revises incentives for private investment in public infrastructure.

Minimum revenue guarantees (MRGs)

PPI is a scheme of risk sharing between the public and private sectors. In periods of recession private companies hesitate to take over the risk from public investment. So, after the Asian financial crisis of 1997, the Korean government introduced MRGs to boost private investment.

MRGs may induce many private investments, but they also bring the danger of inducing private investment with little VFM. MRGs are criticised because they lead to an inflated demand forecast, which will result in increased MRG payments and cause a large budgetary burden. The amount of money due to MRGs was 65.3 billion won in 2002. This tripled to 185.2 billion won in 2006.

The government's financial burden due to MRGs brought about a modification of the MRG mechanism and in 2006 they were abolished for unsolicited projects. For solicited projects the government reduced the guarantee period from 15 years to 10 and also reduced the maximum guarantee limit from 90 per cent of forecast revenue to 75. In addition, to prevent inflated demand forecasts, MRGs apply only to projects with over 50 per cent of the forecast revenue. The modifications to MRGs are summarised in Table 3.6.

The annual number of concession agreements increased after the introduction of MRGs in 1999. However, since MRG support was abolished for unsolicited proposals in 2006, PPI has decreased sharply. In spite of the decrease in PPI, MRG was still severely criticised as a mechanism which caused an excessive budgetary burden. In August 2009, the MOSF announced plans to abolish MRGs and replace them with a new model for guaranteeing the amount of money which private companies spent on PPI projects. The new model is intended to reduce the government's budgetary burden while preventing excessive profit taking from unsolicited proposals.

Table 3.6 Modification of the MRG mechanism

	May 2003–December 2005	Starting in January 2006	
		Solicited projects	Unsolicited projects
Period	15 years	10 years	
Guarantee	First 5 years: 90% Next 5 years: 80% Last 5 years: 70%	First 5 years: 75% Last 5 years: 65%	Abolished
Condition	Revenue > 50% forecast revenue		

Source: Data taken from MOSF and KDI (2008b).

Improvements in the procurement scheme

In Korean PPI, it is often pointed out that the weaknesses of the concession agreements results from their deficient design. A high number of unsolicited projects are the result of the poor capacity of the competent authorities. They are the result of a hurried process and questionable advice, combined with limited experience. In this regard, the importance of regulation with the strongest possible legal grounding cannot be over-emphasised. To improve PPI selection criteria, it is essential both to provide detailed guidelines for initial concession design and to evaluate government support.

It has also been pointed out that the PPI process is complex, time consuming and politically sensitive. UM and Dinghem (2005) proposed the following five measures to improve the procurement of PPI in Korea:

• Make a two-stage bidding process compulsory for large and complex PPI projects to reduce bidding costs and to improve quality of PPI proposals;
• Introduce more stringent regulations on unsolicited proposals to make unsolicited projects not the norm but the exception;
• Introduce more stringent regulation on the formation of consortia to eliminate unnecessary shareholders' conflicts in implementing PPI projects;
• Enhance regulatory oversight on PPI contracts to avoid deficient PPI performance;
• Shift government support from construction firms to project developers in order to foster world class project developers in Korea.

Fostering competition

There has been criticism of the lack of competition in the Korean PPI system. The market is dominated by a few big construction companies.[2] As a result, the average bidding rate tends to be low compared to most industrialised countries.

Competition in the bidding process improves the bargaining position of the government and prevents opportunistic (monopolistic) behaviour on the part of the private bidders. Thus, competition in the bidding process helps a government to attain better VFM. Once a contract is concluded, competition ensures that the private partner delivers the agreed VFM because competition prevents moral hazards and limits the capacity of the private partners to force the government to renegotiate its terms. In the absence of competition, the government may, in effect, continue to carry the risk even when it has been transferred to the private company according to the PPP contract (OECD 2008).

PPI can result in a monopoly situation and higher costs to public users of infrastructure services. To promote competition in PPI, a solid legal framework corresponding to international standards and clear and consistent implementation procedure must be regulated by the PPI Act. Implementation guidelines should be set for fair and equal treatment of domestic and foreign investors.

Since competition in PPI projects is limited due to high tendering costs, in order to boost it, the Korean government simplified the documents required for proposals in 2005 and started to give compensation for project preparation costs in 2007. For solicited projects, the government covers the cost of the feasibility study and preliminary and final designs. For unsolicited projects, a part of the preparation costs of the second-best bidder can be reimbursed. As a result, the average bidding rates rose from 1.2 in 2001, 1.3 in 2003 and 1.8 in 2004 to 3.0 in 2005 and 3.5 in 2007 (Kim 2008).

Maintaining fiscal health

As in other countries, in Korea PPI schemes are accused of transferring the fiscal burden to the next generation. It is claimed that BTO tends to reduce construction costs by utilising future toll revenues. And it is also asserted that BTL is merely a lease contract for future payment. But because these figures do not appear in government budgetary sheets, it is claimed that PPI is a way to shift part of the government's debt off its books, particularly when faced with a fixed ratio of acceptable public sector indebtedness. Thus questions about inter-generational equity are raised frequently.

The Korean government's fiscal commitment to construction subsidy and land acquisition payment amounts to 18.0 trillion won (more than 38 per cent of the total cost) for the 145 BTO projects awarded. Total public financing steadily increased from the early stage of PPI to a peak in 2007.

The MOSF sets the investment ceiling for BTL projects for the current fiscal year and reports this to the National Assembly with the annual budget, since the present value of future payments should be counted in its liabilities. The fiscal implications of PPI projects have to be assessed and incorporated in decisions about the choice between PPIs and traditional government procurement.

The Airport Express that currently links Gimpo Airport to Incheon International Airport has become a black hole for taxpayers' money, operating only near-empty trains since it opened in March 2007. The number of users of the route, which was built by PPI, is less than 10 per cent of what the government had anticipated. This has resulted in the government having to pay hundreds of millions of won every day to private contractors so they can keep the railway operating.

In order to reduce the future financial burden of PPI, in the Five-year National Fiscal Management Plan of 2007–2011, the Korean government set a fiscal rule limiting the size of PPI programme. Following UK practice, the total annual government payment on PPI projects should be less than 2 per cent of total government expenditure. The current forecast on PPI projects suggests that the figure will reach 1.6–1.9 per cent (MOSF and KDI 2008b). Thus government seeks to balance short-term fiscal benefits of concessions and the long-term fiscal costs.

Transparency and political support

It may be claimed that PPPs give private investors the opportunity to make profits by providing services that could be provided more cost effectively by the public sector (Flinders 2005; Yescombe 2007). In fact, considerable risks of 'capture' by private companies can be seen especially in unsolicited proposals.

To ease public notions of 'private profits at public expense', PPI projects must originate from a robust government planning process so that they represent priority investments for the country. To prevent captures, PPI projects must be carried out with long-term national plans in mind. For road projects, they should be checked for whether they are included in the national land development plan or transport plan. The priority among roads needs to be examined, and B/C analysis and VFM test must be published.

A comprehensive disclosure requirement is also needed for PPI projects. PPI projects should be reported to the National Assembly with the Five-year National Fiscal Management Plan.[3] PPI projects may be withdrawn if government annual expenditure fails to comply with the safeguard ceiling. Detailed guidelines for implementing the ceiling and centralised information and management systems should be developed.

Public antipathy towards PPIs is growing in Korea. It is claimed that higher tolls are charged for roads built by BTO and higher fees for halls of residence built by BTL. This antipathy is aggravated by comparing relatively low public infrastructure fees in early PPI projects with generous guarantees.

To address the public's antipathy to PPI projects, strong political commitment and a stabilised institutional framework, with strong leadership, are required to overcome unnecessary antipathy to PPI projects.

Conclusion

In order to provide public services during periods of fiscal stress, public authorities will need to be more innovative in financial matters, possibly relying less on tax revenues and more on utilising the private capital market in financing public investments. PPI schemes were invented as an effective means to expand economic and social infrastructure investments given a limited government budget, through the leverage effects of government incentives.

PPI was developed in the UK as PFI and is now widespread across the world as perhaps the most innovative financing method for public sector capital investment. South Korea has rapidly adopted and developed PPIs and is now the second most active country in applying PPP after the UK.

A significant feature of Korean PPI schemes is the high number of unsolicited projects and MRGs, even though these should be the exception not the norm. The two measures have encouraged projects to be built in order to foster strong economic growth. However, many unsolicited projects with MRGs were commissioned without an adequate VFM test. This resulted in an excessive number of infrastructural investments with low VFM and an unnecessarily high future burden on the public finances. Thus, the Korean government abolished MRGs for unsolicited projects in 2006 and announced the replacement of the MRG mechanism with an alternative cost reimbursement scheme.

Nevertheless, there are still many features of Korea's PPI system that need to be improved for future success. PPI projects must be operated in a legal and regulatory system where transparency is present. Government budgets should provide detailed information on government guarantees and contingent liabilities. Feasibility studies should be taken more seriously in order to reduce the operational risk involved in PPP projects. The government should improve the criteria for selection between PPI projects and traditional public procurement and between solicited projects and unsolicited projects. It must also provide detailed guidelines for initial concession design and evaluate optimal government support.

To cope with changing PPI market situations, the Korean government must continuously revise incentives and the MRG mechanism to encourage private investment in public infrastructure. To boost competition, the government must simplify the documents required for proposals. In order to meet international standards, it should record the values of PFIs/PPPs on the public sector balance sheet to indicate the levels of net public sector debt and the consequential burden on the public finances. To assure strong political support the Korean government should seek to balance short-term fiscal benefits of concessions and the long-term fiscal costs of PPIs.

Notes

1. The exchange rate between the US dollar and the Korean won is US$1 to 1200 won in October 2009.
2. In July 2005 small and medium construction companies warned the central government that they might boycott public-private development projects unless the government changes the rules to make it easier for smaller companies to participate. Many small builders are saying that they will be unable to participate in the bidding process that requires bidders to use their own money to create a proposal, which usually makes up 2–4 per cent of a project's total costs.
3. Since the beginning of April 2009 the European Union has required the values of PFIs/PPPs to be recorded on the public sector balance sheets to indicate the levels of net public sector debt and the consequential burden on the public finances of member states. However, the Korean government had not adopted the measure as of late 2009.

References

Flinders, Matthew (2005) The Politics of Public–Private Partnerships, *The British Journal of Politics and International Relations*, 7 (2): 215–239.

Grimsey, Darrin and Lewis, Mervyn K. (2004) *Public Private Partnerships: The Worldwide Revolution in Infrastructure Provision and Project Finance.* Cheltenham: Edward Elgar.

Kim, Jay-Hyung (2007) *Institutional Settings for Public-Private Partnerships in Korea.* Korea Development Institute.

Kim, Kang-Soo (2008) *PPP Regulation and Promotion in Korea.* PIMAC: Korea Development Institute.

Lee, Myoung Sun (2009) *Private Participation in Infrastructure in Korea.* Republic of Korea: Ministry of Strategy and Finance.

MOSF and KDI (2008a) *Korean BTL: Public – Private Partnerships in Infrastructure.* Ministry of Strategy and Finance and Korea Development Institute.

MOSF and KDI (2008b) *Building a Better Future through Public – Private Partnerships in Infrastructure in Korea.* Ministry of Strategy and Finance and Korea Development Institute.

OECD (2008) *Public-Private partnerships: In Pursuit of Risk Sharing and Value for Money.* OECD.

UM, Paul Noumba and Severine Dinghem (2005) *Private Participation in Infrastructure in the Republic of Korea,* World Bank Policy Research Working Paper 3689.

Yescombe, E. R. (2007) Public-Private Partnerships: Principle of Policy and Finance. London: Elsevier.

4
The Distinctive Financing of Road Infrastructures in Spain: Evolution and Innovation

Basilio Acerete

Introduction

In Spain, as in the majority of Western countries, the development of transport infrastructures, especially roads, has been dependent on public authorities. Nevertheless, the participation of private partners in the construction, financing and management of transport infrastructures is an 'old friend'.

Spain was an early developer of direct toll motorways. This sector has evolved in terms of the financing tools and the corresponding support given by public authorities to make these projects financially sound. In the last decade, direct toll motorways (tolls being paid directly by drivers) have coexisted with shadow toll motorways, for which tolls are paid by the government (and so indirectly by taxpayers) on the basis of the volume of traffic. From the Spanish point of view, shadow tolls seem an innovative method of financing that tries to avoid rejection of direct tolls by citizens. Additionally, the central government and many Spanish autonomous communities have created public entities to carry out public infrastructure projects, trying to utilise private expertise in promoting the public interest and managing financial resources coming from traditional public sector borrowing.

The extensive experience of Spanish companies in the development of direct toll motorways has allowed them to export their know-how to many countries abroad, with projects developed in Europe and Latin and North America. To show the importance of the Spanish toll sector, we can reveal that there are six Spanish concessionaires in the top ten international concession companies (Public Works Financing 2008).

The objective of this chapter is to explore the Spanish case of the financing of roads, analysing each stage of its development and assessing the nature and extent of innovation and the factors driving it. It will focus on the financial tools applied and the engagement of public administrations in providing financing solutions to the problems that arise during this challenging process. Concessionaires of direct toll motorways paid for by drivers guide the content of the chapter, as shadow toll concessions have represented a much smaller part of the Spanish toll sector so far. Given the important implications of transport infrastructures all over the world and the increased interest in the use of private finance, the analysis included in this chapter contributes to an informed study of the use of direct toll motorways, based on the contribution of the Spanish experience to international financing management knowledge.

To analyse the financial aspects of direct toll concessions, we have collected financial information of the Spanish toll motorway sector from either: the financial statements of the companies or the annual report about the sector by the body that represents the central government in its dealings with the concessionaires,[1] an organisation dependent on the Ministry of Public Works. The list of concessionaires analysed is shown in Table 4.1 and includes toll motorways (24) and toll tunnels (4). The parent construction or infrastructure management group that has the controlling interest in each toll concessionaire is also listed.

Figure 4.1 and Table 4.2 show the evolution of the length of high-capacity roads and toll roads in Spain. The length of the network of direct toll motorways and the number of concessionaires has increased since 1969, from one concessionaire and 32 kilometres to 28 concessionaires and nearly 3250 kilometres. The data about the distribution of the shareholding and funding structures of concessionaires are shown in Table 4.3. Table 4.4 includes other commercial and financing data such as the value of annual investment, toll revenues, operating and financing costs, results, returns on equity and other figures interesting for comparative analysis. Dividends paid and their percentages over the share capital and annual profit are included in Table 4.5 and, finally, Table 4.6 shows the classification of international toll operators.

In 1969, the first direct toll motorway was opened. At the time of writing, 2007 is the latest year for which financial information is available. Since the history of the sector started 40 years ago, for the sake of clarity, we have included data only for the most relevant years.

Table 4.1 Toll concessionaires' main characteristics

Parent group	Concessionaire	Length (km)	Date open to traffic
Direct toll motorways			
Abertis	Acesa	541.5	1969
	Iberpistas	69.6	1972
	Aumar	467.6	1974
	Aucat*	56.3	1992
	Castellana	50.8	2002
	AULESA	38.0	2002
Abertis – Sacyr	AVASA	294.4	1978
	Accessos de Madrid	91.5	2003
Sacyr	Guadalcesa	–	–
Itínere	Europistas	84.3	1971
	Aucalsa	86.8	1983
	Audasa	218.9	1979
	Autoestradas*	57.8	1997
	AUDENASA*	112.6	1976
ACS	HENARSA	85.5	2003
	Ciralasa	53.5	2007
Cintra	Ausol	102.2	1999
	AUTEMA*	43.1	1989
	Autopista Madrid-Levante	177.0	2006
	Autopista Madrid-Sur	99.1	2004
Global Via	ACEGA	56.6	2002
	AUCOSTA	114.0	2007
OHL	Autopista Eje-Aeropuerto	8.8	2001
Construction companies	AUSUR	76.6	2005
	Autopista Madrid-Toledo	81.0	2007
Autonomous communities	BIDEGI*	87.4	2003
	INTERBIAK*	36.2	2003
	Total	3191.1	1969
Toll tunnels			
Autonomous comm.	TABASA	16.7	1991
Abertis	Túnel del Cadí	29.7	1985
Itínere	Túneles de Artxanda	3.0	1997
Global Vía	Túnel de Sóller	3.0	2002
	Total	52.4	–

Note: *These concessionaires entered into a contract with autonomous communities; the other contracts were awarded by the central government.

Source: Author.

In the case of public corporations, we have used a descriptive approach to show the process that public administrations follow to establish these entities and the financial implications behind this framework.

Evolution of Spanish toll roads and the establishment of public corporations

The development of transport infrastructures in Spain has traditionally been dependent on public authorities and resources. Nevertheless, the participation of private initiative by means of direct toll concessions paid by users for the financing, construction and management of roads has been so very important that Spain, France and Italy constitute what has been called the 'Europe of toll'.[2] The participation of private initiative has been especially important when the state has suffered a lack of resources to build new infrastructures.

Figure 4.1 shows the length of the direct toll motorway network. It has increased throughout the sample. Nevertheless, there were some years when investment in new projects was brought to a standstill (in 1979–1982, 1985–1988 and the early mid-1990s), so the length did not increase in those years.

In Table 4.2, we see the evolution of the relative importance of direct toll motorways in the framework of Spanish high-capacity roads.[3] Until

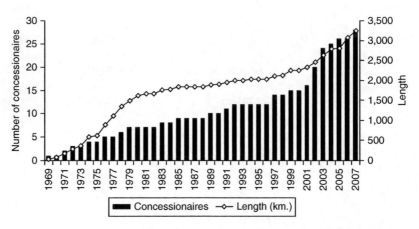

Figure 4.1   Evolution of number of concessionaires and length of direct toll motorways

Source: Based on the annual reports of Delegación del Gobierno en las Sociedades Concesionarias de Autopistas Nacionales de Peaje.

Table 4.2 Importance of direct toll motorways in the Spanish high-capacity road network

Year	Total high capacity roads		Direct toll motorways		
	Length (km)	Variation (%)	Length (km)	Variation	As percentage of high capacity roads (%)
1970	203	–	82	–	40
1975	888	337.4	616	651.2	70
1980	1933	117.7	1622	163.3	79
1985	3170	64.0	1835	13.1	57
1990	5126	61.7	1895	3.3	37
1995	8133	58.7	2033	7.3	25
2000	10480	28.9	2251	10.7	21
2005	13156	25.5	2811	24.9	21
2007	14689	11.7	3244	15.4	21

Source: Based on Anuario Estadístico 2007 del Ministerio de Fomento.

1980, the majority of Spanish motorways were dependent on private initiative, accounting for up to 80 per cent of the length. Thereafter, the percentage starts a decline until 1995, when the total number of kilometres of high-capacity roads was four times the length it had been in 1980 but direct toll motorways represented only 25 per cent. Finally, since the mid-1990s the increase in high-capacity roads and direct toll motorways has maintained a similar path, since high-capacity roads have increased their length by more than 6500 kilometres and direct toll motorways have maintained their relative importance (21 per cent). In Spain, three phases characterise the participation of private initiative in financing and operating high-capacity roads.

The first period runs from the beginning of the Spanish direct toll motorway programme in 1967 to the early 1980s. Although the first reference to toll concessions dates back to 1928, when procurement for the first direct toll motorways was started but not carried out because of the lack of interest of private initiative, it was in the 1960s that concessions of direct toll roads started their 'long journey'. Spain's private toll road programme began with the launch of the *Programme of Spanish National Motorways* to construct 3160 kilometres of motorways. This plan tried to cover the need for better public infrastructures to boost the Spanish economy, which had grown at high rates since the beginning of 1960s, and to maintain and improve these figures. Besides, roads were a key issue for the most important national 'industry', tourism, so the need for high quality roads was a *sine qua non* for maintaining this important source of wealth.

However the Spanish state did not have enough resources to finance the programme. In spite of the economic growth, at that moment the tax system was rather inefficient and the public financing of roads requires an efficient tax system (Bel and Fageda 2009). The Spanish state decided to turn to private finance to get the resources for infrastructures that the state could not provide and, similarly to France and Italy, it decided to turn to the concessions system to carry out those projects. Unlike the French or Italian models where projects were awarded to public entities, in Spain, concessions were given to private companies.[4] The roads that were franchised were the ones most likely to be profitable, but they were isolated concessions, instead of a complete national network, and coexisted alongside free roads.

In 1972, due to the plethora of regulations (a decree was enacted for each new concession) a general law governing concessions for the construction, conservation and operation of motorways by private companies was established.[5] The most important issues included in this law were:

- A minimum equity requirement of 10 per cent (previously, it was 50 per cent);
- State loan and foreign exchange guarantees;
- State subsidies for commercially unviable projects;
- Reimbursable state advances for projects with cash-flow difficulties.

At the same time, the *Programme of Spanish National Motorways* was revised and it included new projects for up to 6340 kilometres of motorways.

Despite the transfer of responsibility to private operators, the state had to maintain some interest in these projects by means of incentives for the privately operated motorways. To a great extent, many of the financial and commercial risks of the projects were not adequately transferred to the private sector and were borne by the state (Bel and Fageda 2005). The effects of the 'exchange rate guarantee' can be highlighted. This provision has been extremely expensive for the Spanish state, as will be seen in later sections.

The economic crisis of the 1970s also affected the progress of the direct toll motorways programme. First, it caused an increase in oil prices and a reduction in the economic activity of the country and, hence, a reduction of traffic on toll motorways. This reduction of traffic was also affected by the lack of realism of the initial traffic forecasts and competition from coexisting free roads. Second, due to the liabilities of private concessionaires in foreign loans, the financial costs rose enormously and many companies in the sector made losses, which threatened their own survival. Third, the construction costs of the projects in progress also increased. As a result, the Spanish toll motorways programme was on the verge of collapsing.

Despite the 1972 plans for more than 3000 kilometres of new motorways, in 1980 only 1900 kilometres were open to traffic; of these, about 1500 kilometres were private direct toll motorways.

The second phase in the Spanish toll model was characterised by 'rationalization and restructuring' (Farrell 1997). It took place from 1982 until the mid-1990s and there was a shift in road policy: the abandonment of private initiative for building high-capacity roads and a return to public financing and management. The share of direct toll motorways within the high-capacity network decreased dramatically during the 1980s (see Table 4.2). The rationale behind this is that the state had more resources with which to finance transport infrastructures.[6] These resources came from the economic growth of the late 1980s, a more efficient tax system that permitted the increase of tax collection and the extensive funds provided by the European Economic Community through its Regional Structural Funds, which benefited the governments of the autonomous communities, especially.

The programme of direct toll motorways came to an end and a new *Plan of Dual Carriageways* was launched, based on traditional public procurement. Instead of constructing new roads, this plan considered the transformation of existing trunk roads into dual carriageways. Nevertheless, during this period, some autonomous communities' governments continued to award concessions for toll motorways.

Finally, the third phase, from the mid-1990s to the present day, can be linked to another important event on the economic scene: the process of European Monetary Union and the adoption of the Maastricht Treaty and the EU's Stability and Growth Pact criteria to comply with budgetary discipline. Both economic regulations entailed constraints in public budgets, which could no longer increase expenditure through debt financing as public procurement of infrastructures traditionally did. So the participation of private initiative in the financing and management of public infrastructures and services came on to the stage once again. In this phase, the use of private finance and tolls runs alongside an expansion of publicly procured and free motorways (see Table 4.2). As a result, by the end of 2007, nearly 3250 kilometres of direct toll motorways and 11,445 kilometres of other high-capacity roads were in operation.

Since the late 1990s, many autonomous community governments have established regulations and entered into contracts with private operators to use the shadow toll model, imported from the UK, to build road infrastructures of regional importance (Pina et al. 2003). Prior to 2001, not a single kilometre of shadow toll motorway was open to traffic, but since then there has been a rapid increase in the use of this method. In 2007, nearly 500 kilometres of shadow toll motorways were opened to traffic or on the point of being so. These concessions are funded by taxpayers on the basis of traffic volumes, so they seem like free motorways and permit the avoidance of unpopular new direct tolls. The reason for this deviation from traditional public procurement or private management was the search for an alternative method of financing new investments, thus both meeting the terms of public deficit and debt established by the Stability and Growth Pact and enabling necessary investments. Shadow toll schemes were a relatively new segment in Spain and many direct toll concessionaires have interests in shadow toll companies. Recently, this method has been extended to other public service sectors, such as hospitals and court buildings, and the central government has also used this method to finance the upgrading of old roads.

Another distinctive system in the Spanish experience of financing public projects is the so called 'Spanish model', which consists of the creation by a public administration of a separate public corporation with a structure similar to a private trading company and whose purpose is the implementation of public projects. These entities are subject to business laws and are totally, or mainly, owned by the public administration, but have the capacity to raise finance separately from the parent public authority. They act according to the mandate of the corresponding public administration and manage the construction of infrastructures and the delivery of services. To recoup the financial resources spent, the public corporation recovers the money from the parent public administration. These payments are linked to the mandate being carried out. Several autonomous communities have set up these entities and the central government has also used similar bodies for developing, for example, high speed trains.

The present *Strategic Plan of Transport Infrastructures*, drawn up by the Ministry of Public Works for the period 2005–2020, looks toward the participation of private initiative in the sector providing up to 20 per cent of funds.

In short, the long Spanish experience in the direct toll concessions' sector and all the vicissitudes mentioned above have led to the appearance of many financial models and tools. Consequently, it is interesting to know the reasons behind this so that other countries can take more informed steps in using direct toll concessions.

The financing of toll motorways in Spain

Funding and shareholding structure of toll concessionaires

Although the government regulation originally imposed a minimum of 50 per cent of equity shareholding in the financing of toll motorway projects, the revision of the regulation reduced this percentage, establishing a minimum of 10 per cent.[7] So, the financing of Spanish toll motorway concessionaires became heavily dependent on debt because loans accounted for more than 80 per cent of the resources used to finance the investments (see Table 4.3).

From the beginning of the 1980s, this situation changed and a more balanced relation between equity and liabilities was gradually achieved. From the mid-1990s, nearly 50 per cent of funds came from shareholders' resources, although, in recent years, external funds have increased again.

Regarding the composition of financing, for many years, foreign loans were crucial to the funding of the investments. The Spanish financial market suffered from a lack of resources, so the state encouraged loans from outside Spain. Until the beginning of the 1990s, foreign loans were the most important source of finance for Spanish concessionaires. For example, in 1985, foreign loans accounted for 62 per cent of the funding structure of the toll concessions' sector. In 2000, only a quarter of the funding structure was provided by finance from abroad and, in the last three years under study, this item has only a symbolic presence, falling below 1.5 per cent.

If we go deeper into the composition of the shareholding structure, we find five main forms of institutional shareholder: banks, savings banks,[8] construction companies, public administrations and toll motorway concessionaires. The degree of participation of each type of shareholder has also varied over the years (see Table 4.3).

Financial institutions (banks and savings banks) were the main shareholders in the early years of toll concessions but, at present, their rate of participation in share equity in this sector has fallen dramatically. Banks reduced their investment in concessionaires since the mid-1980s and, especially, in the late 1990s, curiously, when these companies had restructured and stabilised their commercial situation. Savings banks continued to maintain their level of participation in equity until around the early 2000s. The reason for this timing difference is that the savings

Table 4.3   Shareholding and funding structure

Year	Funding structure (%)				Shareholding structure (%)				
	Share capital	Liabilities	Foreign loans	Banks	Savings banks	Construction companies	Public administrations	Concessionaires	Other share holders
1976	18.4	81.6	47.4	43.0	20.5	18.5	0.6	–	17.4
1985	28.7	71.3	62.0	36.2	17.0	10.3	14.7	–	21.8
1990	36.8	63.2	56.5	17.8	23.6	12.1	21.8	–	24.7
1995	46.6	53.4	39.2	12.0	20.3	13.9	28.2	2.5	23.1
2000	43.8	56.2	25.0	3.8	20.4	20.0	25.2	12.0	18.6
2002	49.9	50.1	8.0	1.7	18.2	20.4	27.0	6.2	26.5
2003	48.6	51.4	3.6	4.0	20.4	30.9	7.6	6.9	30.2
2005	44.7	55.3	1.5	0.5	5.1	71.3	6.9	14.1	2.1
2007	35.4	64.6	0.2	0.2	6.3	66.0	7.7	14.7	5.1

Source: Based on annual reports of Delegación del Gobierno en las Sociedades Concesionarias de Autopistas Nacionales de Peaje.

banks are controlled by the autonomous communities' governments to some extent, so they are closer to policies implemented by regional governments and in the period 1982–1996, the few direct toll motorway projects that were submitted to tender by autonomous communities had the financial support of savings banks. Nevertheless, in the last years under study both banks and savings banks have maintained only a symbolic percentage of shareholdings in the sector.

Conversely, construction companies have recently increased their percentage in the shareholding structure of concessionaires enormously, with over 70 per cent, after nearly 35 years of maintaining only 10–20 per cent of share capital. This increase started in 2003, so a large percentage of the €6300 million invested in new direct toll motorways has been provided by existing concession companies. For many years, toll motorway concessionaires have been independent companies but, in the last decade, we have seen a process of individual companies integrating into major groups for the construction and management of infrastructures. So, as direct toll companies are controlled by construction companies, the huge benefits earned by concessionaires in the last decade have been invested in new projects by their parent groups.

Public administrations have also been a key support of the Spanish direct toll motorways sector, as will be analysed in a later section. In the very early years, public administrations did not participate in the shareholding structure; their contribution to shareholding was below 1 per cent. Nevertheless, after 1983, the participation of public administrations was crucial for the support of the toll sector, when three concessionaires (AUDASA, AUCALSA and AUDENASA) were taken over by the state because they were on the verge of bankruptcy, and new projects were launched by the governments of some autonomous communities. In 2002, 27 per cent of share equity was provided by public administrations but, since 2003, this percentage has dropped dramatically, after the central government privatised the state-held concessionaire.

Until the early 1990s, concessionaires did not maintain investments in other concessionaires (see Table 4.3). Originally, the statutory purpose of these companies was exclusively the planning, construction and operation of motorways. However, during the 1990s, the statutory purpose was extended to the possibility of managing new motorways and other activities such as operating service areas, car parks and logistic depots/hubs. Therefore, similarly to construction companies, toll concessionaires have held share capital of new concessionaires in the sector since regulations have permitted this and they have earned huge profits.

Finally, other shareholders with minority interests in concessionaires had maintained an important stake in the shareholding structure, of 15–30 per cent. But, since 2005, this rate has fallen considerably to a mere 5 per cent.

Results and financial issues of toll concessionaires

Since the very beginning of the study period, the toll revenues of the sector have seen an apparently never-ending increase (Table 4.4). This increase is linked to both the growth of the length of the network of motorways and, hence, traffic and to the annual revisions of tolls, although some initiatives have been taken in order to moderate the increase in rates. In some years, the revision of tolls was not applied and tariffs were frozen or the government individually negotiated a reduction of tolls with concessionaires with the objectives of helping to control inflation and improving the distribution of traffic by encouraging the use of toll motorways, many of which were underused while the alternative free roads were continuously congested.

Nonetheless, profits rose so much that, in 2001, the mechanism for the revision of tariffs was amended; a new formula included a cap as a way of sharing 'excess profits' between concessionaires and users. In any case, the turnover of the sector has continued to increase and, in the last available year, the 28 concessionaires earned more than €2000 million, equal to nearly 9 per cent of the total revenues since 1967, or 140 times the toll revenues of the first available year of the series.

The operating costs of these companies have maintained a moderate performance, with figures that, for most years, represent 25–35 per cent of toll revenues. This has permitted operating results to increase in line with toll revenues.

Financing costs have been one of the most important problems for Spanish toll concessionaires. As said before, initially the financing of the direct toll motorways was heavily dependent on debt, especially in the form of foreign loans. All the loans were raised in currencies such as the US dollar, Japanese yen, Deutschmark, Swiss franc and, years later, European Currency Unit (ECU). Soon after the first concessionaires started to operate, the economic crisis resulted in soaring interest rates. Moreover, the Spanish currency depreciated by 20 per cent, on average, against the majority of foreign currencies, so there was an escalation of the cost of finance. Given that these infrastructures take some years to reach an optimal level of activity and revenues, financing costs were a heavy burden for the concessionaires, threatening their survival.

As can be seen in Table 4.4, financing costs increased from the time concessions were put in place until 1985. During that time, financing costs were equal to or more than toll revenues (in 1974 and 1984, the cost of financing was almost double the toll revenues). There was no room for manoeuvre for these companies; they had to dedicate all their revenues to paying financing costs so, until 1986, the aggregated Profit Before Taxes (PBT) of the toll concessionaires' sector was negative. Some toll concessionaires maintained a negative PBT until the 1990s (AUDASA, Europistas, AUDENASA, Túnel del Cadí and AUTEMA).

From the mid-1980s, financing costs remained at more or less the same annual level, with some fluctuations, although continuously falling as a percentage of revenues. The renegotiation of foreign loans and the restructuring of the sector, with the nationalisation of some companies, permitted financing costs to fall in three years to under 50 per cent of toll revenues. In 1999, the financing expenditure recognized and the percentage of revenues used to cover financing costs dropped significantly. This is explained by a change in the accounting regulations that came into force that year for the Spanish toll roads sector, which will be explained in the next section. Nevertheless, the level of financing costs would have been higher if the state had not established guarantees for foreign loans and exchange rate insurance, which will also be analysed in the next section.

The PBT of the toll concessionaires sector did not achieve a positive value until 1987, almost 20 years after the creation of the first concessionaires. Similarly to toll revenues and operating results, since then the PBT of the sector has increased year after year, reaching more than €1239 million in 2007. If we go deeper into the individual concessionaires, we find that the old concessionaires, created in the 1970s and 1980s, achieved a positive value for PBT, on average, 12 years after their creation. In sharp contrast, some new concessionaires, set up in the 1990s and 2000s, have made profits one or two years after the opening of the toll motorways, although, others have still not achieved them after six years of operation.

Farrell (1997), with data until 1994, referring to the performance to date of the sector said: 'most Spanish motorways will make an acceptable but by no means spectacular rate of return over the whole of the concession period'. Ten years after, this assertion cannot be completely confirmed. The rate of Return on Equity (ROE) of the sector had values between 2.7 and 10.5 per cent between 1987 and 2000, and from 2001 it has maintained values over 11 per cent. The average ROE is 9.3 per cent.

Table 4.4   Financing and operating magnitudes of direct toll concessions sector

Year	Annual investment	Toll revenues	Toll revenues per km	Operating costs	Operating costs over revenues (%)
1974	126,656.7	14,718.8	25.2	3824.2	26.0
1975	207,313.7	22,448.4	36.4	5709.0	25.4
1976	305,119.4	30,607.1	34.7	6050.6	19.8
1977	303,817.0	44,163.0	39.8	13,183.2	29.9
1978	253,719.1	63,066.0	46.8	18,983.0	30.1
1979	177,551.0	79,726.7	53.3	24,392.1	30.6
1980	176,195.7	94,791.0	58.4	34,564.8	36.5
1981	111,285.8	114,986.2	68.9	42,150.2	36.7
1982	166,471.9	141,666.4	84.8	50,179.1	35.4
1983	208,524,8	165,997.7	94.5	57,804.1	34.8
1984	153,297,2	191,377.9	108.2	64,197.1	33.5
1985	56,264,3	238,852.4	130.2	74,307.9	31.1
1986	48,170.5	272,857.1	148.7	74,737.7	27.4
1987	44,950.9	331,314.5	180.6	88,621.0	26.7
1988	28,625.6	388,753.9	210.9	101,889.6	26.2
1989	181,664.3	455,755.3	242.8	117,359.6	25.8
1990	305,845.4	547,472.1	288.9	132,053.2	24.1
1991	343,822.8	623,210.5	319.9	154,702.9	24.8
1992	262,801.6	699,025.8	350.4	187,197.8	26.8
1993	195,952.8	714,477.2	357.2	194,940.1	27.3
1994	130,788.0	766,892.0	377.2	202,297.1	26.4
1995	100,955.0	822,599.3	404.6	209,379.4	25.5
1996	188,344.6	865,386.5	425.7	212,428.9	24.5
1997	430,650.4	929,360.6	440.7	221,256.6	23.8
1998	415,162.9	1,004,415.0	474.2	235,643.0	23.5
1999	316,949.7	1,103,267.7	492.1	277,002.9	25.1
2000	255,945.2	1,185,946.5	526.9	309,005.6	26.1
2001	539,638.7	1,303,239.8	560.1	360,149.9	27.6
2002	1,271,026.8	1,431,594.2	585.0	344,446.7	24.1
2003	1,131,465.7	1,489,037.4	567.5	357,369.4	24.0
2004	896,411.9	1,633,384.9	585.9	398,237.2	24.4
2005	1,127,182.0	1,735,113.7	617.3	422,122.0	24.3
2006	1,180,201.3	1,913,934.1	623.6	430,706.2	22.5
2007	692,967.7	2,090,303.5	644.4	458,362.0	21.9
Total	12,723,449.7	23,509,743.2		5,885,254.1	27.1

Source: Based on annual reports of Delegación del Gobierno en las Sociedades Concesionarias

(€ thousands)

Year	Operating result	Financing costs	Financing costs over revenues (%)	Annual exchange payments	Profit before taxes	Return on equity
1974	10,976.3	26,889.9	182.7	1602.7	–15,912.4	–
1975	16,925.1	32,100.7	143.0	383.7	–15,122.7	–
1976	21,849.8	38,686.5	126.4	16,692.3	–16,827.1	–
1977	31,274.3	56,258.3	127.4	33,922.7	–24,811.0	–
1978	46,287.5	74,366.8	117.9	58,374.0	–28,100.9	–
1979	61,503.4	113,720.5	142.6	66,312.2	–51,710.5	–
1980	66,709.3	144,869.2	152.8	54,217.1	–78,219.9	–
1981	81,805.6	204,966.2	178.3	106,783.3	–123,496.0	–
1982	103,797.6	200,687.6	141.7	137,845.3	–109,622.8	–
1983	121,760.2	181,802.6	109.5	254,723.4	–76,344.8	–
1984	142,361.1	199,317.9	104.1	326,538.3	–83,362.8	–
1985	178,951.4	216,795.9	90.8	501,653.4	–75,956.5	–
1986	212,753.5	194,928.7	71.4	217,004.4	–32,776.2	–
1987	260,479.2	179,814.4	54.3	89,818.3	38,818.8	2.7
1988	305,968.1	165,857.7	42.7	83,197.9	86,643.1	5.5
1989	354,823.7	178,784.3	39.2	45,394.3	126,553.9	8.0
1990	436,223.6	198,338.2	36.2	54,512.6	137,768.2	6.3
1991	488,276.7	191,671.2	30.8	74,435.3	186,164.1	7.0
1992	531,792.9	218,225.1	31.2	80,799.4	186,534.3	6.8
1993	540,373.6	194,468.9	27.2	162,893.9	203,961.9	7.2
1994	586,589.0	196,972.1	25.7	180,501.0	230,129.9	8.0
1995	636,149.7	192,894.2	23.4	192,578.9	311,077.9	10.5
1996	674,457.0	163,994.6	19.0	138,342.5	348,025.7	6.5
1997	731,895.7	143,322.3	15.4	117,392.6	313,738.4	5.7
1998	794,236.9	156,629.8	15.6	196,631.7	303,338.0	5.4
1999	861,357.3	81,360.2	7.4	200,939.0	516,584.9	8.8
2000	923,290.4	89,117.5	7.5	174,307.4	557,838.4	9.3
2001	1,018,598.3	118,745.5	9.1	228,193.6	656,270.8	11.3
2002	1,137,875.1	96,112.4	6.7	389,764.4	756,917.8	13.0
2003	1,192,739.9	76,615.7	5.1	273,713.2	821,723.9	12.6
2004	1,310,420.7	83,625.9	5.1	48,467.4	998,980.5	13.9
2005	1,387,310.4	80,741.2	4.7	127,798.8	1,023,589.1	13.4
2006	1,558,312.5	29,747.1	1.6	123,748.1	1,193,117.7	14.7
2007	1,704,034.4	85,322.0	4.1	529.1	1,239,716.3	18.0
Total	18,532,160.2	4,607,751.1	61.8	4,766,656.2	9,505,230.0	9.3

de Autopistas Nacionales de Peaje.

In 1997, only five companies, all of them being concessionaires set up in the 1960s–1970s, paid dividends to their shareholders. In 2007, 12 concessionaires paid dividends (Table 4.5), those mentioned above, plus those set up in the 1970s and 1980s and one created in the 1990s. In the last 12 years, dividends paid amount to €5007 million, more than the financing costs recorded over 40 years or the payments for exchange rate insurance made by the state. It is clear that it takes a very long time before toll concessionaires can pay dividends to their shareholders, due to the huge losses in the first years.

If we analyse the relation between payments of dividends and share capital since 1996, the average ROE is 17 per cent for the companies that pay dividends, ranging from 2 per cent (AUCALSA) to 68 (Iberpistas). The payout by the companies paying dividends is 85 per cent on average. Most of them maintain a very aggressive policy of payment of dividends; in some years they pay all their profits or more than 90 per cent. Only three concessionaires pay 50 per cent or less of their annual profit in dividends.

Regarding the relation between Spanish toll concessionaires and the stock market, at present, only one concessionaire is listed on the Spanish stock exchange (Europistas). Some of the other toll concessionaires are listed indirectly through their parent groups (Abertis, Cintra and Sacyr). Ten years ago, four companies were listed on the stock exchange (Europistas, Acesa, AUMAR and Iberpistas) but, in 2003, three of them merged to create one of the parent groups.

Regulation and public financial engagement with toll concessionaires

As we have seen in the history of the sector, the beginning of the Spanish toll motorway sector was fraught with difficulties. In an environment of economic crisis and reduction in traffic, with new and costly infrastructures that have no alternative use, the idea of closing the motorways was not an option and the state had to come to the rescue with subsidies for commercially unviable projects. It is difficult to know how much the public authorities have paid as operating grants in the last 40 years but, for example, in the period 2000–2005, about €438 million were paid, about 5 per cent of the toll revenues. In the same period, the state also provided about €50 million as capital grants (Acerete et al. 2009).

Operating grants have been paid not only when traffic volumes did not reach break-even levels, but also when reductions in tariffs have been agreed between the state and concessionaires. In the mid-1990s, some concessions relatively close to their end date were renegotiated. These negotiations entailed a reduction in toll charges; in return, the government compensated by extending the period of concession (usually by 13 years) and/or awarding new projects to existing concessionaires. So, concessionaires will obtain more benefits from the new projects and will continue to earn money from the existing concessions for longer.

Besides these direct payments, in 1984, three companies were nationalised and a public sector company – Empresa National de Autopistas, S.A. (ENAUSA) – was set up. In 1995, another toll concessionaire (Autoestradas) was created within this public holding group. All the concessionaires integrated into ENAUSA were privatised in 2003, so the state was directly engaged with the toll sector as a concessionaire for 20 years.

The burden of financing costs for concessionaires, as seen in the previous section, would have been heavier if the state had not provided guarantees for foreign loans and exchange rate insurance against any increase in the cost of finance raised by international loans. Otherwise, Spanish concessionaires would probably not have been able to undertake negotiations with financial institutions from abroad and toll projects would have had to wait for better times because of the lack of financial resources. The guarantees permitted private concessionaires to raise foreign loans eliminating the exchange risk because the state assumed any increase in the cost of international finance.

This has been very costly for the Spanish government but, at the same time, it has given some breathing space to toll concessionaires (see Table 4.4). The state's payments for foreign loans and exchange rate insurance increased over the years until 1985, when they reached their highest value, at more than €500 million. After that, the annual payments dropped due to renegotiation of debts and, in 1988, this insurance provision was abolished and ensuing foreign loans did not benefit from the exchange guarantee. In the last 15 years, the foreign loans' guarantee has also necessitated significant payments by the state, mainly linked to the cancellation of loans. In 2007, only €529,000 were paid, since only one foreign loan remained.

To appreciate how costly foreign loans insurance has been, the total amount paid by the state over nearly 40 years (€4766 million), amounts to a third of the total investment in toll roads (€12,723 million) (see Table 4.4).

Since 1999, the change in the Spanish accounting regulation relating to toll concessionaires has also influenced the financial costs recorded

Table 4.5   Dividends paid and percentage over annual profit and share capital

	ACESA			Europistas			Iberpistas			Aumar			AVASA			Audasa		
Year	Div.	(1)	(2)	Div.	(1)	(2)	Div.	(1)	(2)	Div.	(1)	(2)	Div.	(1)	(2)	Div.	(1)	(2)
1996	101,950	72	15	25,079	104	94	20,103	116	75	44,772	93	11	14,609	85	9	0	0	0
1997	107,046	72	14	0	0	0	20,103	81	60	35,662	100	9	15,464	197	6	0	0	0
1998	112,397	82	15	0	0	0	20,501	76	61	39,623	100	10	606	100	0	0	0	0
1999	118,021	83	15	0	0	0	20,501	63	61	55,474	82	15	5939	91	3	11,967	45	6
2000	123,918	80	15	11,889	79	4	20,506	67	12	65,374	86	16	0	0	0	0	0	0
2001	131,865	80	15	42,397	92	18	7041	21	4	25,874	100	7	29,730	101	13	14,278	45	7
2002	114,303	100	13	14,132	68	10	20,000	94	40	118,844	100	30	35,100	98	15	30,636	90	16
2003	215,381	100	25	8244	49	14	42,000	98	84	129,092	100	31	40,139	100	17	30,423	90	16
2004	245,039	100	28	49,463	88	86	40,000	85	80	139,244	100	33	45,630	100	20	33,597	90	17
2005	262,433	100	30	14,805	65	22	60,000	99	120	146,710	100	34	42,148	100	18	37,064	90	19
2006	308,134	100	35	14,805	57	22	55,000	91	110	164,935	100	38	56,146	100	24	45,920	90	23
2007	330,047	107	38	3580	39	5	55,000	70	110	165,656	68	38	75,515	88	32	50,823	61	26
Total	2,170,534	90	21	184,394	71	31	380,755	80	68	1,131,260	94	23	361,026	105	14	254,708	75	16

Notes: Div. – dividends paid.
(1) Percentage of dividends paid over annual profits (payout).
(2) Percentage of dividends paid over share capital.
Source: Based on annual reports of Delegación del Gobierno en las Sociedades Concesionarias de Autopistas Nacionales de Peaje.

(Acerete et al. 2006). As in other sectors, financial expenditures generated by funds obtained for financing construction can be incorporated into the value of the asset during the construction period. In the Spanish regulation for toll concessionaires, capitalisation of financial expenditure can continue when the motorway is opened to traffic as deferred expenditure to be recognised as an expense in future years. Therefore, since 1999, financial expenditures recorded in the financial performance statements of Spanish toll concessionaires have been lower than real expenditures, because they are calculated according to the requirements of the accounting regulation.

The explanation behind this particular treatment is that this is a sector where the financial costs are huge at the beginning of the period of concession, due to the high level of debt. Toll revenues, presumably, are lower and will increase as the years of the concession go by and the toll revenues reach an optimum level when the business is consolidated. This accounting rule is important for new toll concessions where financial expenditures are high in the early years of the concession and they can defer their recognition as expenses to later periods when the business is consolidated.

In 1997 a new *Toll Motorways Programme* was launched by the Ministry of Public Works, planning an increase of 50 per cent in the extent of toll

Aucalsa			Ausol			AUDENASA			AUTEMA			AUCAT			Autoestrad			Total		
Div.	(1)	(2)	Div.	(1)	(2)	Div.	(1)	(2)	Div.	(1)	(2)	Div.	(1)	(2)	Div.	(1)	(2)	Div.	(1)	(2)
0	0		0	0	0	0	0	0	0	0	0	0	0	0	0	0	0	206,513	83	14
0	0	0	0	0	0	974	31	1	0	0	0	0	0	0	0	0	0	179,249	82	11
0	0	0	0	0	0	1271	36	1	0	0	0	0	0	0	17	90	0	174,415	83	11
0	0	0	5375	40	4	13,890	90	8	0	0	0	0	0	0	1267	90	5	232,434	75	10
0	0	0	5582	70	4	11,222	90	7	0	0	0	3887	63	5	839	89	3	243,217	68	11
0	0	0	7002	70	5	12,818	90	8	0	0	0	10,814	66	14	1849	90	7	283,668	75	10
4962	90	2	8494	60	6	13,951	92	8	9,205	92	11	19,915	97	34	1508	90	6	391,050	95	14
4343	90	1	6269	28	4	14,971	90	9	6,163	90	8	18,490	100	19	1598	90	6	517,113	94	19
1977	90	1	7203	31	5	18,835	95	11	12,627	90	18	23,298	100	24	1872	90	7	618,785	94	23
5757	90	2	15,043	64	11	18,134	90	9	14,528	90	21	26,678	100	28	2074	90	8	645,374	96	24
10,123	90	3	15,626	70	11	15,938	73	9	15,156	90	22	27,600	85	29	2920	90	11	732,303	95	27
11,505	61	4	15,485	46	11	20,193	93	12	15,255	91	22	36,900	113	38	3181	96	12	783,140	84	29
38,667	85	2	86,079	53	7	142,197	79	8	72,934	90	17	167,582	91	24	17,125	91	6	5,007,261	85	17

motorways by the end of 2010. Nevertheless, support from the public administration would be necessary for many of the new direct toll concessions due to low traffic projections and the consequent low financial performance.[9] To guarantee the financial viability of the projects, the Spanish regulation on toll concessions includes, as other means of initially supporting toll concessionaires, 'refundable advance payments' and 'participative loans'.

Refundable advance payments are resources given to concessionaires that initially have cash-flow problems. They are similar to interest-free loans that are repayable when there is an adequate amount of profit, as occurred with AUCALSA. Another concessionaire, Aulesa, will repay the refundable advance payments received over a period of five years, from the moment it has cancelled all its foreign and national debt. In 2007, toll concessionaires had more than €170 million on their balance sheets within the refundable advance payment item.

The latest incentive used by the government to support new concessions has been participative loans. The name comes from the fact that reimbursement is normally linked to the annual toll revenues, so the government 'participates' in the profits of the concessionaire. In this case the loan pays interest, albeit at lower rates than interest paid on the financial markets. If the business is going really well, repayment of the loan is high. If revenues are low, either the repayment is also low or it can even be deferred until the profit figure is adequate. Examples of the terms of concession contracts referring specifically to conditions for repaying participative loans include:

- The concession must pay dividends;
- The real average daily traffic must be above an established average daily traffic (that expected in the agreement of concession or the break-even traffic).

In 2007, more than €147 million were included on concessionaires' balance sheets in the participative loans item.

International expansion of the Spanish toll sector

In the last decade, the concessionaires have earned huge amounts from the collection of tolls that have secured the stability of the sector and made possible the expansion of their business with new projects in other transport sectors either in Spain or abroad.

Concessionaires have traditionally had a close relationship with the construction industry. This has been crucial in the expansion of the Spanish toll sector all over the world. For many years, direct toll motorway concessionaires were independent companies, with normal processes of merger or commercial alliances as for any economic sector. But, in the last decade, formerly individual companies integrated into groups engaged in the construction and management of transport, mobility and communications infrastructures. As is shown in Table 4.1, five main groups control more than 90 per cent of the share capital of toll motorways concessionaires: Abertis, Itínere, ACS, Cintra and Global Vía.

Taking advantage of the regulation that permitted concession companies to extend their corporate functions to other activities, linked with transport and telecommunication infrastructures, and the huge profits that the sector was earning, these companies started to expand their businesses in Spain and all over the world.

Spanish construction/concession companies are leading international groups in the management of transport and communications infrastructures. They directly manage or have interests in a number of concessions for roads, tunnels and bridges. They also include business units that operate in sectors such as rail, sea ports, airports and car parks and even in the development of logistic platforms.

As noted above, at present, there are six Spanish companies within the top ten positions (according to the volume of investment in

Table 4.6 Top international operators of transport infrastructures

	International investment* (€ thousands)	Projects under construction/ operation	Active proposals
1. Cintra (Spain) *Greece, Ireland, Portugal, Canada, Chile, USA*	52,276,317.6	38	30
2. Macquarie (Australia)	36,102,852.8	44	18
3. ACS (Spain) *Greece, Ireland, Portugal, UK, Argentina, Canada, Chile, USA, South Africa*	25,294,992.4	57	27
4. Vinci-Cofiroute (France)	18,503,670.2	22	23
5. Hochtief (Germany)	17,108,613.0	23	11
6. Sacyr-Itínere (Spain) *Ireland, Portugal, Brazil, Chile, Costa Rica*	15,154,000.0	40	22
7. Abertis (Spain) *France, Italy, Portugal, UK, Argentina, Colombia, Chile, Puerto Rico, South Africa*	14,640,435.0	32	7
8. Bouygues (France)	10,347,951.4	17	16
9. OHL (Spain) *Argentina, Brazil, Chile, Mexico, Peru*	10,041,345.5	28	33
10. Global Vía (Spain) *Ireland, Portugal, Chile, Mexico*	9,619,762.3	33	17

Note: *Since 1985.

Source: Data taken from Public Works Financing (2008).

transport infrastructures or the number of transportation concession/ PPP projects), in the classification elaborated by Public Works Financing (see Table 4.6), toll roads being one of the driving forces behind the growth of these companies. Their investments since 1985 amount to €127,000 million for 228 projects under construction or in operation.

These infrastructure groups are present mainly in Europe (Greece, France, Ireland, Italy Portugal, Spain and the UK), North America (Canada, Mexico and the USA), South America (Argentina, Brazil, Chile, Colombia, Costa Rica, Peru and Puerto Rico) and South Africa. They also have 129 active proposals[10] in these countries, as well as in Eastern European countries.

Public entities for the management of public infrastructures

This model draws together public entities whose purpose is to construct and/or manage public infrastructures, and the services related to them, which are promoted by the corresponding public administration. In this case, the provision of infrastructures is based on the creation of a special purpose public entity that initially does not generate revenue, but that has the capacity to raise funds with the financial support provided by the controlling public administration. This model has been called the 'Spanish model' in contrast to the 'English model' (shadow tolls) or the 'German model' (full price payment).

These entities are like trading companies in which public administrations have interests. Several autonomous communities have created this type of entity to carry out projects of regional interest:

* Gestió d'Infraestructures, S.A. (GISA), Catalonia;
* Gestión de Infraestructuras de Andalucía, S.A. (GIASA), Andalusia;
* Madrid Infraestructuras de Transporte (MINTRA), Madrid;
* Gestión de Infraestructuras de Castilla y León, S.A. (GICALSA), Castilla-León;
* Sociedad Pública de Investimentos de Galicia, S.A. (SPI), Galicia;
* Gestión de Infraestructuras de Castilla-La Mancha, S.A., Castilla-La Mancha.

The central government has also created an entity (Sociedad Estatal de Infraestructuras de Transporte Terrestre) to promote and construct infrastructures all over the country.

The distinctive feature of this model is the existence of a legal entity separate from a public administration. One of the most important arguments that explain the creation of this type of entity is their flexibility in the development of projects, since they are not subject to government restrictions related to personnel and procurement. Nevertheless, they have to comply with the principles of public disclosure and competition that public administrations have to follow in public procurement processes. This feature tries to combine social objectives with the principles of efficiency, effectiveness and economy, so that social benefits can be achieved and public resources reach an optimum level at the same time. These entities are also called 'instrumental' since they are an 'instrument' of the corresponding public administration for carrying out activities related to public infrastructures.

In Figure 4.2, the relationships between the agents involved in this model are shown. The first step is the agreement between the public administration and the special purpose public entity, in which the public administration specifies the work to be done and the terms of the financial support. After this agreement, the public entity can raise funds from financial markets and enter into contracts with construction companies and private service providers at the end of the corresponding tendering process. Although special purpose public entities can enter into a contract with any construction company or service provider, they always act according to an order given by the public administration. When the infrastructure is finished, it is transferred to the parent public administration.

The restrictions on public debt established by the Maastricht Treaty and the Stability and Growth Pact can be circumvented by means of these entities. So, as well as the objective of improving efficiency and effectiveness in the provision of public infrastructures and services, this important feature explains why this model was needed in the 1990s. However, the European System of Accounts (ESA 95) was revised and nowadays it is more difficult to avoid consolidating these entities into the public administration sector. According to the ESA 95, if the sales of a public entity cover more than 50 per cent of its operating expenses, it is included in the corporations sector and its debt is not consolidated

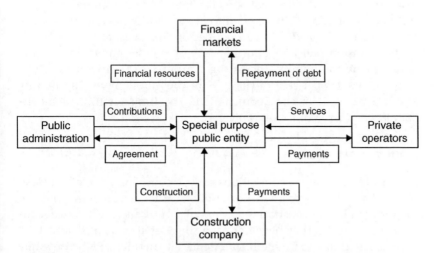

Figure 4.2 Relations between agents and special purpose public entities
Source: Author.

into the public administration sector. Given that these companies receive payments from the government, it has to be proven that these payments are not direct subsidies but, instead, payments in accordance with a certain level of service/availability of the infrastructure. Otherwise, the debt raised by the special purpose public entity will be consolidated into the debt of the public administration.

The Autonomous Community of Madrid created Madrid Infraestructuras de Transporte (MINTRA) to manage the extension of Madrid's underground. This public entity was in charge of all the activities to complete the works. After the finalisation of the infrastructure, MINTRA now operates the new sections, receiving payments from private operators, almost exclusively Metro de Madrid S.A., the company that runs the rest of Madrid's underground network.

The value of the funds raised to finance the investment carried out by MINTRA amounts to €3600 million. Although MINTRA's revenues could be considered sales because they are payments from Metro de Madrid, in 2005, Eurostat classified MINTRA in the public administration sector. The rationale behind this decision is that most of the turnover of MINTRA comes from Metro de Madrid – a public corporation – and payments are fixed in advance and do not correspond to objective features related to the use of the infrastructure. Apart from that, there is a clause in the agreement between MINTRA and Metro de Madrid that states that, in the case of financial difficulties for either company, there will be an adjustment of tariffs so that the company in difficulties can recover its economic balance. For these reasons, the payments received by MINTRA can not be considered as sales.

This decision had an important impact on the public debt of the autonomous community, increasing it from €6200 million to €9800 million, about 3 per cent of the GDP of the Autonomous Community and 0.3 per cent of the Spanish GDP (the limit established by the Stability and Growth Pact is 3 per cent).

Conclusions

Spanish toll motorway concessions can be considered one of the first, if not the earliest, experience of Public-Private Partnerships (PPPs) in modern public administration. Although, in essence, toll concessions are PPPs, in Spain, they have not been considered as such because they arose as a response to financing problems. Furthermore, PPPs also imply a search for the improvement of the management of public infrastructures, and this has not been the main objective of toll concessions in

Spain. The Spanish government's lack of financial resources was the main reason for using this model. Nowadays, although it is stated that PPPs seek to improve efficiency and effectiveness in the provision of public infrastructures and services, at a time of budgetary restrictions for governments the search for financing continues to be the underlying reason for these initiatives. Spanish toll motorways offer a very good service and infrastructure but they have been very expensive for taxpayers and could be cheaper for users, since concessionaires have been earning a lot of money in the last decade.

Ultimately, the Spanish experience in the financing of direct toll motorways is going to be very successful, according to the financial results of the toll concessionaires. Nevertheless, the sector had to struggle with many difficulties in the early years and was even on the verge of collapse because of an extremely adverse economic environment. Specific regulation that fulfils the needs of the toll sector and financial support from the state and public administrations have been crucial for this success. The state has backed the Spanish toll motorway sector in many ways (direct subsidies, exchange rate insurance, loan guarantees, tariff revision, nationalisation of toll concessionaires, refundable advance payments and participative loans). Even the accounting regulation has provided favourable requirements (capitalisation of financial expenditure). In this work, we have analysed these forms of backing for the toll motorway sector, the reasons for their implementation and their impact on operating magnitudes. Support from the public administration was intended to avoid the collapse of the toll motorway sector. It has been very costly but, paradoxically, it has permitted the creation of financially sound companies eager for new projects in Spain and abroad.

The government has changed its policy of supporting the toll sector by replacing direct non-refundable subsidies, limited by public deficit constraints, with funds that back new projects when they are set up (refundable advance payments and participative loans). Furthermore, these methods of support have changed the relationship between public administration and private operators. Now, public administrations are associated with the profits of the private concessionaire instead of being merely a provider of non-refundable finance.

When toll companies pay dividends, they have an aggressive policy of payment; in most years they pay nearly all their annual profit. The rationale for this behaviour is understandable: it has taken a long time (10 years or more, even 18 years) to make profits and investors should be rewarded as soon as possible, once the early difficulties have passed.

Farrell (1997) did not believe that toll concessionaires would achieve high rates of return, according to the data available at that time. Ten years later, the ROE of the toll concessionaires sector is more than acceptable and it is expected to continue to increase during the remaining period of the concessions. Some toll concessionaires have even been paying dividends of over 25 per cent to their shareholders for several years.

Nonetheless, we have to distinguish old concessionaires, set up in the 1960s and 1970s, from newer concessionaires, set up in the late 1980s and 1990s, because profitability comes mainly from the former, as only they pay dividends. However, it is expected that new concessions will not have the same difficulties as the old ones: some of them are even making profits a few years after the opening date. The different economic situation and the experience gained by concessionaires contribute to great expectations for the new concessions.

The know-how gained by toll concessionaires has made it possible for Spanish transport operators to become world leaders in the development of concession projects. Spanish infrastructure management groups have large interests in French and Italian toll concessionaires (countries that have similar experience in toll motorway concessions), showing that Spanish companies have beaten them. They are also carrying out projects in countries where collaboration between the public and private sectors is well known (Canada, the USA and the UK) but also in other countries (in South America) where the economic situation of the state is closer to the situation of the Spanish government in the 1960s, with a lack of public resources, but great potential for economic growth. In this case, the advantage is that the private operators are subsidiaries of well established companies with sufficient financial robustness and experience to avoid difficulties.

In Spain, turning to private finance and management has been a common practice in times when public resources are lacking, for example in the 1960s–1970s. During the 1980s, when the state had funds, the traditional public provision and financing of public infrastructures were mainly used. Then, in the 1990s, budgetary restrictions due to commitments to economic discipline meant a return to private initiative. At that moment, the creation of special purpose public entities with private management features was another model for getting around the shortage of public resources. In addition, these entities require the search for value for money in delivering public services and infrastructures. The EU has been careful to make sure that this objective is carried out, avoiding the possibility of the participation of private finance as just a means for circumventing budgetary discipline in public administrations. The guidance provided by ESA 95 ensures that public monies are not simply subsidies and that there is a real framework for gaining efficiency and effectiveness in both public services and public resources. Although an independent entity is set up to raise debt, the example of MINTRA (although there are voices that claim that the Eurostat decision is incorrect) makes it clear that, if there is no transfer of risks linked to public payments, this entity will be classified as part of the public administration sector and, thus, one of the main reasons for its creation is undermined. So, public administrations have to be more careful in complying with what they are preaching, that is, the value for money of public infrastructures and the services related to them.

Notes

1. Delegación del Gobierno en las Sociedades Concesionarias de Autopistas Nacionales de Peaje.
2. In this chapter, when the word 'toll' is used it is referred to direct tolls paid by drivers.
3. High-capacity roads include toll and free motorways and dual carriageways.
4. Nonetheless, within the privatisation process of public companies during the 1990s, these French and Italian operators were privatised, and Spanish private concessionaires acquired share equity participation.
5. Ley 8/1972, de 10 de mayo, de construcción, conservación y explotación de autopistas en régimen de concesión.
6. There was also an underlying political reason: the Socialist Party won the elections and, because of its ideology, changed Spanish road policy.
7. In some toll concessions, the minimum percentage is higher.
8. Within the financial entities that are shareholders of concessionaires we can distinguish between banks and savings banks. The former are investment banks and divisions of banks dealing with corporate entities. Savings banks have a non-profit nature and a regional scope. They are meant to put their profits into providing works of social importance and other strategic actions to encourage the socioeconomic development of their sphere of action.
9. Izquierdo (1997) expected that half of the projected motorways in the first phase of the programme would require subsidies ranging from 40 to 65 per cent of the total investment.
10. One of the most important infrastructure projects of this century, the extension of the Panama Canal, has been awarded to SACYR.

References

Acerete, B., Stafford, A. and Shaoul, J. (2009) Taking Its Toll: The Private Financing of Roads in Spain, *Public Money & Management*, 29 (1): 19–26.
Acerete, B., Stafford, A. and Stapleton, P. (2006) Accounting for the Use of Private Finance in Roads: The Experiences in the UK and Spain, Paper Presented at

the 4th International Conference on Accounting, Auditing and Management in the *Public Sector*. Siena, Italy, September.

Bel, G. and Fageda, X. (2005) Is a Mixed Funding Model for the Motorway Network Sustainable Over time? The Spanish Case. In G. Ragazzi and W. Rothgatter (eds.) *Procurement and Financing Motorways in Europe, Research in Transportation Economics*, 15. The Netherlands: Elsevier.

Bel, G. and Fageda, X. (2009) Privatization and Regulatory Reform of Toll Motorways in Europe, *Governance: An International Journal of Policy, Administration and Institutions*, 22 (2): 295–318.

Farrell, S. (1997) Financing European Transport Infrastructure: Policies and Practice in Western Europe. Basingstoke: Macmillan.

Izquierdo, R. (1997) *Gestión y financiación de las infraestructuras de transporte terrestre*. Madrid: Asociación Española de la Carretera.

Ministry of Public Works (various years) *Informe sobre el sector de autopistas de peaje en España*. Madrid: Centro de Publicaciones Secretaría General Técnica.

Pina, V., Torres, L. and Acerete, B. (2003) *La Iniciativa Privada en el Sector Público: Externalización de Servicios y Financiación de Infraestructuras*. Madrid: AECA.

Public Works Financing (2008) PWF 2008 International Major Projects Database, *Summary: 2008 International survey of Public-Private Partnerships*, 231. Westfield, NJ: Public Works Financing, October.

5
Public-Private Partnerships in Slovenia: Reverse Financial Innovations Enhancing the Public Role

Nevenka Hrovatin

Introduction

Public-Private Partnership (PPP) is a broad term which covers a comprehensive range of private involvement in the provision of public services or services of general social interest, and involves quite a wide range of cooperation between the public and private sectors. In the broadest sense, it pertains also to privatisation, although in fact in the view of experts in the field this is a misconception, since the private sector does not buy an asset, but rather 'purchases a stream of services under specified conditions' (Grimsey and Lewis 2004, 6). This may also include private financing of public infrastructure, although the emphasis is on the private provision of services which may, of course, also involve construction. Participation of a private party in the project design, construction and management of project delivery and the collection of financial streams (including risk bearing) is a distinctive feature of PPP versus the traditional procurement type of contractual agreements.

The EU has adopted a broader definition of PPPs than that outlined above, although EU law itself does not lay down any provisions on them. To clarify some issues regarding the PPP practice, the EU adopted the Green Paper in 2004 (EC 2004a). It differentiates between two types of PPPs.

The first type is a *purely contractual PPP*, of which there are two forms: (1) procurement arrangements for the private delivery of goods, construction of works or services, and (2) concessions, where the concessionaire gets the exclusive right to deliver a commercial public service or other activity, which may also include the construction of facilities (concession partnership). However, in the academic literature there is much confusion about the definition of concessions. Hall (2008), for example, confines concession PPPs to only those where a company (concessionaire) is paid from user charges (such as water charges and toll roads). PPPs where the private company is paid from public money and which involve construction are known as Private Finance Initiative (PFIs). This form has been widely used in the UK since 2000. The EU places both types under the same umbrella of concession. A distinctive feature of PFIs compared to other types of PPPs is that the private party (concessionaire), which usually provides financing for the project, should also bear the risk.

While traditional purely contractual procurement-type PPPs are regulated by a special EU directive, the procedures and principles for awarding concessions are not laid down in EU secondary legislation, only in Articles 43–49 of the EU Treaty. They generally require that principles of transparency, equality of treatment, proportionality an mutual recognition be respected (EC 2004a; 2005a).

The second type of PPP in the EU legislation is the *institutional PPP* (IPPP) which involves the cooperation of public and private sectors within a distinct entity. This pertains to jointly owned undertakings providing public services, including cases where the private sector takes control of an existing public undertaking (EC 2005b). Public enterprises (i.e. enterprises with majority public ownership) belong to this type of PPP, which is much more broadly defined than the usual perception among academics and practitioners of what PPP stands for.

This chapter concentrates in particular on the scope of concession-type PPPs in Slovenia. The focus is on PPPs in the broader sense, where the private party constructs the facilities, provides the service and bears the risk regardless of the method of payment (from user charges or from public budgets). This involves concession-type PPPs of continental Europe and the British PFI-type of concessions. The objective is to determine the significance of PPPs in the construction of networks and facilities for services of general economic interest in Slovenia in comparison with other European countries, and the reasons for their potential under- or over-participation in investment financing in Slovenia.

The chapter provides a comparative overview of PPPs in Slovenia at the state and municipality levels. After noting their infancy in Slovenia, it tries to find reasons for and discuss the drivers of their growing public role in public service construction and delivery. Several reasons are suggested and analysed, such as the lack of legislation and political will, the dominant traditional model of public financing enabled by macroeconomic fiscal stability, the pattern of ownership transformation that created public enterprises in most utilities, the current reorganisation of public enterprises inspired by EU legislation and practice that has led to the withdrawal of private ownership participation in public enterprises and, finally, failures of PPPs in Slovenia.

The very limited presence of PPPs in Slovenia

Slovenia's huge infrastructure investment needs in the 1990s could not be covered from public sources (Table 5.1). These needs amounted to around €4 billion in just four major network industries (energy, transport including highways and railways, communications and municipal infrastructure), amounting to 8.7 per cent of GDP (Hrovatin 1999a; Mrak 1998). All sources of finance envisaged to cover investments, public and private, would provide less than 60 per cent of total needs. This would create a financial investment gap of 3.6 per cent of GDP that could not be covered from public sources.[1] The solution suggested by Slovenian economists and accepted by politicians was to fill the gap by using various forms of PPP.[2] However, although there was the political

Table 5.1 Infrastructural investment needs and gaps in infrastructural financing in Slovenia, 1997–2000 (€ millions, 1996 prices)

	Investment needs		Financial sources		Financial investment gap	
	Value	% GDP	Value	% GDP	Value	% GDP
Energy	1012.3	2.2	559.6	1.2	452.8	1.0
• Electricity	(688.1)	(1.5)	(419.8)	(0.9)	(268.3)	(0.6)
Transport and communications	2203.7	4.7	1632.5	3.5	571.3	1.2
• Transport	(1705.1)	(3.6)	(1212.6)	(2.6)	492.4	(1.0)
–Highways	(1012.3)					
–Railways	(195.3)					
• Communications	(498.7)	(1.1)	(419.8)	(0.9)	(78.9)	(0.2)
Municipal Infrastructure	829.6	1.8	186.5	0.4	643.0	1.4
Total	4045.6	8.7	2378.6	5.1	1667.1	3.6

Note: The official exchange rate on 1 January 1999, when Slovenia joined the EU, is used (€1 = SIT 239.64).

Source: Hrovatin (1999a) based on study by Mrak (1998).

will, it took almost ten years to pass legislation that would enhance the role of PPPs in practice.

In spite of the large investment gap requiring greater private sector participation, the current scope of PPPs in Slovenia is still disappointing, as Tables 5.2, 5.3 and 5.4 indicate.

Concessions as defined in the ministerial report (MF 2009a) are not in compliance with Public-Private Partnership Act (2006), which defines concessions as those contractual PPPs where the private sector bears the risk. Some services and works are financed from public budgets and the state bears the risk. In addition some concessions were granted to public firms and therefore do not represent the PPP type of service construction and provision, such as the construction of highways where the concession is given to the 100 per cent state-owned company DARS. The situation is similar in the energy sector, with concessions given to majority state-owned large hydropower plants and with maintenance of the port of Luka Koper, where the state is also the majority owner.

PFI-type concessions involve private construction and operation of new facilities and, in continental Europe, are often financed from charges rather than public budgets (EIB 2007). However, when comparing Slovenian PPPs with European practice it is interesting to note that in Slovenia the number of PFI-type of concessions is almost negligible at the national level (Table 5.2). Municipalities are also quite reluctant to use the private sector for constructing and delivering services. Almost a third of them have not granted a concession and almost a quarter have granted only one (Table 5.3). As at the state level most concessions are of the service type with no construction of new facilities (Table 5.4). The exceptions are gas distribution utilities (where 19 concessions have been granted to 12 companies) and waste-water treatment plants, with 16 concessions, where some of them may also be a PPP type (i.e. if the public enterprise is the concessionaire). In other sectors there are only few attempts to start with private sector involvement.[3]

This picture is in sharp contrast with the presence of PFI-type PPPs in other European countries and, in particular, in the UK which has 76 per cent of European PPPs by number (EIB 2007). By mid-2009 the UK had signed 641 projects worth £63.804 billion, with another 116 worth £12.4 billion in the procurement pipeline (HM Treasury 2009a; 2009b). The UK, Spain (the second biggest PPP country), France, Germany, Italy and Portugal together account for 95 per cent of the total European PPP market (EIB 2007).[4] In terms of value, the share of the UK is lower (56 per cent) and the share of the other five countries is around one third. This indicates that the UK's sectoral distribution

Table 5.2 Concessions in Slovenia granted by the state (as at 2008)

Sector	Number	Type	Duration (years)	Sector	Number	Type	Duration (years)
Education	–	Service concession	3 (or at least the length of the study of the accredited study programme)	Use of natural resources	136	Service concession	–
Primary, secondary, professional high[a]	16	Service concession	n.a.	Social services	–	–	–
Tertiary	13 institutions (28 concessions)	Service concession	n.a.	Institutional care of the elderly (dormitories)	26	Works and service concession	40 (for 24)
Health	–	–	–	Job search for students (student service)	55	Service concession	–
Secondary health care – specialists clinics	319	Service concession	n.a.	Job search for others	51	Service concession	–
Energy	–	–	–	Job search and rehabilitation of disabled	12	Service concession	4
Small hydropower plants (up to 10 MW)	498	Works and service concession	n.a.	Special concessions for leadership, care and employment under special circumstances	11	Service concession	7–20

Continued

Table 5.2 Continued

Sector	Number	Type	Duration (years)	Sector	Number	Type	Duration (years)
Large hydropower plants	6	Service concession (granted to public enterprises)	n.a.	Others	–	–	–
Tourism	–	–	–	Chimney sweeping	90	Service concessions	–
Construction of ski lifts	35	Works and service concession	20–40	Old motor vehicles and tyres	6	Service concessions	–
Transport	–	–	–	Labelling and registration of animals	68	Service concession	–
Public intercity bus transport	49	Service concession	5.33	Public veterinary service	169	Service concession	10
Highways	1 (public enterprise DARS)	Works concession	Min. 20, max: duration of highway construction (from 29 April 2004)[b]	Veterinary control	4	Service concession	–
Maintenance of the port of Luka Koper	1 (Port Luka Koper)	Service concession (to the IPPP)	From the second half of 2008	Organisations for animal breeding	14	Service concession	1
Maintenance of the infrastructure for safe sailing	1	Service concession	10	–	–	–	–

Notes: [a] 85 per cent state financing: 13 institutions; 100 per cent state financing: three institutions.
[b] Time needed to complete the construction of highways in Slovenia as planned in ReNPIA (2004).

Source: Data taken from MF (2009a).

Table 5.3 Concessions in Slovenia granted by municipalities (as at 2008)

Number of concessions	Number of municipalities	% of municipalities
0	69	32.9
1	52	24.8
2–14	76	36.2
No evidence	13	6.2
Total	210	100.0

Source: Data taken from MF (2009a).

of PPPs is different than in continental countries and favours many smaller projects.

Slovenia accounts for only 0.1 per cent of PPPs by number with 0 per cent by value. This places Slovenia last in Europe, together with Denmark, Latvia and the Slovak Republic. The majority of PPPs in mainland Europe are in the transport sector (60 per cent), which is also the largest sector in value terms (84 per cent). In the transport sector, road projects prevail (60 per cent by number and 67 per cent by value) indicating that construction of large highways takes this form. Transport is also the first in value terms (36 per cent) in the UK while projects providing social and other state-operated services dominate in number, namely hospitals (31 per cent), schools (25 per cent) other buildings such as nursing homes, communal housing, government, police and military buildings and prisons (14 per cent).

In spite of the lower share of transport PPPs in the UK than in mainland Europe, it is worth noting that their significance is much greater in total financing than in mainland Europe. Transport sector PPPs account for 60 per cent of all investments in transport, storage and communication in the UK but for less than 5 per cent in mainland Europe. The same is true for the health and education sectors.

As Slovenia has the lowest presence of PPPs among EU member states, it is instructive to see why this innovative form of financing for network industries and public services generally has not gained more popularity in Slovenia. So, the key impediments to PPPs are now outlined.

Lack of legislation and institutional support for PPPs

Specific legislation, in particular a special law on PPPs, together with a government strategy and institutional support, is seen as one of the

Table 5.4 Concessions in Slovenia granted by municipalities by sector (as at 2008)

Activity	Number of concessions	Type of PPP	Activity	Number of concessions	Type of PPP
Refuse collection and disposal	42 (22; 8; 2.86)[a]	Service concession	Maintenance of public lightening	11	Service concession
Funeral services	54 (32; 8; 1.67)[a]	Service concession	Public passengers city road transport	10	Service concession
Distribution of natural gas	58 (19)[b] (12; 14; 4.83)[a]	19 works concessions	Operation of district heating	10 (1)[c]	Service concession (9)
Water supply, sewerage and waste-water treatment[d]	40	Service concession	Primary health care	1575	Service concession
Waste-water treatment (cleaning) and waste-water treatment plants	16	Service and works concession	Others for construction	12[e]	Works and service concession
Street cleaning and maintenance of public outdoor premises	41[f] (25; n.a.; 1.64)[a]	Service concession	Others for operation and maintenance	77	Service concession

Notes: [a] Numbers in parenthesis stand for: the number of companies that obtained concessions, the maximum number of concessions per company and average number of concessions per company respectively;

[b] 19 out of 58 also for construction of the distribution network in addition to its operation;

[c] 1 for construction and operation;

[d] 18 only for water supply, 10 for water supply and sewerage and waste-water treatment, 1 also for refuse collection and disposal and for street lightening;

[e] Construction of parking garages (1), construction and operation of cable networks (4), construction and operation of flats for elderly people (1), construction of sports stadiums (1), construction and operation of city cable car (Ljubljana) (1), construction of public parking garages (1), construction of ski lifts (1), construction of multipurpose blocks of flats (1) and construction of (local) port infrastructure and construction of tourist buildings (1);

[f] 2 only for cleaning of forest roads.

Source: Data taken from MF (2009a).

key prerequisites for the faster development of PPPs (Mrak 2006). The significance of this factor was recognised in the strategy for the economic development of Slovenia 2001–2006 (IMAD 2001, 83). An academic and government advisor on Slovenia's financial arrangements with the EU called for appropriate legislation and an institutional set-up more than ten years ago (Mrak 1998) and Slovenia eventually adopted the Public-Private Partnership Act (2006). The act strictly follows the EU Green Paper regarding PPP definitions and recommended projects. Slovenia is thus one of the very few countries that have laid down detailed rules for the award of works and service concessions in accordance with the EU Green Paper. Like the EU, Slovenian law also distinguishes between contractual and institutional PPPs (later named equity partnerships in Slovenian law). Contractual partnerships consist of the public procurement type of PPPs and concessions are either works or service concessions. With the integration of EU court practice (i.e. the Stadt Halle case) into the provisions of the 2006 PPP Act, Slovenia went beyond EU law in governing the tendering procedure (see below).

There are three institutional forms for PPP procedures and activities (Mrak 2006):

- A centralised form – where all public duties regarding PPPs are carried out by one central (state or regional) specialised institution (e.g. in Ontario, Canada);
- A decentralised form – where line ministries and local authorities autonomously carry out all PPP duties (e.g. Portugal);
- A mixed form – where there is a central PPP unit, usually within the Ministry of Finance with sectoral PPP units at the level of line ministries, whose main duty is the identification and development of the projects, and various other institutions like advisory bodies representing business, experts and civil society.

Mrak (2006) strongly opted for the mixed model as the most appropriate for Slovenia. Nevertheless, Slovenia decided to adopt the centralised approach with one special organisational unit within the Ministry of Finance, assisted by experts and representatives from other ministries and by the government's PPP council (headed by the Minister of Finance but with members who are independent experts in the economic, legal and other areas of PPPs). However, as regards procedures, a decentralised model exists in Slovenia. In addition to central government, local authorities are authorised to initiate PPPs and to launch public calls for tender ending in the selection of the most appropriate bidder based on a local act being adopted beforehand.

In spite of adequate legislation on and institutionalisation of PPPs in Slovenia, it seems that this is not sufficient to foster their development. The missing prerequisites are:

- A government strategy for PPPs;
- Identification of PPP projects;
- Experts in the field who would work in the organisational unit within the Ministry of Finance to establish standardised structures and procedures for PPPs, to educate and inform the public sector about PPPs, to cooperate with line ministries, to inform the public about the usefulness of PPPs and to regularly monitor PPP projects.

It is clear that legislation on and institutionalisation of PPPs per se are not sufficient. Besides de jure institutionalisation, de facto institutionalisation is required, implying that the effective work of institutions is even more important than the legislation. Slovenia is only at the initial phase of de facto institutionalisation, which is one of the reasons why PPPs have not gained a more significant role in financing infrastructure and social services facilities.

Public financing of infrastructure construction

Many EU countries with urgent needs for infrastructure construction and upgrading switched to PPPs because their public finances were constrained by the requirements of the EU Stability and Growth Pact (see Chapter 1). According to McQuaid and Scherrer (2008, 26), this macroeconomic budgetary driver was even more important in some continental European countries (e.g. Germany and Austria) than the microeconomic driver in introducing commercial disciplines for delivering more efficient and effective public services. Unlike many continental European countries with budgetary (or fiscal) pressures, Slovenia found itself in a quite favourable condition when its decision to join the European Monetary Union (EMU) was taken. Its public debt amounted to only 27.2 per cent of GDP and its budget deficit to only 2.2 per cent, both well below the Maastricht criteria thresholds for joining the EU (MF 2009b).

Consequently Slovenia had a lot of freedom to use public financing for infrastructure investments, rather than seeking private involvement through PPPs. This is one of the important reasons why Slovenia did not make widespread use of PPPs in the transport sector, which accounts for the greatest share in value of PPPs in continental Europe. However, in spite of some bad practices with highway PPPs in Europe,[5] Slovenia could not avoid the inefficiencies resulting from relying on the traditional mode of construction.

In 1995 Slovenia adopted a national programme for the construction of highways until 2004 (NPIA 1996). This envisaged the construction of a 'highway cross' to speed up transport movements on the main road links in Slovenia. The management of construction was entrusted to the 100 per cent state-owned company DARS, which, through public procurement, selected bidders for construction contracts. The majority of the finance would come from the special excise duty on petrol, with loans as the second and user charges as the third source. However, from 1994 to 2002 only 45.5 per cent of planned highways were constructed with 54.4 per cent in value. So, in 2004 the resolution for the national programme for construction of highways was adopted to address the lack of fulfilment of the goals stated in the national programme (ReNPIA 2004). The planned value of the investment was also increased by 27 per cent and construction was extended to 2013.

In 2009 the Court of Audit of the Republic of Slovenia (CARS) evaluated the construction and financing of roads and found inefficiencies for which the Ministry of Transport and DARS were held accountable.

First, DARS was first founded as a public enterprise and then reorganised into a company subject to corporate law with the state as the sole owner. The Ministry of Transport's intention was for this reorganisation to enable private sector participation and to enable DARS to use credit financing, and which therefore would not be treated as a public debt. CARS concluded that the reorganisation had not fulfilled its intention. DARS as a concessionaire remained entirely a public (not private) partner after the reorganisation and all loans raised are on the account of (and guaranteed by) the Slovenian state.

Second, DARS did not create separate accounts for the construction of highways and their finances as required by law. Instead, its reports also include its results for its other duties (i.e. the maintenance of roads and collection of tolls). Hence, accounting errors were made as a result of reorganisation.

Third, the concession arrangements between the state and DARS are not clear and rather peculiar. The concession contract does not define the length of contract. It also states that the state should buy all the assets and equipment of the concession at market prices after its expiry. This leaves a lot of ambiguity about the exact assets to be purchased and about the rationality of the provision to purchase the assets. Financial payments between DARS and the state are not adequately arranged. It is also peculiar that DARS as a concessionaire does not bear the risk. On the contrary, it is entitled to a normal return on capital employed.

Fourth, there is also an unclear distribution of tasks in the construction of highways between DARS and the state-owned company DCC. DCC was founded by the Slovenian state to conduct most activities in the construction and maintenance of highways and other roads. As such it is one of the main subcontractors of DARS. DARS is therefore merely an intermediary between the Ministry of Transport and DCC for planning, implementing and reporting the construction of highways that, in the view of CARS, unjustifiably bears all the responsibility (ReNPIA 2004).

Fifth, there are serious doubts about the long-run financial and economic sustainability of the comprehensive highway construction project. Its cost has increased by 252 per cent compared to NPIA (1996) or by 96 per cent compared to the amendments of the NPIA in 1998. The main reason for the increased costs is the extension of the programme from 2013 to 2033, which substantially increases the cost of debt-financing credits and government bonds. Additionally, inclusion of a 1.5 per cent rate of return on investment was not previously accounted for. In 2004–2007, DARS exceeded the planned hiring of credits and issue of bonds by 33 per cent and long-term debt increased by 130 per cent from the end of 2004 to 2007. Moreover, annual spending on construction did not correspond to state plans. The discrepancy (higher spending) amounted to an average of 20 per cent annually between 2004 and 2007.

The increase in annual debt repayments in 2004–2007 meant that the concession fee would not suffice to service the debt without higher toll charges, more budget funds or new credits (credit refinancing). This was recognised by DARS, which outsourced the study of the financial viability of the project and this demonstrated negative net present value (NPV) by 2003. DARS rejected the proposal to raise new loans for payment of those that had expired and opted instead for toll collection in the toll-free period and an increase in toll charges of 2 per cent annually over the next five years. The Ministry of Transport did not respond to this proposal and consequently did not try to upgrade the ReNPIA (2004) to account for the financial gap. It was therefore accused by CARS of not enabling an efficient and transparent system of road planning, construction and financing including the rational and transparent use of financial resources.

As the Ministry for Transport has not accounted for all necessary financial resources for the completion of the highway construction programme, CARS (2009a, 5) anticipates that *'the actual time for its completion will be substantially more than planned (year 2033) and it will be postponed until 2050'*. Starting in 1994 and finishing in 2050, it will be spread over 55 years – well beyond a typical PPP-type road project. CARS also expressed some criticism of the ministry for not trying to implement PPP-type construction. This lack of political will at the ministerial level may also explain why both an EBRD-assisted project investigating private investment in the maintenance of the national road network and development of a private finance concession-based highway maintenance scheme as a planned pilot for PPPs in Slovenia (reported by Grimsey and Lewis 2004) did not take place.

Huge investment needs are also faced by obsolete infrastructure networks including the Slovenian Railways (SR) in order to upgrade them to European standards. SR is not economically sustainable even for its current operation and needs to upgrade its rolling stock. Consequently, in 2004 legislation was adopted so the government could guarantee €146 million of the railway's loans and repay €20.8 million of expired loans from the budget. Payment was switched to the ownership share of the state in the company and €8.2 million were given to the company for redundancies and human resources restructuring (ABRHSR 2004). In spite of this state assistance, in 2007 SR operated at a loss attributable to its infrastructure and rolling stock. By 2007 only 25 per cent of the planned investments of the national programme on railways development were realised. As a result, the transport infrastructure deteriorated, slowing the trains down and allowing foreign railways to bypass Slovenia in their transit activities (SR 2007).

The estimated investments required for the upgrading and renewal of the railway infrastructure, together with necessary new construction, amount to more than €6.2 billion (Romih et al. 2007, 70). If this is done by PPP the length of the concession contract that would allow an adequate financial revenue stream should be 35 years (2005–2040), although the construction would be completed by 2020 (Romih et al. 2007). This does not seem to be excessively long for a transport project. However, the state has not taken any action in this direction, instead relying on the traditional model of financing. It will be interesting to see how long the government can afford the traditional mode of financing, bearing in mind the increase in public sector debt from €4.79

billion in 2000 to €7.39 billion in 2007. Although debt fell as a share of GDP from 26.3 per cent to 22 per cent during this period (MF 2008), the 2007–2009 global credit crunch has started to pull in the opposite direction (see Chapter 1).

In 2009 the government had to prepare two rebalances of the general budget, which changed the planned budget deficit from 0.3 per cent to 5 per cent of GDP. Since this exceeds the allowed EMU threshold (3 per cent) this may constrain the ability of the Slovenian state to seek credit financing for urgent infrastructure projects in the future. It is, nevertheless, not clear whether this will enhance PPP-type construction since the possibilities for private sector financing are also limited with banks being very cautious in providing credit and because of the general lack of resources in the banking sector. Thus, the credit crunch has brought countries with different approaches to infrastructure financing (such as the UK and Slovenia) to a more similar situation than one would desire and has brought into question one of the two principal advantages of PPP, namely the macroeconomic driver of overcoming budgetary constraints. If the strict Eurostat definition of government debt is adopted, the indebtedness problem becomes even more severe since all concessions where the concessionaire does not bear all the risk should be counted as public sector debt.

Public enterprises

One of the most obvious reasons for the low representation of PPPs in infrastructure financing in Slovenia is the predominance of state ownership of infrastructure, either directly or through public enterprises. Public enterprises were not subject to the usual process of ownership transformation when Slovenia launched its mass privatisation programme. A special law was passed in June 1993 requiring the transfer of infrastructure to the founders of the companies (i.e. to the state or to the local communities). This was followed by the partial transfer of remaining assets to state funds and to employees, whether free of charge or at discounted values. For railways, electricity generation and transmission systems and other large networks, infrastructure represented the majority of assets and legislation was adopted to make these 100 per cent state-owned. Notwithstanding minor sales of residual assets to fill the 'privatisation gap',[6] all main electricity generation utilities remained majority state owned.

The same is true for telecommunications, the post office, port of Koper and the main airport in Ljubljana. The government had unfulfilled plans for the privatisation of electricity distribution utilities but the only serious attempt was privatisation of the main telecom incumbent (Telekom Slovenija). Even this did not materialise since, among other reasons, the government could not find an appropriate stra-tegic inves-tor. In fact one of the main reasons for the failure was that attempted privatisation in 2007 came too late to exploit the potential benefits. Liberalisation of the European telecoms markets substantially reduced the attractiveness of fixed telecoms incumbents: previously monopo-lies, they were now being exposed to competitive pressure. In addition to its high ownership participation in network industries, with the exception of natural gas, the state is also heavily involved indirectly in the ownership of many other business firms (i.e. through state funds and cross-ownership of companies).

At the local level, public enterprises also became the principal form of delivery of local services. Communal multi-utility type enterprises majority-owned by local communities were created in many areas. Private investors appeared only in gas distribution where out of 17 companies, seven are public enterprises and ten are majority-owned by private investors, with the latter operating under concessions. Private companies with concessions also operate in waste disposal and in water supply and waste-water treatment.

The data on PPPs in Table 5.2 do not distinguish between concessions given to public enterprises and private firms. Nevertheless, the high presence of public enterprises in the provision of local public services is a significant argument against the widespread use of PPPs at the local level. Due to the low prices of local services caused by state or local control in the past, local networks are highly deteriorated and obsol-ete, causing the waste of resources, especially in water supply. Another obstacle to reconstruction and new investment is legislative constraints on local community borrowings. Raised loans should not exceed 20 per cent of the local community's annual budget. This is one of the reasons why some local communities decided to attract private capital in the construction of waste-water treatment plants. However, the reorganisa-tion of public enterprises required by the Public-Private Partnership Act (2006) further fosters public ownership and the withdrawal of private investors from jointly owned firms (i.e. mixed enterprises with local community dominance). This is more thoroughly elaborated in the next section.

Reorganisation of companies driven by EU legislation and practice

According to the PPP Act 2006, all Slovenian public companies that perform commercial public services have to transform into one of the two possible types of companies:

- A commercial company in compliance with the act regulating commercial companies; or
- A public company in compliance with the special law.

Former public trading companies where private investors hold shares (under private law) have to convert to commercial companies. Former public trading companies wanting to remain as public companies have to arrange the transfer of ownership of private investors' shares either to the Slovenian state (if the company delivers a national public service) or local community (if the public delivers a local public service). Another possibility is that private ownership is terminated in some other way (such as proprietary shares). The decision on the type of transformation should be taken by the founder of the company within three years. This arrangement regarding public enterprises could be seen as a step back. Formerly the criterion defining a public enterprise was majority public ownership in the assets excluding infrastructure, the latter automatically being 100 per cent public. Under the new regime the status of a public enterprise requires 100 per cent public ownership.

Even more profound and decisive for the transformation of public enterprises is the provision of the PPP Act, which requires that commercial companies, being created from public enterprises, should obtain concessions if they want to continue their trading operations. A concession should be awarded by the founder of the firm (i.e. the state or the local community) as a result of the bidding process on public tender. This should be done within one year of the transformation.

In contrast, public enterprises that maintain their status (but without private ownership after their transformation) could be awarded a concession by the founder without a public tender.

This dual legislative solution on public tender is based on EU provisions and the European Court practice in the Stadt Halle case (EC 2005b; SCGOW 2007). The consequence of these provisions, which in the case of Slovenia increases public ownership and control, can be demonstrated in two cases: the electricity distribution sector and communal public utilities.

Reorganisation of electricity distribution utilities

Slovenian electricity distribution and distribution service operations were carried out by five utilities as owners of the networks. To comply with the PPP Act so that public tendering could be avoided (allowing the utilities to continue their business without being exposed to potential competition), the government decided to create a new entirely state-owned firm (SODO) in 2007.

SODO was awarded the concession to operate the distribution system. Since it did not have any assets, the five distribution companies were forced to lease their networks to SODO. Additionally, since SODO did not have its own staff to conduct the business, it signed contracts with each company to provide electricity distribution services (operation and maintenance of the system). SODO pays a rental to the companies, which covers the costs of operation in line with the use-of-network charges set by the regulator, the Energy Agency.

This is a rather peculiar situation, where the owners of the assets, that is, electricity distribution companies, lease the assets to another firm (SODO) and then contractually conduct the business with their own assets. The principal task of the owners, that is, the operation (management) of the system, which should be done by electricity distribution companies, is in this way performed by another company (SODO) as a non-owner (lessee) of the assets.

This arrangement is also in sharp contrast to the UK practice as, for example, the ENW (Electricity North West) case demonstrates. As the owner and operator of the distribution system, ENW delegated the tasks of conducting distribution services and of maintaining the networks to UUES (United Utilities Electricity Services Limited) on the basis of the *Asset Services Agreement* (ENW 2008). The Slovenian case is the exact opposite since the owner cannot manage (operate) its own assets and cannot take strategic decisions. It also implies that SODO (rather than the distribution companies) is now subject to regulation and in direct contact with the Energy Agency. Since SODO is not adequately equipped with staff or resources, the ten-year investment plans (which should be updated every two years) and all required regulatory data are still supplied by the commercial companies themselves. It is clear that this division of tasks and ownership rights cannot work effectively in practice.

CARS (2009b) has already questioned this solution which, in its view, allows the unjustified transfer of profits (via the use-of-network charge) into private hands, as the distribution companies are 20.5 per cent owned by private investors. Criticism was also addressed to the Ministry of Economy, which began reorganising the electricity distribution sector without preparing the strategy for its efficient restructuring in compliance with EU law. As a response to these criticisms the government has prepared plans for the phased restructuring of the electricity distribution business. It will eventually (by 2020) lead to the merger of the five distribution companies and SODO into a single 100 per cent state-owned company with trading activities being divested. By squeezing private investors out of the compulsory public service of electricity distribution operations, the fully state-owned company could continue to operate without any competitive bidding pressures. This will not be an easy task, however, since the envisaged transfer of employees to SODO and resulting potential redundancies have already encountered the vociferous opposition of sectoral trade unions, which announced strikes.

Reorganisation of communal utilities

Because of the PPP Act (2006) communal utilities faced the same fear of losing their right to continue their business on public tenders as the electricity distribution companies unless they were transferred to 100 per cent local community ownership. This is why the majority of companies maintained their status as public enterprises with no private ownership. In response to a questionnaire (with a 25 per cent response rate), two-thirds of companies stated that avoidance of public tendering for the award of the concession was the main reason for their decision not to change their public enterprise status (Šen Kreže 2009).

Some companies with mixed ownership have not yet transformed, in spite of their desire to withdraw private ownership in order to transform into 100 per cent public enterprises with a guaranteed concession without a public tender. Private investors have not agreed to give up their ownership rights in some companies and some local utilities do not have enough resources to buy their shares. Currently 47 companies are owned by one or more local utilities, two by local community and employees, 12 are in mixed public-private ownership and seven are privately owned.

Public enterprises also benefit from being able to conduct all in-house contractual construction works without public tender as long as 'their price is equal to or lower than the market price' (APC 2006). This accords with EU guidelines allowing delivery of contracts (to the units over which the public bodies exercise the same control as their own departments) without a public tender, provided they are entirely publicly owned and offer services exclusively to the regional authority that holds their shares (EC 2004a; SCGOW 2007).

In this way, the construction of facilities by public enterprises rather than PPPs is favoured at the local community level. In spite of many advantages being reported in favour of PPP-type construction, public enterprises in Slovenia advocate the advantages of in-house or public construction work (Šen Kreže 2009) as follows:

- Quicker work since their is no need for public tender;
- Better utilisation of labour and capital in public enterprises since they conduct other constructions in addition to their core business;
- Better organisation of work in public enterprises;
- Better cooperation between local community and the company in coordinating the interests in construction works;
- Higher quality of materials used and works done since the public company is responsible for the maintenance of buildings and equipment after their construction.

Nevertheless, one of the main disadvantages of in-house provision is that the procedure to determine whether the public enterprise offers a market or lower-than-market price is not clearly specified and therefore left to local communities. Potential private competitors are often not motivated to bid. High transaction costs for bid preparation and awareness of the existence of public enterprises for these kinds of works may deter them from tendering. On the other hand they may offer a predatory pricing bid if there is a possibility that the long-run contract could be signed. Thus, the competitive pressure from the private sector does not necessarily lower the cost of in-house provision.

Lessons from reorganisation of electricity distribution and communal utilities

The two cases of the reorganisation of electricity and communal companies clearly demonstrate how EU court practice may inspire organisational changes in the delivery of public services that increase the government role through higher public ownership rather than competition for concessions. As the Slovenian case demonstrates, member states might protect their domestic companies by reorganisation into 100 per cent publicly owned enterprises in order to avoid competition from domestic private or foreign firms. This would save them having to deal with redundancies and social and political pressures caused by public enterprises losing the right to provide the service after public tenders. Conflicts with powerful trade unions are not welcomed by any government. Such an enhancement of public ownership was definitely not envisaged by the EU policy. It is also not economically rational, since a private presence in public enterprises can be expected (and was intended) to lead to greater efficiency through competition rather than to diminish their efficiency or effectiveness. On the contrary, both efficiency and effectiveness could be reduced now public enterprises are not subject to competitive pressures and have no private shareholders who would require rational behaviour in terms of cost savings.

Although Slovenia may have rushed too fast into the reorganisation of communal enterprises, mandatory tendering may not always bring about workable competitive tendering and therefore may not guarantee greater economic efficiency. Big international oligopolistic firms may restrict competition through collusive and market-hindering behaviour. Local communities lack the experienced and skilled staff needed for carrying out and monitoring tendering procedures. High transaction costs for the preparation of tenders, closure of contracts and monitoring of their execution, together with higher prices, lower quality and redundancies, may not offset the potential benefits of lower costs in private provision of public services.

German municipal firms (*stadtwerke*) face a situation similar to that in Slovenia with mixed ownership and required mandatory tendering. Instead of starting reorganisation or mandatory tendering, German municipal firms claim that EU tendering provisions for services of public interest jeopardise its system of local service provision based on local self-government, including the right of municipalities to choose the organisational form of their provision, whether public, mixed or private (SCGOW 2007).

German utilities call for the legislation envisaged by the EU draft Urban Transport Regulation, where in-house provision should be judged on a case-by-case basis. Effective control by the local community should be checked, the provision of services should be limited to the local authority or several cooperating authorities and the right to award the contract without tendering should be extended to mixed enterprises (i.e. institutional PPPs). Since Slovenia faced the same situation it should perhaps have joined German endeavours to shape the EU legislation rather than prematurely transposing EU court practice into Slovenian legislation, which requires economically irrational solutions for the delivery of public services at the state and local levels. Having assessed the European Commission's provisions on concessions, the European Parliament called on it to 'give serious consideration to regional self-government interests and to involve representatives of regional as well as local interests in drawing up future rules' (EP 2006, 4–5). Moreover, it also 'favours transitional periods for existing contracts that have been concluded in good faith in accordance with national law, in order to avoid legal uncertainty' (EP 2006, 5).

Negative demonstration effects: PPP failures

PPP failures in Slovenia also contributed to the under-representation of PPPs in the construction of networks.[7] A pioneering BOT project for the construction of a waste-water cleaning plant serves as an illustration. In 1998 the city council of Maribor awarded the concession, after international public tender, to a consortium led by Suez-Lyonnaise des Eaux and Degremont (a subsidiary of Suez) with two partners (subsidiaries of the Austrian company Steweag). The 22-year concession contract was signed in July 1998 between the municipality of Maribor and the project company Aquasystems (Mrak 2005). The project was 75 per cent financed by structural credit from the EBRD and 25 per cent by sponsors' equity. The revenues of Aquasystems would come from the city of Maribor's collection of water taxes (charges) at a special local budget account. If there were a lack of financial resources, the city of Maribor would have to pay the concessionaire from its own funds. In 2006, two years after construction, the accumulated debt of the city of Maribor to Aquasystems amounted to €8.3 million.

After negotiations between the two contractual parties a compromise was reached whereby Aqasystems agreed to the repayment of decreased debt (a reduction of normal and overdue interest), higher charges and amendments to the original concession contract (CLCM 2007).[8] On the other hand, this agreement negatively impacted on the operation of the public enterprise Nigrad, which supplies the city's drinking water. Since the increase in both charges (for water supply and waste-water treatment) would be seen as an excessively high burden for consumers, Nigrad could not raised its low water charges.

Another example demonstrating the lack of government will to support PPP projects is the planned BOT-type construction of five hydro-electric plants on the river Sava. Although the concessionaire was selected in 1994, in 1998 the government decided not to sign the contract as the electricity price required by the concessionaire could not be guaranteed due to the uncertain effects of the liberalisation of EU electricity markets (Hrovatin 1999a). Another example of avoiding the BOT-type construction is the thermal power plant in Trbovlje, where the feasibility study rejected this type of financing since it 'significantly raises the price of electricity' (TPPT 1995).

Inefficiencies in the award and operation of concessions are also present in the health sector where the Ministry of Health was subjected to severe criticism by CARS (2008). An opaque and uncoordinated system for awarding concessions for primary health care by local communities jeopardised the economic and financial viability of publicly owned health care facilities. A similar scenario, with unfair competition of private schools with public (state) schools can also be seen in tertiary education. However, a more detailed analysis of problems in these two sectors would go beyond the aim of this chapter.

Conclusions

The evolution of PPPs and public enterprises in Slovenia clearly shows that Slovenia went 'retro' in the public provision and construction of public services. The large infrastructure financing gap and the urgent need to upgrade the railways, water utilities, prisons and many other municipalities' projects demonstrate that the resulting outcome may be worse than if it had followed other countries and made widespread use of PPPs. Even if PPPs in other countries have sometimes (or even often) led to unnecessarily high costs via collusion, higher interest rates, unnecessarily high transaction costs, political corruption and fraud (as well as being contrary to the public service ethos), it could be argued that at least new infrastructure was provided with resultant economic and social benefits.

By wider use of PPPs, Slovenia could have avoided delays in infrastructure construction. On the other hand, by relying on the traditional model of financing it could have avoided the principal inefficiencies of PPPs. However, the implementation of highway construction via the traditional mode revealed enormous cost over-runs, inefficient and non-transparent allocation of tasks among the public bodies involved, huge extensions of deadlines (substantial over-runs of construction time) and incomplete financial schemes. These problems may require excessive increases in tolls or in the money required from taxpayers. Proper public scrutiny and opportunity for meaningful control can provide superior value for money in the public sector rather than private provision, but they were definitely absent in Slovenian highway construction (Hall 2008).

It is also reasonable to conclude that the Slovenian public sector is to a large extent responsible for PPP failures. In the Maribor wastewater treatment plant case, the underestimation of future demand resulting in lack of revenue flows, avoidance of agreed continuous increases in water prices, political priorities caused by local elections and subsidisation without provision in the local budget all point to a lack of public accountability in contract design and implementation. Moreover, the lack of strategy and administrative support at the state level severely hinders the wider use of PPPs.

Development of Slovenia's infrastructure seems to be falling far behind the rest of the EU and the financial investment gap could be seriously damaging Slovenia's economic prospects. In other words, tactical short-term concerns about avoiding excessive profits and costs have over-ridden the strategic long-term needs of the economy. This recently became clear as Slovenia encountered macroeconomic (budgetary) limits in public financing as a result of the financial crisis. It is not surprising that the Slovenian government has recently started to talk about the potential use of PPPs and private partners for the Slovenian railways and similar infrastructure projects.

Nevertheless, PPP is not a panacea for public service provision. Many cases where public and private companies operate in the same industry show that public provision of services may be cheaper and more efficient.[9] It is therefore rational to recommend allowing the coexistence of the two models on a case-by-case basis. An innovation in enhancing both PPP and public sector performance could be to apply yardstick competition to the two models in the same industry. Charges for PPP service provision should be linked to public sector prices or vice versa, whichever is the more efficient. Provisions on yardstick competition to determine the level of prices should be part of the concession contracts.

Moreover, some deficiencies of PPPs (such as the high cost of capital) could be eliminated by profit-sharing between public and private sectors if the profitability of a PPP exceeds the contractually predetermined level. To avoid high transaction costs and their duplication, Slovenia could set up a professional PPP body at the state level that would provide skills and expertise to ministries and municipalities for the entire PPP proced-ure. As regards uncertainty, the solution is to apply a cautious and conservative approach to feasibility studies, to use appropriate risk allocation among stakeholders and, where possible, to be insured against the risk. As Slovenian experiences with highway construction show, dealing with uncertainty is not an easy task even in traditional public financing.

In conclusion, the consequences of innovation failures, albeit high profile ones, are likely to be dwarfed both by the successes arising from innovation and by the consequences of the failure to innovate, the latter being the Slovenian case.

Notes

1. The gap of around 3 per cent of GDP is also acknowledged in the Strategy for the Economic Development of Slovenia (2001, 1).
2. Mrak (2006) notes that there were talks in support of PPPs in the coalition agreement after the parliamentary elections in 2000 and that PPPs also received significant attention in the coalition agreement after the 2004 parliamentary elections.
3. See note 5 in Table 5.4.
4. Only PPPs involving private construction and private risk bearing.
5. See, for example, the Hungarian cases (EC 2004b).
6. The 'privatisation gap' is the result of overestimation of social assets that were subject to ownership transformation at the start of privatisation process. Since the government issued vouchers according to the overestimated assets, it turned out that there was not enough social property (i.e. company shares) to be exchanged for vouchers. This lack of social property is called 'the privatisation gap' and it mostly accumulated in privatisation investment funds (PIFs) that gathered vouchers from citizens and exchanged them for company shares. After long negotiations with PIFs, the government filled in the 'gap' by giving them its shares in some state-owned companies. In this way 10 per cent of shares in electricity distribution companies, in Slovenian Telekom and other companies were given to PIFs free of charge. For more on this see Hrovatin (1999b) and Simonetti et al. (2004).
7. For other cases of PPP failures worldwide see ESSU (2009a).
8. Other cases in the water sector worldwide, where the contracts were terminated or cancelled, are reported by ESSU (2009b). See also the lessons to be drawn from selected PPP projects in water and waste-water treatment projects in Europe (EC 2004b).
9. See for example Hall's (2008) evidence for French water utilities and other cases. A good review on the empirical evidence on privatisation's effectiveness is provided in Megginson (2005).

References

Act on the Business Rehabilitation of the Holding Slovenian Railways, Public Limited Company (ABRHSR) (2004) (In Slovene: *Zakon o poslovni sanaciji Holdinga Slovenske železnice, d.o.o.* (ZPSHSZ)). Official Journal RS, 45/2004.

Act on Public Procurement (APC) (2006) (In Slovene: *Zakon o javnem naročanju – ZNJ 2*). Official Journal RS, 128/2006.

City Local Community Maribor (CLCM) (2007) Report on the Solving of Expired Liabilities of the City Local Community Maribor to the Company Aquasystems (In Slovene: *Poročilo o reševanju zapadlih obveznosti Mestne občine Maribor do družbe Aquasystems*). Maribor, 15 November, http://www.maribor.si/povezava.aspx?pid=3395 (accessed 2 September 2009).

Court of Audit of the Republic of Slovenia (CARS) (2008) Summary Report. Awarding Concessions in Health Sector (In Slovene: *Zbirno poročilo. Podeljevanje koncesij v zdravstvu*) Ljubljana, 22 December.

Court of Audit of the Republic of Slovenia (CARS) (2009a) *Audit Report. Implementing and Financing of the Programme for the Construction of Highways.* (In Slovene: *Revizijsko poročilo. Izvajanje in financiranje programa gradnje avtocest*). Ljubljana, 10 March 2009.

Court of Audit of the Republic of Slovenia (CARS) (2009b) *After Audit Report. Correcting Measures of the Ministry for the Economy and the Company SODO, the Electricity Distribution System Operator* (In Slovene: *Porevizijsko poročilo. Popravljalni ukrepi Ministrstva za gospodarstvo in družbe SODO, sistemski operater distribucijskega omrežja električne energije*). Maribor, 24 July 2009.

European Commission (EC) (2004a) *Green Paper on Public-Private Partnerships and Community Law on Public Contracts and Concessions.* Brussels, COM(2004) 327 final.

European Commission (EC) (2004b) *Resource Book On PPP Case Studies*, http://www.pppcentrum.cz/res/data/001/000228.pdf (accessed 2 September 2009).

European Commission (EC) (2005a) *Communication from the Commission to the European Parliament, the Council, the European Economic and Social Committee and the Committee of the Regions on Public-Private Partnerships and Community Law on Public Procurement and Concessions.* Brussels, COM(2005)569 final.

European Commission (EC) (2005b) *Frequently Asked Questions (FAQs) on Public Procurement: Commission Proposes Clarification of EU Rules on Public-Private Partnerships.* Memo/05/431. Brussels, 17 November 2005, http://www.cream-europe.eu/en/documents/memo_05_431_en.pdf (accessed 20 August 2009).

European Investment Bank (EIB) (2007) *Public – Private Partnerships in Europe. Economic and Financial Report 2007/3* (By Bland-Brude F., Goldsmith, H. and Välilä, T.).

European Parliament (EP) (2006) *Report on Public-Private Partnerships and Community Law on Public Procurement and Concessions.* Final A6–0363/2006, http://www.cream-europe.eu/en/documents/eu_report_ppp_en.pdf (accessed 20 August 2009).

Electricity North West Limited (ENW) (2008) *Regulatory Financial Statements, 31 March 2008*, http://www.enwltd.co.uk/_common/pdf/Electricity_North_West_Limited_Regulatory_Accounts-31_March_2008.pdf (accessed 2 September 2009).

European Services Strategies Unit (ESSU) (2009a) Contract and Privatisation Failures, http://www.european-services-strategy.org.uk/outsourcing-library/contract-and-privatisation-failures/ (accessed 2 September 2009).

European Services Strategies Unit (ESSU) (2009b) *37 Failed Privatisation Projects in Water Supply and Sanitation*, http://www.european-services-strategy.org.uk/outsourcing-library/contract-and-privatisation-failures/37-failed-privatisation-projects-in-water-supp/ (accessed 2 September 2009).

Grimsey, D. and Lewis, M. K. (2004) *Public Private Partnerships: The Worldwide Revolution in Infrastructure Provision and Project Finance.* Cheltenham, UK; Northampton, MA: Edward Elgar.

Hall, D. (2008) *PPPs in the EU – A Critical Appraisal.* Paper presented at ASPE conference St. Petersburg October-November 2008, http://www.google.si/search?hl=sl&q=PPPs+in+the+EU+%E2%80%93+a+critical+appraisal&btnG=Iskanje&meta (accessed 12 August 2009).

HM Treasury (2009a) PFI Signed Projects List – April 2009 (Excel 478KB), http://www.hm-treasury.gov.uk/ppp_pfi_stats.htm (accessed 21 August 2009).

HM Treasury (2009b) PFI Projects in Procurement – June 2009 (Excel 46KB), http://www.hm-treasury.gov.uk/ppp_pfi_stats.htm (accessed 21 August 2009).

Hrovatin, N. (1999a) Public-Private Sector Partnerships in Providing Infrastructural Services: The Need for Further Development in Slovenia. In L. Montanheiro, B. Haigh, D. Morris and M. Linehan (eds) *Public Private Sector Partnerships: Furthering Development*. Sheffield: Sheffield Hallam University Press.

Hrovatin, N. (1999b) Industrial Structure and Privatisation of the Slovenian Electricity Industry, *Economia delle fonti di energia e dell'ambiente*, 42 (2): 143–183.

IMAD (Institute for Macroeconomic Analysis and Development) (2001) *Slovenia in the EU. Strategy for the Economic Development of Slovenia 2001–2006* (In Slovene: *Slovenija v Evropski uniji. Strategija gospodarskega razvoja Slovenije 2001–2006*). Ljubljana: IMAD (In Slovene: *Urad Republike Slovenije za makroekonomske analize in razvoj*).

McQuaid, R. W. and Scherrer, W. (2008) Public Private Partnership in the European Union: Experiences in the UK, Germany and Austria, *Uprava (Administration)*, VI (2): 7–31.

Megginson, L. W. (2005) *The Financial Economics of Privatization*. Oxford: Oxford University Press.

Ministry of Finance of the Republic of Slovenia (MF) (2008) *Report on the Management of Debt of the State Budget of the Republic of Slovenia for 2007* (In Slovene: *Poročilo o upravljanju z dolgom državnega proračuna republike Slovenije leta 2007*).

Ministry of Finance of the Republic of Slovenia (MF) (2009a) *Report on the Signed Contracts on Public-Private Partnership in the Republic of Slovenia in 2008* (In Slovene: *Poročilo o sklenjenih oblikah javno-zasebnega partnerstva v republiki Sloveniji v letu 2008*).

Ministry of Finance of the Republic of Slovenia (MF) (2009b) *Report on the State Deficit and Debt – April 2009 – According to the ESA 95 Methodology* (In Slovene: *Poročilo o primanjkljaju in dolgu države – April 2009 – pripravljeno na osnovi metodologije ESA 95*).

Mrak, M. (1998) How to Reduce the Funding Gap for Infrastructure Financing: The Case of Slovenia. In L. Montanheiro, D. Morris, and N. Hrovatin (eds) *Public and Private Sector Partnerships: Fostering Enterprise*. Sheffield: Sheffield Hallam University Press, 383–395.

Mrak, M. (ed.) (2005) *Project Financing* (In Slovene: *Projektno financiranje*) (Ljubljana: Služba vlade RS za lokalno samoupravo in regionalno politiko (Body of the Government of RS for Local Self-Governance and Regional Policy)).

Mrak, M. (2006) Institutionalisation of Public-Private Partnership: Experiences Across the World and Basic Outlines for Slovenia (In Slovene: *Institucionalizacija javno-zasebnega partnerstva: izkušnje v svetu ter osnovne konture predloga za Slovenijo*). Uprava (*Administration*), IV (1): 105–123.

NPIA (*National Programme on the Construction of Highways in the Republic of Slovenia*) (1996) (In Slovene: *Nacionalni program izgradnje avtocest v Republiki Sloveniji*). Official Journal RS, 13/96.

Public-Private Partnership Act (PPP Act) (2006) (In Slovene: *Zakon o javno-zaseb-nem partnerstvu – ZJZP*). Official Journal RS, 127/2006.

ReNPIA (*Resolution on National Programme for Highways Construction in the Republic of Slovenia*) (2004) (In Slovene: *Resolucija o nacionalnem programu izgradnje avtocest v Republiki Sloveniji ReNPIA*). Official Journal RS, 50/2004.

Romih, D., Oplotnik, Ž. J. and Križanič, F. (2007) Project Financing of Railway Infrastructure (In Slovene: *Projektno financiranje železniške infrastructure*). *Naše gospodarstvo* (*Our Economy*), 53 (1–2): 66–74.

Šen Kreže, B. (2009) The Impact of Public-Private Partnership Act on the Operation of Municipal Companies (In Slovene: *Vplivi zakona o javno-zasebnem partnerstvu na delovanje komunalnih podjetij*). Ljubljana: Faculty of Economics, University of Ljubljana. Masters Thesis.

Simonetti, M., Rojec, M. and Gregorič, A. (2004) Privatization, Restructuring and Corporate Governance of the Enterprise Sector. In M. Mrak, M. Rojec, C. Silva-Jáuregui (eds) *Slovenia: From Yugoslavia to the European Union*. Washington, DC: The World Bank.

SR (Slovenian Railways, In Slovene: *Slovenske železnice* (SŽ)) (2007) *Annual Report* (In Slovene: *Letno poročilo*) (SŽ: Ljubljana).

The Scientific Council of the Gesellschaft für öffentliche Wirtschaft (SCGOW) (2007): *Tendering of Direct Awarding of Public Services – Plea for the Right to Choose for Territorial Authorities. On the Need for Legal Provisions on the In-house Concept in the European Union. Statement of the Scientific Council of the Gesellschaft für öffentiliche Wirtschaft*. Berlin, May, http://goew.de/pdf/c.1.9.goew.pdf (accessed 20 September 2009).

TPPT (Thermal Power Plant Trbovlje, In Slovene: *Termoelektrarna Trbovlje*) (1995) *A Feasibility Study of Building a Replacement Unit TET3* (In Slovene: *Termoelektrarna Trbovlje: Študija izvedljivosti nadomestne enote TET3*). Ljubljana: IBE.

6
Local Government Funding Agencies: Lessons from Success and Failure

Nicholas Anderson, Stephen J. Bailey and Hartwig Pautz

Introduction

Governments have traditionally used bond markets to finance their huge infrastructure investments. These markets are the largest branch of the global financial markets. Institutional investors invest substantial amounts of pension funds and other long-term savings in these markets. Financial intermediaries and companies also use these markets to take and hedge risks. Bond markets are a cornerstone of the financial markets because government bonds:

- Generally have the highest credit ratings in their respective countries, so investors can be sure that their savings are securely invested;
- Normally provide a reasonable real return to investors over the long term;
- Are the most liquid forms of investments, allowing investors and financial intermediaries to buy and sell them with very low trading costs.

The public sector has tried to keep the financial costs as low as possible with payment structures spread evenly over 10 to 20 years at the most advantageous rates. Fixed-rate and floating-rate 'bullet' bond issuance (bonds with a single repayment of the principal at the final maturity of the bond) in the capital markets is normally the cheapest mode of borrowing at any given time. Fixed-rate bond issues that provide predictable cash flows have been used more than floating-rate financing. The latter is used more for short-term liquidity needs except when interest rates are at very high levels. Central governments can construct smooth cash flows of their regular bullet bonds by issuing bullet bonds with varying maturities regularly each year. A portfolio of loans is generally regarded to be less risky if 60–70 per cent is denominated in fixed-rate loans and the remainder is debt with a floating rate of interest.

Over the last 20 years or so, many governments moved away from traditional financing methods in order to get their borrowing off their public sector balance sheets. They increasingly made use of Private Finance Initiatives (PFIs) and Public-Private Partnerships (PPPs), whereby consortia of private companies supply finance, build the physical public sector infrastructure and, thereafter, provide and manage the related public services.

However, the 2007–2009 credit crunch resulted in many banks and monoline insurance companies being in financial crisis and unable to lend to public sector infrastructure projects (Bailey et al. 2009a; 2009b). Some banks depend on government support and are now unwilling to support public sector projects outside their national boundaries. Banks are much more risk averse and are likely to remain so for the foreseeable future. Long-term credit has become short in supply and very costly. Lending will be for shorter maturities and require more equity and more conservative debt levels. The banks' cost of funding will remain high with elevated capital adequacy requirements. Higher returns will be needed on this capital to cover increased credit losses and to pay off government support.

Simultaneously with the shortage of commercial credit, governments are committing themselves to invest in huge public infrastructure projects. Together with these direct investments and other forms of support packages, governments are, and will continue, issuing record amounts of bonds. This may increase interest rates in all bond markets from their historically low levels of mid-2009. This borrowing may crowd out other borrowers, who will continue to pay higher premiums. Industrial and financial sponsors of such projects will thus be challenged to find sufficiently long-term funding at attractive absolute levels. Banks will be less inclined to allow dividend payments.

These private financing problems highlight the need for new approaches to private sector involvement in public infrastructure because governments will take over the procurement of many more new infrastructure investments in an effort to get their respective economies rolling again. This chapter therefore examines tried and well tested innovations in the financing of municipal infrastructure in the

Nordic countries and compares them with similar but largely unsuccessful initiatives in several European countries.

The local government funding agency (LGFA) model

In the Nordic countries, the leading role in investing and maintaining public infrastructure for services is taken by regional (rather than central) government. The relative lack of adequate procurement resources, political expediency and a weak system of local government in the UK and France have meant that central government has had little alternative but to resort to PFI/PPP solutions in order to upgrade and construct new infrastructure. However, the PFI/PPP model has rarely been used in the Nordic region because procurement practices and technical competence for infrastructure procurement are well developed at both central and regional government levels.

While not adopting the formal PFI/PPP model, partnerships between the public and private sectors in the broadest sense have always been the norm in the Nordic markets. Contract management (CM) is a well tested Nordic partnership solution. In this model the procuring body employs an engineering consultant (project manager) to manage the project from the planning stage onwards until it reaches the final operating stage. Many recent big infrastructure projects in Finland have been executed using CM contracts (Kiiras et al. 2002). There are many examples, including the Kerava-Helsinki urban railway line project, the Leppävaara-Helsinki urban railway line project and the Kerava-Lahti railway line project.

The largest infrastructure projects in Scandinavia have also been managed in a similar manner by the public sector. These are the rail and motorway bridges and tunnels linking Sweden and Denmark, the Oresund link and the Great Belt Bridge in Denmark. The same management team of professionals has also continued with a new town development and the metro between Copenhagen Airport and the centre of Copenhagen. This latter development company is owned jointly by the city and the kingdom of Denmark. The Arlanda Express project in Sweden received generous public grants, low-cost loans and tax concessions from the government (Bengtson and Bursjö 2002).

Local government funding agencies (LGFAs) have developed from traditional solutions, have replicated the efficiencies of government bond markets and have been a haven of security for their beneficiaries, regional governments, during the financial crisis of 2007–2009. Central government has also benefited from their cost efficiencies and from having self-discipline imposed from within strong local government.

These investments are generally handled in the same manner as by the central government but with one difference: central government normally contributes to a minor part of the investment and operating costs through grants and subsidies. The remaining costs must be covered in much the same way as by central government with tax revenues, user charges and by borrowing.

On their own, few of the large regional entities, like states and large cities, have the same advantageous access to the bond markets as central governments. They seldom have the necessary resources, skills and size to operate in these markets. They have therefore innovated by creating their own surrogate agencies, LGFAs, to finance this infrastructure and by developing more efficient contractual arrangements for infrastructure procurement.

LGFAs are cost-effective compared with traditional procurement and typical PFI/PPP solutions because they:

- Replicate the government bond market;
- Compete with loans provided by the banking system;
- Are more flexible;
- Utilise the best possible project management;
- Secure the lowest possible funding costs;
- Allow the easy replication of knowledge and good implementation practices within the public sector;
- Are based on cooperation between the private and public sectors.

Four Nordic LGFAs: Lessons from success

Although established at different times, all four Nordic LGFAs were created to give better access to more competitively priced funding. When Finland's LGFA was founded in 1989, the country faced a disastrous economic downturn that was amplified by the regime change in Russia in the early 1990s. GNP fell by more than 10 per cent in one year with record levels of unemployment. There was volatility in interest rates and in the external value of the Finnish currency. This was followed by the worst-ever banking crisis in the history of the country. Following a recent deregulation of the financial markets, many municipalities had imprudently borrowed in foreign currencies. Devaluation of the Finnish currency brought extraordinary losses, of which the banks took advantage without hesitation.

The LGFAs in Norway and Denmark were also both established in conditions of economic stress, in 1926 and 1898 respectively. In Sweden, the LGFA was established in 1986, before Sweden's financial crisis of the early 1990s.

Other similar institutions are established in the Netherlands, Germany, France, Italy, Canada and the USA but only the Netherlands has achieved the same sustainable solution that is exclusively focused on the funding needs of regional government. The two LGFAs in the Netherlands are Bank Nederlandse Gemeenten and Nederlandse Waterschapsbank. The other institutions have been modelled as banks and have substantial activities in the commercial markets with clients outside the public sector. In the USA and Canada a number of regional 'Bond Banks' have been established but they operate on a very narrow scope and further discussion of their activities is outside the remit of this chapter.

The LGFAs are efficient replications of the government bond markets in that they are able to fund themselves at the same or nearly the same costs as their own governments. They can do this because they:

- Are sufficiently large and efficient;
- Enjoy the same ratings as their respective governments;
- Operate only for the benefit of their clients: regional governments;
- Provide finance as well as advisory services (Table 6.1).

Their diversified sources of funding allow them to offer their clients (regional government entities) the loans that best match their funding requirements in order to finance the construction and maintenance of their infrastructure investments.

The best solutions have withstood the test of time and remained robust even during the recent 2007–2009 financial crisis. In fact, LGFAs are now being used aggressively by many governments to pull their economies out of the deep economic recession. New social housing projects and other basic infrastructure have been kick-started during 2009.

Explaining the success of the four Nordic LGFAs

Nordic experience has shown that there are minimum prerequisites necessary for the continued success of an LGFA. First, municipalities should be a self-governing part of the national government, preferably with this enshrined in the nation's constitution. This is a common feature of all the Nordic LGFAs.

Table 6.1   The four Nordic LGFAs

Country	Sweden	Denmark	Finland	Norway
Name	Kommun invest	Kommune Kredit	Municipality Finance	Kommunal banken
Established	1986	1898	1989	1926
Ownership	100% municipal	100% municipal	80% municipal and 20% government	84% municipal and 16% government
Main services for local governments	Finance and advisory	Finance and leasing	Finance and advisory	Finance
Balance Sheet size (€ billions) 2009	15	17	12	25
Net profit (€ millions) 2009	1	34	3	65
Market share (estimated) (%)	50	96	45	45
Employees	44	50	48	43
Rating	AAA/Aaa	AAA/Aaa	AAA/Aaa	AAA/Aaa
Main competitors	Commercial banks	Commercial banks	Commercial banks	Commercial banks

Sources: Financial reports from each LGFA: www.kommuninvest.se; http://kommunekredit.dk; www.munifin.fi; www.kommunalbanken.no

Second, the responsibilities of the municipalities to provide the basic services like health care, social services, education and child day care should be clearly defined and set out in under a Municipal Act or other similar legislation. This ensures that municipalities are empowered and responsible for this capital-intensive activity, for which they then have the right to tax residents or the right to receive payments to finance the provision of these services.

Third, it is essential to have strong support from large groups of municipalities to form a joint funding system, being between 80 per cent and 100 per cent municipally owned (Table 6.1). This is extremely challenging to achieve especially when there are significant political, social and geographical differences. The Nordic countries have recognised the considerable economic and financial management benefits and they have overcome vested interests and massive lobbying efforts from the banks to prevent the passage of these proposals. In both Sweden and Finland the respective banking associations lodged unsuccessful complaints against the LGFAs based on claims that they were supported by illegal state aid.

Fourth, LGFAs should operate without having to maximise profits. They should seek to attain a result that enables growth of the balance sheet in the same fashion as other cooperative business models. Dividends should not be a primary objective of this exercise and should not be paid before the operations are sufficiently robust. This has allowed the four Nordic LGFAs to accumulate substantial balance sheets of between €12 and €25 billion (Table 6.1).

Fifth, in all the Nordic countries the key to financial management is to have experienced professionals who enjoy excellent working relationships with banks and institutional investors on the global markets. It is imperative to have personal contacts and the necessary negotiating skills to deal with banks and investors on behalf of the ultimate borrowers. This is possible in these relatively small and compact LGFAs, none of which has more than 50 staff (Table 6.1). Their proven track record is evidence of their success in both handling the manifold relationships with the global financial markets and serving the needs of the large numbers of domestic entities that typify the local government sector. The cost savings in attaining this level of efficiency with such small organisations can be enormous.

Sixth, LGFAs, as managed by the Nordic countries, lead to a reduction of monopoly power of the commercial banks, their main competitors (Table 6.1). The annual cost savings that were envisaged by Kommuninvest and Municipality Finance when they were created were in the region of 1 per cent of the new loans made by the LGFA. At the time the commercial banks were able to charge a 1 per cent margin above the London Inter-Bank Offer Rate (LIBOR) interest rate when lending to individual municipalities. This was a perverse situation since the municipal sectors in all four countries as a whole enjoy AAA and AA ratings higher than the ratings of the individual commercial banks (Table 6.1). This interest rate difference totally disappeared with the entry of the LGFAs, which also opened up the markets to fair and transparent competitive bidding for all loans at market prices. All loan procurements are subject to negotiated bidding processes in accordance with EU competition law.

In their early days, few believed that these LGFAs could develop to their present size with their substantial market shares (Table 6.1). Prior to the 2007–2009 financial crisis only the KommuneKredit in Denmark had a market share in excess of 60 per cent of the total loans borrowed by regional governments. In the other countries the market shares ranged between 30 and 60 per cent.

Since the financial crisis, their market shares have risen to over 80 per cent of all new loans and to no less than two-fifths of all loans (Table 6.1). The annual interest rate savings are much larger because the market share of lending by LGFAs has risen, so increasing the benefits of such cost efficiencies for the public sector. As stated above, in all the Nordic countries, LGFAs do not seek to maximise profits but, instead, to remain profitable and sustainable over the long term. Table 6.1 demonstrates profits even during 2009.

LGFAs have the same credit rating as the sovereign state, have professional staff, maintain healthy competition and provide local governments with a secure source of long-term financing for basic infrastructure. Such a system has also been a key factor in permitting governments to stimulate the economy with new infrastructure projects. Another source of cost efficiencies has been good financial management from the member entities. This has taken place as a result of training and the replication of best practices, but also it is a result of peer pressure. Self-interest creates peer pressure to stop poor financial management practices by individual members since this will threaten the stability of the ratings of the system as a whole.

Seventh, the LGFA is a centre of knowledge. Kommuninvest and Municipality Finance both have advisory units and both have regular professional training and seminars for members. Local politicians are on the board of both agencies. Members are invited to AGMs and the conferences that are arranged around the countries.

Finally the activities of all the LGFAs are restricted to providing credit exclusively for the municipal sector. Because of this restriction, the ability of the Finnish LGFA (Kuntarahoitus) to repay debt is supported by the Municipal Guarantee Board (MGB). Although not an insurance company as such, the MGB is a form of municipal mutual pool (see Chapter 7). This means that member municipalities would provide financial support to prevent default by the LGFA. Hence, its bond issues are very low risk for buyers and that is why it is rated AAA (see Table 6.1).

More generally, in not being allowed to finance business in the competitive markets outside the remit of the municipal sector, the four Nordic LGFAs are able to borrow money at relatively low rates of interest. This was not the case with the two organisations mentioned in the following section.

Unsuccessful LGFAs in Belgium and France

It is instructive to consider the unhappy fate in 2009 of two municipal banks, Dexia from France/Belgium and Depfa from Germany/Ireland. Each of these banks found its roots with Napoleon, who created the Caisse des Depots in 1806 after the French Revolution to ensure liquidity for French regional governments. Regional government developed rapidly in France and Credit Locale, a strong LGFA, was created to fund infrastructure projects throughout the whole country. Napoleon's exploits in other parts of Europe and those of his successors led eventually to the formation of the German states and the creation of the first Landesbanks in the 1850s. These were a mixture of LGFAs and savings banks for the small and medium-sized enterprises (SMEs).

At the turn of the twentieth century the Belgian government and its municipalities created Credit Communale de Belgique, another LGFA based on the French model. Dexia was formed some 20 years ago from a merger between France's Credit Locale and Credit Communale de Belgique. The Belgian government urgently needed to reduce its debt and meet the Maastricht criteria (Bailey and Fingland 2008). Formation of Dexia was a quick fix that the French were happy to perform since they purchased the Belgian assets at an extraordinary low price. Dexia then went to the stock exchange to raise more capital, after which it embarked on a series of massive acquisitions and geographical expansions. It wanted to be a global leader in public finance with innovative financial solutions. Depfa went through a similar but less dramatic privatisation process in the global markets.

The two banks (Dexia and Depfa) provided long-term finance for large projects of regional governments. They relied heavily on the availability of long-term funding from the bond markets to fund these long-term commitments on favourable terms. However, the financial crisis closed down this source and the cost of alternative funding was far in excess of the income from their loan books. Both banks were then saved from bankruptcy by their respective governments in 2009. The lesson is that financial innovation must be based on matched and conservative funding and not on an uncontrolled mismatching of assets and liabilities.

The problematic development of an LGFA in Scotland: The Scottish Futures Trust

The devolved Scottish government has attempted to establish a form of LGFA, the initiative having been taken by the Scottish National

Party (SNP) rather than by Scottish local governments themselves. Establishment of Scotland's LGFA has been a long drawn out and rather tortuous process and the success of the initiative is not yet apparent. It is used here not as an example of failure but, instead, as a detailed illustration of the need to adopt a consensus-seeking approach amongst all affected parties and of the difficulties faced in the search for a credible alternative to PFIs/PPPs.

In May 1999, Scotland held elections to its first parliament since 1707. A few months before these elections the SNP proposed a new policy instrument to replace PFIs/PPPs: the Scottish Public Service Trust (Salmond 1999a). Devised to be a cheaper and more accountable alternative to PFIs/PPPs, various trusts – each set up to service a different sector such as housing or health – would be established as limited and non-profit-making companies and would be overseen by a board of experts and trustees drawn from the new Scottish Parliament and local authorities.

The trusts would seek finance from the private sector in exchange for bonds they would issue and through bank loans with relatively low interest rates – lower than those for PFIs/PPPs borrowing as the trusts were operating on a not-for-profit basis. With little risk attached to them, trusts would bid for contracts alongside private consortia for building hospitals and schools. Once a school or hospital was built, it would be owned by the trust so the infrastructural project would not pass into private control. Borrowing from the private sector would mean that the trusts would be excluded from the heavily constrained public sector borrowing requirement. Because the proposed trusts would find it cheaper to raise money, have permanent in-house expertise and would not be obliged to make profits, the SNP expected them to slowly crowd out PFI consortia (Swinney 1999b).

When the idea was launched in February 1999 it was, first, characterised by rhetoric that was strongly directed against private profits stemming from public infrastructure projects. The SNP declared that the trust would serve the interest of the public rather 'than private companies helping themselves at the public's expense' (Swinney 1999a) so that public money would no longer 'line[s] the coffers of fat cats' (Swinney 1999b). It was argued that PFI was driven by private profiteering which endangered jobs and pay levels, and private companies had proved to be no more efficient than the public sector (Swinney 1999b). Therefore, to end 'profiteering from the public purse', the trust would be the best way to circumvent PPPs within the constraints of the devolution settlement in order to address the crisis in public investment (Neil

1999). Second, the SNP embedded the trust in the SNP's long-standing campaign for a sovereign (i.e. independent rather than devolved) Scottish state. The trust was a sign of the SNP's commitment to developing new policies for the new Scotland.

The harsh language directed against private capital caused dismay and concern in the Scottish business community. Few supporting voices could be made out (Buxton 1999) – certainly not from the finance industry, which feared it could lose the profits from PFIs/PPPs. The Bank of Scotland – one of the leading PFI/PPP financers in Scotland – described the trust as 'unworkable as it stands' (Horsburgh 1999). The Scottish print media, mostly hostile to the SNP and independence until the run-up to the 2007 elections (McNair 2008), quoted numerous business people and PFI/PPP experts who doubted that the trust would allow money to be raised more cheaply or that it could be used to keep money off the government's balance sheet (Fraser 1999; Deerin 1999).

Possibly as a reaction to the critique, the SNP's election manifesto of April 1999 adopted a slightly more moderate tone for describing the trust and its aims. The SNP no longer lambasted private involvement in the provision of public infrastructure per se, but now argued that 'the expertise of the private sector can be harnessed for the public's good, and [.] competitive rates of finance can deliver high value investment' (SNP 1999, 6). Nonetheless, the proposed trusts could achieve the objectives of PFIs/PPPs 'in the public interest in a far better way' because they would 'hold the assets in trust for the nation while they are under construction and in operation, handing them back to the public at the end of the contract period' [and would] 'eliminate the waste, expense, excessive profit and inefficiency of PFI' (SNP 1999, 6).

The SNP lost the 1999 elections and the trust was resurrected for the 2003 election manifesto as 'Not-for-Profit Trusts'. This policy proposal did not differ substantially from that made in 1999 and was no more concrete than its predecessor. Having lost the 2003 elections, in the run-up to the 2007 Scottish elections, the SNP again advocated its alternative to PFIs/PPPs, the Scottish Futures Trust (SFT) (Smith 2006).

The SFT would be open to institutions and the public to invest in and would save £116 million a year from within existing PFI/PPP deals. Capital would be raised, following a US example, by issuing public bonds. With assets held 'in trust for the nation without the unnecessary private profit that is an integral part of PFI [...] the SNP will act to end the crippling cost of PFI borrowing' (Sturgeon 2007).

The SNP advocated the SFT as a 'better value option for future infrastructure funding' and vowed that they would 'match the current hospital building programme brick for brick' (Dinwoodie 2007a; Robison 2007). The SNP's 2007 election manifesto called PFI/PPP 'costly and flawed' and advocated the SFT (SNP 2007). Distrust in the private sector's profit motive in relation to public projects was as important for the discourse in this document as it had been for the earlier incarnations of the SFT.

The SNP in government: Developing and implementing the SFT

The SNP became the strongest party in the 2007 elections to the Scottish Parliament but failed to achieve a majority of seats. It formed a minority government, which meant that its policy-making powers were limited by the necessity to find – changing – majorities with the other parties and independent parliamentarians. However, as the SFT did not require any legislation, its implementation was not hampered by the SNP government's minority status and would not have to be based on consensus between political forces.

The SFT became a key policy instrument for the Scottish government's strategy to finance development of Scotland's public sector infrastructure in place of PFIs and PPPs and so, in July 2007, the new government set up a small working group to turn the SFT into an effective policy instrument. The group consisted of government officials, a political advisor and members of Partnerships UK (PUK) – an organisation set up by the UK Treasury to promote the effective use of PPP by providing expertise (Chinyio and Gameson 2009). In October 2007 a steering group was formed. It was chaired by the Chief Economic Advisor to the Scottish Executive/Government and had representatives on board from the Society of Local Authority Chief Executives, from PUK and from the Scottish government's Council of Economic Advisors: in short, mostly actors in favour of PPP/PFI financing.

The SNP government, the SFT delivery team and those working on the SFT's Strategic Business Case (SBC) had, by November 2007, accepted that the proposed bond scheme could not function as a mechanism to fund the SFT after the UK Treasury had told the Scottish government that month that it did not have the powers to replace PPPs with a local tax-exempt US-style bond scheme (Haldane 2007; Scott 2007).

In parallel with the establishment of the delivery team, the Scottish government published a consultation paper (Scottish Government 2007). The paper set out the principal aims of the SFT as, first, being a channel for public and private capital into infrastructure investment programmes and projects and, second, providing other services such as investment planning, project delivery and asset management. The document maintained the SNP's critical stance towards private finance in public projects but only in so far as 'excess profits' were made (Scottish Government 2007; Swinney 2007).

While it had been indicated earlier that SFT would be in the public realm, now it was envisaged to be a limited private sector organisation with a 'public interest ethos' (Scottish Government 2007, 8). However, following publication of the consultation document, criticism from all sides of the government's scheme grew. PFI critics thought that SFT was 'nothing new' (Pollock 2007), and the public sector workers' trade union Unison said that it was 'sceptical that a private company such as the proposed SFT can have a genuine public interest ethos' (Davidson 2007). Criticism also came from the UK government, which pointed out that what was known of the proposal so far had not clarified the fundamental question of whether the SFT was a public or private body and that it was doubtful that the UK Treasury could be persuaded of the legality of the scheme.

Speculation emerged in the media that the Scottish government simply wanted to use the SFT to raise to prominence the issue of its limited financial powers and thus increase the frustration in Scotland about the lack of financial autonomy (Dinwoodie 2007b). While the consultations were ongoing, criticism of the feasibility of the trust was growing louder. In January 2008, SNP leader Alex Salmond proposed that inheritance tax relief should be given to those who bought bonds as part of SFT – another policy field that is reserved to Westminster and therefore another policy proposal which could not be made to work (Hutcheson 2008, 25).

Despite all the criticism and the obvious constraints of the 1999 devolution settlement on the SFT the Scottish government continued developing it, even though by now it was taking forms which had less and less resemblance to the financing vehicle the SNP had envisaged before the 2007 Scottish parliamentary elections. In May 2008, the SBC (Scottish Government 2008) presented the SFT as a further development of the non-profit distributing (NPD) programmes used in Scotland since 2002. Unlike PFI, the SFT's NPD projects would be 100 per cent debt financed so that there would be no uncapped equity returns and any surpluses in the delivery would flow into a charitable body for community use. The scope for uncapped investor returns as in PFI was to be discontinued and would only be considered in rare circumstances, namely where the risks involved in a project would be exceptionally high.

The Scottish government expected the financial benefit of establishing the SFT in the target benefit range of 3–5 per cent (Scottish Government 2008, 14). As an organisation the SFT would have a staff of fewer than 10 and then increase to 20 'senior and experienced infrastructure professionals' over three to four years (Scottish Government 2008, 40).

The SFT was split into two separate parts: first, the SFT as an investment partner, quality assurer, developer and deliverer of projects and, second, the SFT as a finance arranger or investor in projects. The first, SFT Development and Delivery (SFT D&D), would be located in the public sector. The second, SFT Finance and Investment (SFT F&I), would sit in the private sector and would be a joint venture between the private and public sectors (Scottish Government 2008, 13).

The first branch being easier to establish, it was given the responsibility of devising more concrete plans for the second branch. SFT D&D was to be launched in autumn 2009 and SFT F&I should be established in autumn 2010 (Scottish Government 2008, 44). In the first phase SFT D&D would mostly keep busy by making its own business plan (Scottish Government 2008, 45). Despite the public-private split, the SFT would continue to be '"owned" by the public sector in its widest sense' (Scottish Government 2008, 28). The SFT would initially be under direct oversight of Scottish Ministers but later be potentially overseen by an Infrastructure Board for Scotland of senior representatives of the public sector and chaired by the Cabinet Secretary for Finance.

The Scottish government had to admit that its originally envisaged own-bond scheme – central to the capital raising efforts of the SFT – was impossible to implement. Different arrangements for the SFT to build up capital were proposed: the UK's Prudential Borrowing Framework (Bailey et al. 2010) and access to funding by local authorities via the Public Works Loan Board (part of the UK government's Debt Management Office) or through commercial lenders. This meant that until the SFT was allowed to issue its own bonds, its sole role would be to help local government to drive efficiency 'to make available resources go further', that is, the SFT would be a mere advisor for local government borrowing from already existing and already used sources.

Unsurprisingly, the SBC was criticised by all sides while the government continued to make slow progress with getting SFT up and running. Therefore, it is not an easy undertaking to say what the SFT actually is today. The actual legal form of SFT differs to some extent from what the SBC envisaged and it is still unclear how money will be raised. The SNP leader remained bullish about the SFT and said in March 2009 that it 'has been extremely properly thought-out' and that 'its time has come' – while at the same time demanding that the UK government should give the Scottish government the right to borrow (Salmond 2009a).

At present, however, the Scottish government's ability to find new ways to fund public service and infrastructure investments is severely limited by the 1999 devolution settlement. No Scottish mainstream party has said that it would use Scotland's very limited income tax raising powers to generate additional public monies and that power has not been used during the first ten years of Scotland's devolved state.

Issuing bonds and abolishing inheritance tax were beyond the powers of the Scottish Parliament. The subsequent idea of a cluster of councils issuing bonds to attract private finance for the building of infrastructure was criticised because for the last 33 years of having these powers barely a council has made use of them. Eventually, the SNP had to accept another form of PPP – NPD models – as the main game in town for financing new public infrastructure and services projects.

Despite its long-standing rejection of PFI/PPPs, the SNP also started to appreciate their utility in terms of electoral logic: after all, PPPs made it possible to finance public projects while the real costs would bite later (Shaw 2004, 73). And because the SNP had promised that it would match the previous Labour/Liberal Democrat government's school-building programme 'brick by brick' when in government itself (e.g. Dinwoodie 2007a) it needed to produce success even if that meant using a quasi-PPP model such as NPD.

The PFI/PPP programme had delivered investment of £5.9 billion up to 2009 in Scotland (Hellowell 2007; Scottish Government 2009). Even though it had also created a public sector cash liability of £22.3 billion, the SNP began to acknowledge the contributions that the private sector could make to public infrastructure and services, if only 'excess profits' were curtailed.

In government, the SNP has not been able to devise an alternative funding mechanism which actually works. Between 1999 and 2009, the SFT evolved from the initial radical proposal for a public sector, non-profit vehicle that would borrow its own cash from the City and deliver increased investment more cheaply, into a watered-down version only giving advice to help local authorities and the Scottish NHS to strike better PFI deals. There had continued to be a considerable degree of opposition to the SNP minority government's evolving incarnations of the SFT and even its final form was not built on a consensus.

The SNP had been repeatedly forced into defensive positions as criticisms were made of the various versions of the trust concept (Scottish

Public Services Trust, non-profit, NPD and SFT). Although a version of the SFT was proposed in 1999, the NPD model was resurrected in the 2003 SNP manifesto and again in 2006 prior to the 2007 election. There was still little progress more than a year after the consultation process finished. The resulting planning blight (while awaiting its adoption and implementation) meant that, at worst, the SFT proposal created considerable negative value or, at best, low value added. The repeated watering down of this anti-PFI/PPP proposal has arguably caused any potential value added to diminish over time.

A better consensus-seeking process might have averted some of the widely alleged negative impacts of the SFT and rejection of PFIs/PPPs on public infrastructure construction in the midst of a global recession (Penman 2009). The long drawn out saga of the SFT seriously damaged the economic reputation of the SNP government, certainly among opinion formers in the media and within the business community. Notwithstanding the SNP's commitment to match the school-building programme promised by the previous Labour/Liberal Democrat Scottish government, no money was forthcoming via the SFT to build new schools in Scotland within the SNP's first two years in office.

In spring 2009, the Scottish government published yet another new idea relating to public sector investment. Alex Salmond announced that a Scottish Investment Bank would be set up to 'support Scotland's economic recovery' (Currie 2009; Salmond 2009b). This bank, initially based on money from the European Regional Development Fund, Scottish Enterprise's existing Scottish Co-operative Investment Fund, Scottish Venture Fund and Scottish Seed Fund, might become the recipient of capital from local government – possibly raised through local bonds – and thus serve as a National Municipal Bank in conjunction with SFT.

Even by late 2009, the SFT was still an evolving policy instrument in terms of its aims, arrangements for governance and accountability, operation, how it engages with business and local authorities, planned expenditures and the sectors in which those expenditures are taking place. Clearly, the search for a credible alternative to PFIs/PPPs has proven highly problematic in Scotland.

Lessons from the SFT experience for other LGFAs

The SFT differs from the Nordic version of LGFAs in a number of respects.

- The SFT is an element of the SNP's stance of 'standing up for Scotland's interests', which is part of the SNP's *raison d'être* (Johns et al. 2009, 212; Macleod 2007). The motives behind the SFT are therefore very different from those behind Nordic LGFAs, with the SFT being 'imposed' upon local authorities.
- As a policy instrument, the SFT could not work within the Scottish devolution settlement because the Scottish government has no powers to borrow – unlike the UK central government and local authorities throughout Scotland, the rest of the UK and the Nordic countries. It therefore has no credit rating, unlike the AAA ratings of the Nordic LGFAs.
- Unlike the Nordic LGFAs, the SFT has no assets of its own and hence no balance sheet to underpin its financial transactions.
- Having no powers to raise its own finance, the SFT does not seek to compete with commercial banks – unlike the Nordic LGFAs.
- The SFT is a purely advisory agency whereas the Nordic LGFAs provide both finance and advice.
- The SFT has a much lower market share than Nordic LGFAs, limited in 2009 to the Hub initiative in Scotland (see Chapter 2).
- The SFT does not have strong support from Scottish local governments, upon whom it depends to raise finance for infrastructure projects. Nordic LGFAs have strong support from their municipalities and so have been able to overcome the vested interests and negative lobbying of commercial banks.
- More generally, the SFT is not built on a consensus between the SNP and policy-field stakeholders from industry, the financial sector, trade unions, local authorities and national government. The Nordic experience of LGFAs is based on consensus between municipalities and central government.
- The SFT's Hub initiative allows profits to be split between the public and private sector partners whereas the Nordic LGFAs retain profits that would otherwise have gone to commercial banks.

Conclusions

The Nordic LGFA model is an important innovation in the municipal financing of public sector infrastructure and could be adopted much more widely. A financial innovation by the public (rather than private) sector, it has weathered the storm of the 2007–2009 financial crisis much better than a large part of the commercial banking sector. The crisis revealed the weakness of the many poorly constructed financial innovations: solutions that have not been driven by cost efficiencies for the benefit of the public sector have seen their use curtailed. Thus it can be argued that this financial crisis has had the beneficial effect of removing inefficient solutions and allowing the continued development of more sustainable methods of financing public sector infrastructure projects.

Taking the majority of municipalities into a group that becomes effectively jointly liable for the debts of an LGFA can result in the same credit rating as the sovereign government. Based on such conditions, local government debt should therefore not need any other form of credit enhancement to improve their creditworthiness either from the state or third parties (e.g. monoline insurance companies) or by securing debt with other collateral or receivables. It is also important to note that an LGFA does require a substantial equity base in order to be credible and that a relatively small proportion of equity is an insignificant cost for the public sector compared with the cost savings over time of efficient funding.

The short and troubled history of Scotland's LGFA owes much to the fact that it did not persuade the majority of municipalities to form a group that would have become jointly liable for the debts of the SFT. It has been imposed upon them by the Scottish government and has forced them to continue with a version of the formal PFI/PPP model which many of them oppose. Lacking its own finances and assets, the SFT is finding it very difficult to develop its own major public sector infrastructure programmes and its future success remains in doubt.

The long successful history of Nordic LGFAs makes clear that they could be very effective during periods when the parent countries were much weaker than they are today. In Norway, Kommunalbanken was created when Norway had the lowest GDP per capita in a poor Europe. Denmark's KommuneKredit was created more than 100 years ago when Denmark was certainly less developed than any of the new member states. The same argument works for France, Germany and the Netherlands.

With hindsight of the 2007–2009 financial crisis, it can be seen that LGFAs are a resilient and sustainable solution for regional governments. They are in fact one of the only remaining cost-competitive sources of funding for regional government. As is well known, many banks have sought the protection and support of their national governments. Others, along with many of the monoline insurance companies, have closed down or have stepped away from the regional government loan market. LGFAs have continued to perform well and in most countries they continue to operate successfully, with the glaring exceptions of France, Belgium, the UK and Germany [Press reports in 2009 indicate that French municipalities are considering establishing their own LGFA once again].

The fact that LGFAs have survived the financial crisis so well is evidence that there are few structural weaknesses in the LGFA model. Obviously they are small and vulnerable to accidents. Their net income is tiny compared to their balance sheet size and capital. However, increased margins will only increase the costs to their beneficiaries and owners. The same argument applies to their capital base. It is small and if it were increased it would increase the effective cost of borrowing for its beneficiaries and owners: the municipal sector.

LGFAs have evolved over 100 years or so and the Nordic model appears to be a well defined and well developed funding agency that operates well because it is transparent and subject to enormous peer pressure from owners, banks and investors. This model can easily be replicated, as has been seen with both the Swedish and Finnish LGFAs, which have grown up from nothing during the last two to three decades.

References

Bailey, S. J., Asenova, D. and Beck, M. (2009a) UK Public Private Partnerships and the Credit Crunch: A Case Of Risk Contagion? *Journal of Risk and Governance*, 1(3): 26.

Bailey, S. J., Asenova, D. and Hood, J. (2009b) Making More Use of Local Government Bonds in Scotland? *Public Money and Management*, 29 (1): 11–18.

Bailey, S. J., Asenova, D., Hood, J. and Manochin, M. (2010) An Exploratory Study of the Utilisation of the UK's Prudential Borrowing Framework, *Public Policy and Administration*, 25 (forthcoming).

Bailey, S. J. and Fingland, L. (2008) The Stability and Growth Pact: Its Credibility and Sustainability, *Public Money and Management*, 28 (4): 223–230.

Bengtson, M. and Bursjö, R. (2002) *Arlandabanan på villovägar. Samhällsekonomiska.* Uppsala Universitet Sweden: Stockholm.

Buxton, James (1999) Concern over PFI Plan, *Financial Times*, 17 February, 8.

Chinyio, Ezekiel and Gameson, Rod (2009) Private Finance Initiative in Use. In Akintoye Akintola and Matthias Beck (eds) *Policy, Finance & Management for Public-Private Partnerships*. London : Wiley-Blackwell, 3–26.

Currie, Brian (2009) Scottish Investment Bank to Help Fund Innovation, The Herald. 22 April, www.theherald.co.uk/politics/news/display. var.2503460.0.Scottish_Investment_Bank_to_help_fund_innovation.php (accessed 16 April 2009).

Davidson, Lorraine (2007) Unison Condemns Successor to Private Finance Initiatives, *The Times*, 21 December, 9.

Deerin, Chris (1999) Salmond's Big Idea is Savaged by Bosses: Public Cash Plan in Tatters, *Daily Record*, 18 February.

Dinwoodie, Robbie (2007a) Labour's Promise of 150 More Schools Matched by the SNP. *The Herald*, 30 January, 9.

Dinwoodie, Robbie (2007b) Treasury Set to Block Swinney's Public Finance Plan, *The Herald*, 21 December, 6.

Fraser, Ian (1999) Public Row over Future of Private Finance, *Sunday Herald*, 21 February, 14.

Haldane, Juliet (2007) Scottish Futures Trust – The Way Forward for Scotland? November, The Scotsman, http://www.shepwedd.co.uk/knowledge/published-articles/article/117/scottish-futures-Trust-the-way-forward-for-scotland-/1/

Hellowell, Mark (2007) Written Evidence to the Finance Committee of the Scottish Parliament with Regards to Its Inquiry into the Funding of Capital Investment, University of Edinburgh. http://www.health.ed.ac.uk/CIPHP/Documents/ScottishFinanceCommittee.pdf (accessed 29 April 2009).

Horsburgh, Frances (1999) Salmond Defends SNP's Funding Plans as Liddell Goes on Attack, *The Herald*, 19 February, 6.

Hutcheson, Paul (2008) SNP Unveil Tax Perk to Finance Schools and Hospitals, *Sunday Herald*, 20 January 2008, 25.

Johns, R., Mitchell, J., Denver, D. and Pattie, C. (2009) Valence Politics in Scotland: Towards an Explanation of the 2007 Election, *Political Studies*, 57 (1): 207–234.

Kiiras, J., Stenroos, V. and Oyegoke, A. S. (2002) CM Forms in Finland. Helsinki University of Technology, Construction Economics and Management. Espoo, Finland, Working Paper No. 44.

Macleod (2007) Salmond is on the Road to Tax and Turmoil, *The Times*, 22 March, 7.

McNair, Brian (2008) The Scottish Media and Politics. In Neil Blain and Hutchinson Neil (eds) *The Media in Scotland*. Edinburgh: Edinburgh University Press, 227–242.

Neil, Alex (1999) SNP's Trusts are Shot Down, *The Herald*, 17 February, 6.

Penman, John (2009) Scottish Agenda: The SFT Must Stop Talking and Start Building, *The Sunday Times*, 15 February.

Pollock, A. (2007) Quoted in *The Herald*, 21 December.

Robison, Shona (2007) Protest as NHS Set to Confirm Private Partnership hospital, quoted in Moss, Lyndsay, *The Scotsman*, 30 January, 8.

Salmond, Alex (1999) Deerin, Chris. Salmond's Big Idea is Savaged by Bosses: Public Cash Plan in Tatters, *Daily Record*, 18 February.

Salmond, Alex (2009a) Staying Power, 13 March, quoted in Scott, David, http://www.publicfinance.co.uk/features_details.cfm?News_id=59907.

Salmond, Alex (2009b) SNP Appoints PFI Expert Barry White to Head Futures Trust, quoted in Macleod, Angus. *The Times*, 6 April.

Scott, David (2007) Scottish Government May Drop Bond Plan for Non-profit PPPs, *Public Finance*, 9 November, 10.

Scottish Government (2007) Consultation on the Role of a Scottish Futures Trust in Infrastructure Investment in Scotland. Edinburgh: Scottish Government.

Scottish Government (2008) Taking Forward the Scottish Futures Trust: The Strategic Business Case. Edinburgh: Scottish Government.

Scottish Government (2009) Total Number of PPP and NPD Projects and their Capital Value Figures – 5 February, http://www.scotland.gov.uk/Resource/Doc/919/0077358.xls

Shaw, Eric (2004) What Matters is What Works: The Third Way and the Private Finance Initiative. In S. Hale, and W. Leggett (eds) *The Third Way and Beyond*. Manchester: University Press.

Smith, Mark (2006) Salmond: My Vision. *Daily Mirror*, 10 April, 26.

SNP (1999) Scotland's Party: Manifesto for the 1999 Parliament Elections, http://www.psr.keele.ac.uk/area/uk/ass/snp/man99.pdf

SNP (2007) Scottish National Party: Election Manifesto, http://www.snp.org/node/13534 (accessed 11 March).

Sturgeon, Nicola (2007) Nicola Sturgeon Q & A, 26 October 2006, http://news.bbc.co.uk/1/hi/programmes/question_time/6046338.stm for Sturgeon comment.

Swinney, John (1999a) Public Row Over Future of Private Finance, *Sunday Herald*, 21 February, 14.

Swinney, John (1999b) Saving Your Money is a Matter of Trust, *Evening News*, 18 February, 10.

Swinney, John (2007) Foreword. Consultation on the Role of a Scottish Futures Trust in Infrastructure Investment in Scotland.

7
Innovation in Local Government Risk Financing: Lessons from the UK and Nordic Experiences

John Hood, Bill Stein and Pekka Valkama

Introduction

Key developments in the public sectors of many countries over the past two decades have been the notion of 'modernisation', generally meaning a shift from a traditional public sector ethos to a more private sector approach, and its corollary 'innovation' (Bovaird and Löffler 2003; Flynn 2007). Innovation was, in the past, anathema to many in the public sector as, by its very nature, it introduced risk into what was a risk-averse environment. For example, in the UK, central government does not wish to see other parts of the public sector taking excessive risks, or taking risks which may be acceptable in the private sector but are regarded as not being within the public domain. The mantra is one of 'balanced' or 'well managed' risk taking. How, therefore, can public bodies construct a system to exploit fully private sector knowledge of the possibilities for the management of risk, especially for the financing of risk, yet comply with rules and regulations relating to the risks they are allowed to take? Risk financing, in this context, refers to the mechanisms in place to ensure that funds are available to meet the financial consequences of unforeseen losses.

UK local authorities, as a significant part of the wider public sector, have traditionally been both limited and cautious in their choice of mechanisms for financing the complex set of risks that they face, especially those that are insurable (ALARM 2005; Fone and Young 2005; Hood and Young 2005). In reality, the financing mechanism of choice for insurable risks has been the purchase of commercially available insurance cover, often by means of an 'insurance fund' (LASAAC 2005).

The utilisation of insurance would square with the lower rung of 'Stewart's ladder' (Stewart 1984), which is concerned with different levels of accountability within (especially public) organisations, whereby those accountable for financing risk could, by sanctioning the purchase of insurance, satisfy criteria on legality and probity. Yet, as we will explain, although still highly significant as a mechanism to treat risks, traditional insurance is not without its weaknesses. For UK local authorities, the existence of rules, regulations and constraints imposed by central government has created barriers to the use of innovative alternatives to insurance. By contrast, many large private sector organisations have not been subject to the same fiscal and regulatory regimes and, as a consequence, have experimented with a range of risk-financing methods. Not all of these methods have been successful and some of them remain inappropriate for local authorities. Detailed analysis of the applicability of alternative risk-financing mechanisms for local authorities has been an under-researched area and this work seeks to help address this knowledge gap. Specifically, we investigate the risk-financing method known as mutuals, or pooling. Mutual risk pooling is an activity whereby a number of, generally, homogenous entities unite to form a separate entity, which will provide risk financing to members of the pool. It operates in similar form to conventional insurance, although the pool as 'insurer' is owned by its policy-holders and not shareholders.

The legislative landscape for UK local authorities seemed set for change in 2007 with the creation of the London Authorities Mutual Limited (LAML). Its members were confident that risk pooling would no longer be dismissed as *ultra vires,* that is, beyond the powers granted to them. LAML is a risk pool formed by a number of London boroughs, the City Corporation of London and the Greater London Authority. At around the same time, the Fire and Rescue Mutual Limited (FRAML) was launched and plans also announced for the creation of the Councils' Alternative Risk & Insurance Group (CARIG). Against the background of these developments, we examine in detail a proposal for a pool of Scottish local authorities, which was rejected following a feasibility study, and we compare this with the LAML case. As will be seen, the events surrounding LAML would suggest that the local government environment in the UK is not as conducive to mutual risk pools as it is in other European, specifically Nordic, countries.

History of UK local authority insurance purchasing

The case for and against heavy reliance on insurance by any organisation has been well covered in the literature (see for example De Mey 2003; Nawaz and Stein 1998; Punter 2002). Until 1992, however, UK local authorities relied almost exclusively on Municipal Mutual Insurance (MMI) to provide cover against the vast majority of their insurable risks. MMI had been in existence since 1903 and by the 1970s it was providing insurance to over 90 per cent of UK local authorities (Fone and Young 2005). Due to a number of factors, including increased claims, a flawed diversification strategy and the constraints of mutuality in raising capital, MMI collapsed in 1992 and the staff and renewal rights were absorbed into the Zurich Insurance Group to become Zurich Municipal Insurance (ZMI). After MMI's demise, an adequate, although limited, commercial insurance market emerged for local authorities, which was itself affected by a downturn in the underwriting cycle, a significant decline in investment returns and a number of other problems, such as terrorism concerns, which all converged in late 2001 (Hood and Acc-Nikmehr (2006)).

A number of commentators (ALARM, 2005; Gollier 2001; 2003; Gollier and Pratt 1996) have questioned the rationale for insurance being such a central plank of local authorities' risk-financing strategy and practice. They have raised the idea of over-reliance on commercially purchased insurance being a potentially flawed strategy and have explored a number of issues surrounding both the insurance market and variations on the basic theme of insurance.

Although, like all public sector organisations, local authorities have been under increasing pressure to be more 'business-like', it is often unclear what being 'business-like' really entails. Christopher Hood (1991) in his seminal exposition of 'New Public Management' identifies one of its 'doctrinal components' as the adoption of a 'private sector' management style. In the context of risk financing this could, arguably, point to a more challenging attitude to the status quo and a greater exploration of the alternatives to insurance which have been developed over the past 20 years or so.

Figure 7.1 outlines the various risk-financing options that, at least in theory, exist for local authorities. These include no insurance, own insurance, private sector insurance and mutual insurance. The last has three alternative forms: a Guaranteed Indemnity Mutual (GIM), a Discretionary Mutual (DM) or a 'captive' insurance company (owned by a group of authorities).

The reality, at least in the UK, however, is that despite some convergence between private and public management techniques, local authorities have substantially eschewed the alternative risk-financing techniques which the private sector has embraced. It should be recognised, therefore, that conventional insurance might fit well with the risk appetite of

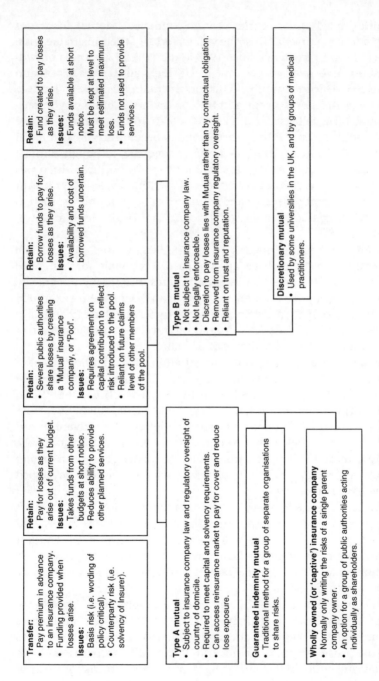

Transfer:
- Pay premium in advance to an insurance company.
- Funding provided when losses arise.

Issues:
- Basis risk (i.e. wording of policy critical).
- Counterparty risk (i.e. solvency of Insurer).

Retain:
- Pay for losses as they arise out of current budget.

Issues:
- Takes funds from other budgets at short notice.
- Reduces ability to provide other planned services.

Retain:
- Several public authorities share losses by creating a 'Mutual' insurance company, or 'Pool'.

Issues:
- Requires agreement on capital contribution to reflect risk introduced to the pool.
- Reliant on future claims level of other members of the pool.

Retain:
- Borrow funds to pay for losses as they arise.

Issues:
- Availability and cost of borrowed funds uncertain.

Retain:
- Fund created to pay losses as they arise.

Issues:
- Funds available at short notice.
- Must be kept at level to meet estimated maximum loss.
- Funds not used to provide services.

Type A mutual
- Subject to insurance company law and regulatory oversight of country of domicile.
- Required to meet capital and solvency requirements.
- Can access reinsurance market to pay for cover and reduce loss exposure.

Guaranteed indemnity mutual
- Traditional method for a group of separate organisations to share risks.

Wholly owned (or 'captive') insurance company
- Normally only writing the risks of a single parent company owner.
- An option for a group of public authorities acting individually as shareholders.

Type B mutual
- Not subject to insurance company law.
- Not legally enforceable.
- Discretion to pay losses lies with Mutual rather than by contractual obligation.
- Removed from insurance company regulatory oversight.
- Reliant on trust and reputation.

Discretionary mutual
- Used by some universities in the UK, and by groups of medical practitioners.

Figure 7.1 Alternative options for municipal risk financing

local authorities. In addition to this cautious approach, it must always be borne in mind that there are constraints on the activities of local authorities, which do not apply to private sector organisations. In effect, authorities have traditionally only been able to act in accordance with very specific powers given to them by central government and have not had the freedoms and flexibilities found in the private sector.

Notwithstanding all of these factors, and given the questions raised against conventional insurance by those such as Gollier, there is a sustainable argument that UK local authorities should, at least, explore the feasibility and viability of those alternatives which are *intra vires*, that is, within their powers.

Risk pooling

The specific issue of local authority risk mutuals or pools has not been explicitly addressed by UK central government, but it is interesting to note that the Cabinet Office has produced a report (Cabinet Office 2002, 37–38) containing material relevant to local authorities which is clear on the related, wider issue of risk financing: 'We recommend that the Treasury should consider running a pilot of the use of captive[1] insurance arrangements in government.' Additionally, a Labour government minister has suggested, in a wide-ranging speech on reducing the public finance deficit, that there is a place for mutual insurers in local government, although at this stage very little specific detail is provided (Guardian 2009). Given central government's 'modernisation' agenda, the public finance crisis and the inherent problems of the conventional insurance market, it seems strange that there has been, until only very recently, little movement among local authorities towards risk pooling, although there is some evidence of increased interest (FRAML 2007; London Centre of Excellence 2007).

Risk pooling, at a basic level, is an example of local authorities co-operating in risk spreading and taking advantage of economies of scale. To a certain degree, precedents for this exist in the well understood ideas of consortium purchasing and the National Procurement Strategy (Dept of Communities and Local Government 2006). In reality, however, risk pooling is more complex than authorities simply cooperating in the purchase of services and capital equipment as it raises issues of risk and liability sharing. As our Scottish case study will demonstrate, there may also be concerns in local authorities over how pooling can, in the short term, satisfy central government requirements on Best Value in a competitive environment where commercial insurers may offer reduced premiums to retain business. Despite these difficulties it is, however, a valid, feasible and highly relevant alternative to traditional insurance procurement and is worthy of exploration.

On a global basis, public sector risk-financing mutuals or pools are not new, with some government pools in, for example, Japan having their origins in the 1920s and earlier (Young et al. 1999). Although there appears to be no publicly accessible European database, there is sufficient evidence that the local government mutual concept has been grasped in a number of countries, examples being Ethias in Belgium and S:t Erik Försäkring in Sweden. In addition, responses to enquiries to the Association of Mutual Insurers and Insurance Cooperatives in Europe (AMICE) (http://www.amice-eu.org) indicated that the European Municipal Insurance Group is a loose network of municipal insurers, most of which are mutuals and also members of AMICE. Further research is needed into such factors as the political and legislative environments in which other European local authorities operate, the nature of the commercial insurance market and the historical attitude towards mutuals and pools. Nonetheless, the general evidence would suggest that the concept has been grasped much more enthusiastically outside the UK.

In the UK, where these types of insurance/risk-financing pools have existed, they have been traditionally referred to as mutuals, that is, they are mutually owned and utilised by their members. It is important to bear in mind that issues surrounding *intra* and *ultra vires*, that is, acting within the limitations of powers and acting outside those limitations, must be addressed. It would be *ultra vires* for a local authority to share or accept the risks of another local authority. However, mutual risk pools do not involve the actual risks themselves being shared, it is the negative financial consequences of these risks coming to fruition that are shared by members of the pool, which appears, based on the Cabinet Office (2002) guidance, to be *intra vires*. For example, local authorities would not be assuming the legal liability of a fellow pool member that has failed to protect a vulnerable adult in its care, but if there was a financial consequence of this failure to protect, that is, the vulnerable adult was awarded compensation by the courts, the risk pool would pay this compensation. In that respect, the risk-financing arrangements are no different from conventional insurance.

Although found in all branches of insurance, the origins of UK mutuals lie in the life insurance sector and this sector still has some in existence. However, difficulties in accessing fresh capital have favoured demutualisation to obtain a status where share capital can be raised and to release assets or profits to the founding or current members. Mutual insurance companies have no capital stock and are owned by policy-holders. The earnings of the company, over and above the payments of the losses, operating expenses and reserves, are the property of the policy-holders. The origins of mutual insurance as a form of risk financing in the UK go back to the establishment of trade guilds centuries ago.

Today, they are usually formed when insurance is either expensive or unobtainable, that is, they are influenced by the underwriting cycle (Cummings and Outreville 1987; Winter 1989), with hard-market conditions being an ideal breeding ground for risk pooling. Allied to the problems associated with the cyclical 'hard-market/soft market', many traditional insurers are demonstrably cautious about new and developing areas of risk and they tend to focus on excluding them rather than thinking about ways to cover them (ALARM 2005). When pools are formed to overcome these market problems, the aim is usually to write a specific risk or number of risks, for example employers' liability, rather than to replace the commercial insurance market for all insurance needs. In addition to overcoming availability and affordability problems, there may be more direct benefits from concerted risk-mitigation actions, particularly if attitudes are shared by fellow mutual owners. As indicated earlier, the insurance market can be highly problematic and local authorities have experienced many of the market-related problems which would point to risk pooling being a creditable financing mechanism.

To pool or not to pool?

There are a number of macro and micro differences between local authorities in Scotland and England. For all practical purposes, however, the insurable risks to which they are exposed and the main methods available to finance those risks are substantially the same. That being the case, it is valid to compare and contrast the decisions taken in forming the LAML and those taken to abandon the creation of a pool by 16 Scottish authorities.

The London Authorities Mutual Limited (LAML)

In 2005 a feasibility study was carried out by 28 London local authorities into the creation of a GIM. The detailed figures are not publicly available, but LAML (2007a) asserts that the conclusion was that '*a mutual insurance company owned by London authorities could generate significant premium savings and, in the medium term, generate a substantial operating surplus for its members'.* LAML commenced business on 1 April 2007, and as a GIM is subject to authorisation and regulation by the Financial Services Authority (FSA). A one-off payment from members, in addition to their premium contribution, was required to meet the capitalisation requirements. As noted in Figure 7.1, there are additional burdens on GIMs when compared to DMs, but the literature from LAML is silent on why this form of mutual was utilised. The processes behind this decision would be a useful and interesting area for further research.

Although, unsurprisingly, LAML does not disclose the precise figures that its members used in their decision-making process, it does identify a number of key points to support its business case:

- Legal opinion confirmed that the mutual was *intra vires*;
- Robust financial modelling of possible losses indicated a significant surplus over the first five years of trading;
- Concerns over lack of choice in the insurance marketplace and over premium costs in relation to claims costs;
- Premium savings of 15 per cent would be achieved;
- Cover would be equal to, or greater than, that available in the conventional market;
- 'Consortium' purchasing would result in increased leverage with reinsurers;
- Standard & Poor's (S&P) 'A' rated reinsurers would provide appropriate protection;
- The mutual would be tax efficient and underwriting profit would be used for the benefit of members.
- A mutual insurance company owned by London authorities could generate significant premium savings and, in the medium term, generate a substantial operating surplus for its members.

In many respects, therefore, their feasibility study supported the advantages of pools experienced in other countries. In addition, The London Centre of Excellence (2007), a partnership of public bodies which aims to optimise the governance and operation of London's public sector, claimed that LAML *'will provide a much better deal for local government than we have seen to date'*. Davies (2007) identified that, in addition to achieving better value for money, the catalysts for the creation of the LAML included the Gershon Efficiency Review and central government's Shared Services Agenda. In April 2008 four additional

London authorities joined the ten original subscribing members of LAML, suggesting that the first-year experiences of these members had been positive, that the financial position was robust and that the conventional insurance market was unwilling, or unable, to match the LAML on price, cover or service levels. Indeed, three members have been identified as having had premium savings of £278,000 in the first year (Municipal Journal 2008). An expectation was formed that, as their current insurance contracts expired, more London authorities would move to LAML during 2008 and 2009.

Although LAML was confident of its legal position, having taken advice and been subject to rigorous review by the FSA and the Audit Commission (LAML 2007b), one insurance provider, concerned that it was being excluded from the public sector insurance market, commenced court action in May 2007 to challenge the existence of such mutuals (Municipal Journal 2008). The case was brought by Risk Management Partners Limited, a London-based general managing agency owned by the US company Arthur J. Gallacher and with insurance capacity provided by American International Group. A complaint was brought against one LAML member, the London Borough of Brent, although LAML joined the legal action in support of Brent.

The complaint challenged whether Brent, under its statutory powers, had the right to join the mutual insurer LAML, and whether it should have followed European rules that require public sector entities to put large procurement contracts out to open tender. In two separate decisions (delivered in April and May 2008) the judge upheld Risk Management Partners' complaints, finding that the London Borough of Brent had acted *ultra vires*. Lord Justice Brunton, who heard the case, said he would focus on the *'fundamental difference between ... participation in LAML and normal commercial insurance'*. By participating in the mutual, Brent was not only buying insurance for itself but also providing liability cover to other members participating in the scheme. Brent had paid a £160,500 capitalisation charge to LAML, and had taken on potentially unlimited liabilities to cover LAML in the event of future shortfalls.

The judge also found that even if it was *intra vires*, it was not entitled to disregard the Public Contracts Regulations 2006, which require contracts of this size to be put to open tender. It is not clear whether Risk Management Partners would have beaten LAML in open tender, but the point is that Brent failed to give them the opportunity to do so. Clearly, in the future such procedural niceties should be observed to the letter and LAML be required to win in open tender.

The judge gave leave to appeal against the *ultra vires* ruling. In June 2009, the Court of Appeal also ruled that the participation of local authorities in an insurance mutual in the manner of LAML was *ultra vires* (Royal Courts of Justice 2009). The Court of Appeal also ruled that Brent had acted in breach of the Procurement Regulations 2006 when it awarded its insurance contracts to LAML. The Chairman of LAML summed up the implications of this Court of Appeal judgement by stating that the judgement 'takes us back to the late eighties and there will be enhanced nervousness about the extent of a local authority's powers – the very thing the introduction of wellbeing powers was intended to resolve' (LAML 2009).

Although the Court of Appeal judgement forced LAML to close for business and to go into a 'run-off' position, this may not be the end of the story in the longer term. In the immediate aftermath of the judgement, supporters of LAML pressed for central government to change the law and broaden the powers of local government. This may or may not happen and is clearly dependent on much wider political developments. At this time, however, the existing judgements on the Brent case do provide helpful insights into the issues surrounding local authority mutuals.

The Scottish experience

A feasibility study on the viability of insurance pooling was carried out between April 2003 and January 2005, on behalf of 16 (out of a total of 32) Scottish local authorities. The impetus for the project came from the significant increases in the costs of property insurance since 2001, which had resulted in a combination of higher premiums and increased policy excesses (deductibles). Also, there was recognition that historically the prevailing property insurance market conditions meant there was little effective competition to ZMI in the market (Heath Lambert Group 2007), and so local authorities were unable to demonstrate value for money (VFM) in the procurement of property insurance. Also, the potential existed for significant upwards cost fluctuations (premiums increased by 91 per cent in a two-year period from 2002) in the insurance market and the subsequent knock-on impact on the resources available to deliver front line services. As a consequence of the substantial price increases being encountered, the Chartered Institute of Public Finance and Accountancy (CIPFA) Scotland Directors of Finance Section set up a subgroup to undertake a feasibility study on the viability of insurance facility options. The study had the main objectives of stabilising the existing volatile market, introducing market competition and customer choice, providing greater predictability and budget certainty and allowing VFM to be evidenced through market competition or peer comparison. The feasibility study was carried out in three phases between April 2003 and February 2005.

Phase 1: Preliminary Feasibility Study. This involved 16 local authorities and concluded that insurance pooling was viable and offered the potential for cost savings and greater budget stability.

Phase 2: Structure and Legality. This considered the best structure for the risk-financing vehicle and concluded that the optimum way forwards was for the local authorities to establish a risk-pooling vehicle in the form of a limited liability company incorporated in the Isle of Man. Legal opinion was sought, which confirmed that Scottish local authorities could enter into such arrangements by virtue of their power.

Phase 3: Premium Tendering Exercise. This involved the mutual standing in open competition against other insurance companies in two stages: first, a consortium tender to cover all of the property risks of the local authority participants, and second, tenders to meet the risks of individual authorities. In the first (consortium) stage only the mutual tendered for the consortium's insurances and its price of £7.5 million represented a 9 per cent saving on the current premiums. In the second stage, individual member local authorities sought quotations from the mutual and from the commercial insurance market. This second stage produced total premium quotes of £7.3 million, which represented an overall reduction of 11.9 per cent on the previous year's total premiums for the members of the mutual.

Clearly, one of the main objectives of creating market competition was thus met, with all participants receiving a minimum of two quotes and some attracting more. Within the average reduction in premiums (11.9 per cent) there were considerable variations, with large authorities obtaining reductions of 8–29 per cent, while smaller authorities were faced with increases of 4–13 per cent in their property insurance premiums. It seems clear that insurance companies had introduced selective pricing and had targeted reductions at the larger local authorities to, perhaps, reduce the chances of the mutual's success and destabilise the participants' consensus. Early in 2005, the participants had to consider the way forwards and, in particular, decide whether or not to proceed. Due to the extremely favourable renewal terms offered to four of the larger authorities, the number of potential participants fell to eight (only 25 per cent of Scottish local authorities) and a loss of critical mass was emerging.

The project got as far as submitting a bid to the Scottish Executive's Efficient Government fund for £1.5 million to provide initial capital for the insurance company justified by an annual turnover of £7.5 million and average profit of £300,000 per annum. However, sufficient support could not be mustered for the April 2005 start-up and the project did not proceed (Scottish Executive 2006), although in the light of the English court's decision on LAML that may have been a sensible decision.

The European and Nordic perspective

Given the outcome of the LAML litigation, the development of local authority mutuals in the UK can now only be taken forwards by central government legislation. In the short term, this would seem to be unlikely.

The situation in many European countries is, however, quite different (Eurofi 2008). Since 1973, initially under the auspices of the International Union of Local Authorities, a group has existed to promote the use of local authority mutuals. This group, now known as European Municipal Insurance Group (EMIG), has members from six European countries: Belgium, Denmark, France, Germany, Ireland and Norway. We will focus on the two Nordic country members, that is, Denmark and Norway, as well as Sweden and Finland who are not EMIG members. Information on this topic is not widely available in the public domain, but we have been able to access an unpublished report by EMIG (2008). Furthermore, it would be inappropriate to draw direct comparisons between countries due to such factors as differing government systems, different powers and responsibilities of local authorities and the historical relationship between local authorities and the insurance market. This section simply, therefore, provides an insight into what is happening in local authority risk financing in Denmark, Norway Sweden and Finland.

Denmark

Denmark has a long history of local authority mutual insurance companies (Henriksen and Bundesen 2004), three being founded in the early twentieth century. The time of formation and the reasons for the formation, the fact that the costs versus benefits of commercially available transactions were weighted against the local authorities, were not dissimilar to the MMI in the UK. In 1971, the three companies merged to form the KommuneForsikring.

Most, but not all, *amtskommuner* (provinces or counties) and *kommuner* (urban and rural municipalities) buy insurance from KommuneForsikring, and some of those that do also purchase some cover from the commercial market. The company provides all types of insurance to local authorities, as well as to other selected sectors, for example, transport bodies and to the employees of the organisations it insures. Again, therefore, similarities exist between its business model and that of the MMI.

Where, however, KommuneForsikring differs from many mutuals is its expansion into wider areas of risk management. This expansion has been achieved through its wholly owned subsidiary, the European Institute for Risk Management, which provides research and training material, as well as having an educational aspect (EIRM 2009). Although, therefore, these services are not directly provided by the mutual itself, what is being offered makes KommuneForsikring more like the 'risk management pools' into which many US mutuals have evolved (see Young 1989 for a detailed history of US risk-pool development).

The position of KommuneForsikring has, however, changed in recent years. In 2007 it was purchased by the Gjensidige group, Norway's largest insurance company. Gjensidige is not a purely mutual company, with 25 per cent of its capital allocated to 'Equity Certificate' holders and the remaining 75 per cent held by its customers. It seems, therefore, that the ultimate owner of KommuneForsikring is a hybrid of a mutual and publicly quoted company. Its 2008 annual report (KommuneForsikring 2009) suggests that, although the company is still heavily committed to insuring the public sector, it may be moving towards a broader portfolio of public and private sector clients. This possible market expansion is not outlined in detail by the company and the strategy and tactics inherent in such a diversification would represent an interesting topic for future research.

Norway

The main mutual company in Norway is Kommunal Landspensjonkasse (KLP), which is owned by *kommuner* (municipalities), *fylker* (counties) and health authorities and is a major provider of pensions. KLP has a number of subsidiaries, transacting business in such areas as property, asset and fund management and mortgage provision. Its subsidiary company, KLP Skadeforsikring, formed in 1994 as a continuation of the mutual company Kommunal Ulykkesforsikring, is a non-life insurance company offering insurance to the public sector and companies closely involved with it. The company claims that it insures more than 360 of the country's municipalities and more than 1300 companies, and its interim report for the first quarter of 2009 suggests that the company's premium income has grown and its non-life insurance business has been profitable (KLP 2009).

The capital of Norway, Oslo, has had its own captive insurance company since 1996. According to the Oslo city council, the purpose of creating the company was to improve risk management, increase loss-avoidance activities and reduce the insurance expenses of the city government. The city also converted its pension fund into the captive insurance company four years later on (Standard and Poor's 2000).

Sweden

Swedish local governments for many decades used to arrange risk funding through internal risk funds and commercial insurance. Compared with external risk pools or funds, one benefit of internal risk funds has been that a possible surplus could be used immediately for local purposes. In some cases, municipal experiences of these funds combined with internal risk-management training and preventive actions have been positive. Nevertheless, local governments' handling of risks ranged widely between individual municipalities, especially among those local governments which used private insurance. The reputation of local governments deteriorated notably during the 1990s, and commercial insurance companies became cautious with regard to the local government sector. The insurance companies considered the number of municipal accidents and the costs too high. Competition between companies dried up, because the insurance companies lost interest in municipal insurance markets at the beginning of the new millennium. When local governments needed to organise public procurement of commercial insurances, some received no bids from the companies. This development launched a new era of municipal mutual risk pools in Sweden (Carlsund and Bohman 2006, 2; Helander 2005, 12; Svenska Kommunförbudet 1997, 36).

As a reaction to the diminished competition, several Swedish local governments established mutual risk pools. For example, 30 local governments in south Sweden established a mutual insurance company in 2005. The aim of the mutual company (Kommunassurans Syd Försäkring AB) is to increase competition and to guarantee bidding for municipal shareholders when they want to buy insurance. Out of 26 local governments, 20 from the capital region created a regional mutual insurance company in 2008. The company (Stockholmsregionens Försäkring AB) grants insurance not only for shareholding municipalities but also for municipal limited companies in the capital region. At the beginning of 2008, a group of 23 small local governments established their own mutual risk pool (Förenade Småkommuners Försäkrings Aktiebolag). These local governments were dissatisfied with rising insurance costs and deteriorating terms of commercial insurance contracts.

The first municipal captive insurance company (S:t Erik Försäkrings AB) was established in 1986 by the city of Stockholm. The company serves agencies of the capital and limited companies owned by the city by helping them to identify risks and limit damage and providing insurance cover for them. The city owns the captive company through a holding company (the Stockholm Stadshus AB Group), because the city has delegated the functions of capital corporate ownership to its own placement company. The second biggest city in Sweden, Gothenburg, founded its own municipal captive insurance company (Försäkrings AB Göta Lejon) in 1990. The company not only passively takes care of the city's insurance but also actively carries out risk-management operations. The selection of types of insurance offered is wide, including, for example, motor-vehicle, fire, damage liability, theft, medical claims and travel insurance. Risk-management activities involve information campaigns, training, exercises, technical protection systems, etc. (Svenska Kommunförbudet 1997, 39).

Svenska Kommun Försäkrings AB is an interesting mutual risk pool, because its owners are both Swedish and Norwegian. Nine of the owners of this captive company are Swedish local governments, but one is the Norwegian city of Trondheim. Other local governments from Norway and Denmark have been interested in this company, but the company has not seen any need to increase the number of its shareholders (Helander 2005, 12).

Most pensions for local government sector personnel are taken care of by a joint-venture insurance company (KPA Insurance), which is 40 per cent owned by the Swedish Association of Local Authorities and Regions and 60 per cent by a private sector mutual insurance company. Housing companies for the public good, which are predominantly municipal enterprises, have an association as an umbrella organisation, and this is the owner of a mutual property insurance company granting insurance not only to municipal but also to private housing corporations (Svenska Kommunförbudet 1997, 40–41).

Finland

In contrast to Denmark, Norway and Sweden, in Finland, there are no similar mutual insurance companies owned by local governments or operating only in municipal markets. Most local governments use commercial insurance purchased through competitive tendering from private sector insurance companies, which are listed or non-listed limited companies and companies operating on the basis of mutuality. These mutual insurance companies are more or less like conventional insurance companies offering insurance and other financial services not only for local governments but also for households and private enterprises and industries. Some local governments also cooperate through joint purchasing arrangements, and they organise competitive tendering of insurance companies jointly. Although there are not very many insurance companies competing for local government customers, the insurance market for local governments has been competitive and, so far, the local government sector has not seen much need for municipal mutual companies (Enberg 2009; Kivistö 1994, 22).

Large and some medium-sized Finnish cities are exceptions in not using voluntary insurances because they have adopted an internal pooling policy. These cities have damage funds as internal insurance pools (see Figure 7.2), into which all city bureaux and agencies have to pay annual fees and from which financial compensation is provided in case of accident or damage. Some city governments run funds only for material damages but some funds also cover other kinds of risks, for example liabilities.

All Finnish local governments and joint municipal boards are members of the Local Government Pensions Institution, which is a

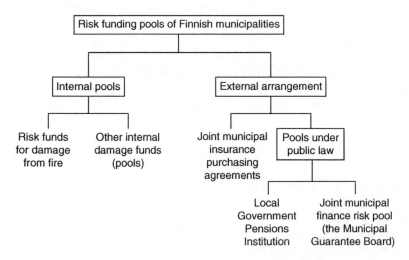

Figure 7.2   Main types of municipal risk funding pools in Finland

municipal pension insurance corporation regulated by a special public law. Municipalities need to arrange statutory employment pension
insurances through the corporation for local government officeholders
and employees. Municipally owned limited companies and associations
can also utilise pension schemes provided by the corporation.

There is also one more special mutual pool, which was created in
order to give guarantees for financial risks of the local government sector. The Municipal Guarantee Board was established in 1996 by an Act
of Parliament, and the legal form of the organisation is a body under
public law. Membership of the board was voluntary for local governments but the vast majority decided to join. The Guarantee Board
grants guarantees for funding collected by credit institutions directly
or indirectly owned or controlled by municipalities. These guarantees
may be granted if the funding is going to be used for lending to municipalities, joint municipal boards and municipally owned or controlled
limited companies.

Discussion and conclusion

LAML and the Scottish case have provided us with a wealth of material from which to extract the key issues underlying recent attempts
to revive the concept of local authority mutuals in the UK. The Scottish
case was weakened by the actions of the commercial insurance market
in tendering highly competitive premiums to selected potential members of the mutual. LAML has apparently been killed off, on account
of legal action by a single commercial insurer challenging its legality.
Although we did not consider them in detail in this chapter, it may
be noted that the LAML court ruling led to immediate suspension of
FRAML and to a delay in the launch of CARIG. At the time of writing (October 2009), it appears that in the contest between the new UK
mutuals and the traditional insurance industry, the latter has won an
easy victory. The key forces at play in this struggle have now certainly
been made very clear. For clarity, we now set these out under a number
of sub-headings.

The legislative framework may be changed

First, let us deal with the recent legal wrangling. It is quite possible that
the current legal arguments will be merely a temporary stumble in the
revival of local authority mutuals in the UK. If there are rules regarding a competitive tendering process then clearly they must be obeyed
and local authorities will be more careful in the future. The *ultra/intra*

vires issue has certainly been resolved by the Appeal Court judgement. Given that central government's strategy for local government has been to deliver efficiencies and savings through innovation, shared working and using its enhanced powers, it may be persuaded to act to amend the law.

Evidence that mutuals can deliver attractive cost savings

Notwithstanding the subsequent legal challenge from RMP, the formation of LAML appears to suggest that there is a sustainable case in the UK for innovation, especially in the context of risk pooling. Greater primary research would be needed into LAML to examine, in depth, its financial modelling and their decision to form in the way that it did. Notwithstanding that, the early evidence would suggest that the pool has delivered on cost savings and is attractive to authorities.

New confidence in risk-management expertise softens traditional conservatism

Local authorities are faced with a complex set of risks but have, traditionally, been very conservative in the mechanisms they use to finance them – often due to a combination of legal constraints and risk aversion. Many large commercial organisations have developed risk-financing strategies that help smooth out relatively predictable fluctuations in property and liability loss, and experience and mechanisms such as captives are at a high state of development. Simultaneously with these private sector developments, other countries have seen advancements in risk pooling as an effective addition to the public sector-risk financing armoury. There appears to be no reason why the UK's local authorities cannot do the same. Only recently have we seen some UK local authorities experimenting with the wide range of less conservative risk financing techniques that are now available and, indeed, used widely in the private sector (ALARM 2005, London Centre of Excellence 2007).

As the level of professionalism of local authority risk managers has increased, greater expertise and confidence may have played a part in the recent attempts at the formation of mutuals. The evidence from the Scottish experience, however, would point to an innate conservatism and a continuing reliance on the conventional insurance market and, mainly, on one major insurer in that market. The caution and conservatism of directors of finance is understandable and well grounded in long-established custom and practice. It is our contention, however, that there is a low-risk alternative to this conservatism which, in the medium to long term, could prove advantageous to local authorities (i.e. greater utilisation of risk pooling by the formation of mutuals). The formation, after apparently rigorous appraisal of options, of LAML and FRAML demonstrates that examples of innovation and balanced risk taking do exist in the local authority sphere.

It may also be the case that some local authorities would see risk pooling as being little different from MMI, and are conscious of the collapse of that organisation. That would, however, be a flawed view. MMI, as a mutual, was a form of risk pool but its precise form and its strategic and operational approach to insurance principles and practice was quite different from that of contemporary risk-pooling arrangements.

The legislative framework must take a medium- to long-term view

Insurance is a business where success cannot be measured in the short term – certainly not in a single year. Catastrophe risks such as fire and weather, and legal liabilities, are subject to much year-by-year variability and, in the case of legal liabilities, to a long tail before all claims arise and are settled. Local authority mutuals are no different from other insurers in that they must be judged in the medium- to long term, rather than just in a single year. Unless the law allows for this they will most certainly be fatally weakened. The legislative framework under which local authorities operate would have to accept that the value delivered by any mutual could not be calculated on a single year's experience. If central government were minded to alter the legislative framework it would need to realise that local authorities must be prepared to spend money in the short term (the capital injection into a new mutual) to save money in the medium to longer term (in the savings in premiums made and the related risk-management focus). The current fiscal climate may not be right for that for some time yet, but there is evidence to suggest that UK mutuals will not go away.

Mutual members must take a medium- to long-term view

Given that the underwriting cycle is part and parcel of the insurance market, the inevitable outcome of this will be periods of low market capacity and high premiums and vice versa. In a situation of open tendering, the cycles of the insurance market will tend to produce mutual-beating premiums from time to time, at least for some of its members. Moreover, it would be naive to imagine that insurers are not capable of deliberately underpricing as a tactical measure to win new business – with the hope that windfall profits can be reaped in subsequent years.

Insurers can make life difficult for the mutual

The initiation of court action by an insurer would indicate that the conventional market sees it as an innovation challenging their historical supremacy. The rational behaviour of traditional insurers will be, as appears to have been the case in the Scottish project, to offer short-term incentives to authorities which undermine the financial viability of pooling. In our view, authorities taking this short-term view are missing a longer-term opportunity and are, perhaps, placing too much emphasis on lower-rung accountability. There is also the danger that consortiums explore pooling, satisfy themselves as to its viability and sustainability and then succumb to the short-term inducements of the insurance companies. This may only succeed in removing pooling from the risk-financing agenda for the foreseeable future.

Mutuals and insurers may coexist happily

Risk pooling need not be an 'all or nothing' venture. There is no reason why local authorities could not form a pool to finance a specific form of risk, for example fire damage to property, and, at the same time, use their preferred method of risk financing, that is, insurance, for all their other insurable risks. This heuristic approach would allow authorities to benefit from the advantages of risk pooling, gain experience in the organisation and administration of pooling and develop relationships with reinsurers. At the same time, in recognition of any downside risks, their potential liabilities would be limited by the restricted nature of this exploratory venture. If, as the evidence from other domains would suggest, the pool proved to be viable, economical and sustainable, the framework and organisation would then be in place for wider utilisation. As is common practice amongst captive insurance companies, mutuals would also wish to make use of the reinsurance market for protection against higher levels of losses.

The same problems are faced by any industry mutual

It would be wrong to leave the impression that all problems faced by a local authority mutual would come from external forces such as regulation and the insurance industry. They face the same problems as any 'industry' mutual, such as those formed by members of the oil or pharmaceutical industries. Industry mutuals, for example, because they are all engaged in the same range of activities, are likely to face a concentration of the same types of risk. This may lead to claims from many members if specific types of loss arise. Industry mutuals work best when members are of a similar 'quality' and tensions may arise when some members with excellent risk management and claims record feel they are subsidising less well managed authorities (Punter 2007).

Summing up

It could be argued, on an a priori basis, that the incentives which local authorities have towards more effective risk management may differ between buying insurance from private sector companies, an element of contracting out and financing risk through either self-insurance or mutual insurance, that is, keeping the risk financing fully or partly 'in house'. If authorities, either individually or through a mutual pooling arrangement, bear the risk that otherwise could have been transferred to an insurer then there is an incentive for them to be much more proactive in minimising the risk.

Given, however, that insurance is not available for all risks and that it will seldom pay the full cost of those risks that are insured, it would be fundamentally flawed to say that there is little risk-management incentive when insurance is purchased through the market. Even so, for individual authority self-insurance, financial risk is effectively transferred to those who pay local taxes and so local politicians and officers bear only political and reputational risk respectively. So this approach to insurance is not free of perverse incentives and unwelcome consequences.

Mutual risk-pooling weakens the incentives provided by individual authority self-insurance, but may still provide more incentive to be proactive in reducing risk through robust risk-management practices than simply buying insurance from the private sector. Being more proactive in respect of financial risk may have spinoff benefits for management of other forms of risk in nourishing a risk-management culture and cost-effective risk-management practices across all categories of risk.

In terms of a way forwards, we recognise that UK local authorities are fundamentally different from large private sector companies and we are not suggesting that they totally abandon their traditional approach to risk financing and embark on wholesale 'alternative' programmes. Given, however, the apparent problems associated with the traditionally cyclical insurance market in terms of capacity and price, we consider that authorities should at least consider the alternatives if they are free to do so following the resolution of the legal issues and the diffi-culties associated with demonstrating value in any single year.

It is clear from our, albeit limited, investigation of the local government risk-financing arrangements in some Nordic countries that mutual risk pools can be a useful part of the strategic and operational environment. It is inappropriate to draw direct comparisons between the UK and the Nordic countries, as, for example the *intra/ultra vires* issue is not similar and, in the main, the Nordic countries have more flexibility and freedom in the decision-making process. The differences between them may reflect different attitudes to 'rolling back the frontiers of the state', innovation and liberalisation of markets.

Despite the UK being seen as being at the forefront in Western Europe vis-à-vis such policies, its position as regards local authority risk financing appears to be conservative and very much based in long-standing custom and practice. Given the global nature of the insurance market, it is unlikely that there are significant and unique differences between the commercial insurance buying problems of local authorities across Western Europe. That being the case, and accepting that national differences would need to be factored in, we argue that if the UK government is serious in its attempt to encourage innovation in local authorities, it should look to the Nordic countries as an example of innovative, but prudent, risk-financing mechanisms.

Note

1. A captive insurance company is one that is set up by a, generally non-insurance, organisation to insure its own risks.

References

ALARM (2005) Alternative Risk Financing: Guidance on Alternatives to Traditional Insurance Market Products. Exmouth: Association of Local Authority Risk Managers.

Bovaird, T. and Löffler, E. (2003) *Public Management & Governance*. London: Routledge.

Cabinet Office (2002) Risk: Improving Government's Capability to Handle Risk and Uncertainty. London: The Strategy Unit.

Carlsund, A. and Bohman, G. (2006) Samarbete för bra försäkring. Kommunförbundet Stockholms län. Erik Langby & Lennart Dahlberg: Gemensamt försäkringsbolag för kommuner I Stockholms län. Rekommendation 2006-06-15.

Cummings, J. D. and Outreville, J. F. (1987) An International Analysis of Underwriting Cycles, *Journal of Risk and Insurance*, 54 (2): 246–262.

Davies, M. (2007) Establishment of the London Authorities' Mutual Ltd: A Case Study. London: Centre of Excellence.

De Mey (2003) The Aftermath of September 11: The Impact on and Systemic Risk to the Insurance Industry, *The Geneva Papers on Risk and Insurance*, 28 (1): 65–70.

Department of Communities and Local Government (2006) The National Procurement Strategy for Local Government: Two Years On. London: DCLG.

EIRM (2009) www.eirm.net

Enberg, M. (2009) Development Chief, Finnish Association of Local Governments: A telephone interview 7th October.

Eurofi (2008) *Future Outlook for EU Mutual Insurance Groups*, www.eurofi.net.

Flynn, N. (2007) *Public Sector Management*. (5th edition) London: Sage.

Fone, M. and Young, P. (2005) *Managing Risks in Public Organisations*. Leicester: Perpetuity Press.

FRAML (2007) *Insurance Mutual Now Open for Business*, Fire and Rescue Authorities Mutual Ltd, http://www.framl.co.uk/view/archives/ (accessed 10 April 2008).

The Guardian (2009) *Labour Drive to Make Services More Efficient*, http://www.guardian.co.uk/society/2009/oct/20/john-denham-public-finances-services (accessed 28 October 2009).

Gollier, C. (2001) *The Economics of Risk and Time*. Cambridge (USA): MIT Press.

Gollier, C. (2003) To Insure or Not to Insure?: An Insurance Puzzle, *The Geneva Papers on Risk and Insurance Theory*, 28: 5–24.

Gollier, C. and Pratt, J. (1996) Risk Vulnerability and the Tampering Effect of Background Risk, *Econometrica*, 64: 1109–1124.

Heath Lambert Group (2007) Public Sector, State of the Market: Special Report. London.

Helander, M. (2005) Kommuner sparer pengar genom försäkringssamverkan. *Kommunal ekonomi*, 1: 12–13.

Henriksen, L. S. and Bundesen, P. (2004) The Moving Frontier in Denmark: Voluntary-State Relationships Since 1850, *Journal of Social Policy*, 33 (4): 605–625.

Hood, C. (1991) A Public Management for all Seasons, *Public Administration*, 69 (1): 3–19.

Hood, J. and Acc-Nikmehr, N. (2006) Local Authorities and the Financing of the Employers' Liability Risk, *Public Money and Management*, 26 (4): 243–250.

Hood, J. and Young, P. (2005) Risk Financing in UK Local Authorities: Is There a Case for Risk Pooling?' *International Journal of Public Sector Management*, 18, parts 6 and 7.

Kivistö, R. (1993) Vakuuttaminen tärkeä riskienhallinnan osa. *Kuntalehti*, 7: 22–23.

158   *John Hood, Bill Stein and Pekka Valkama*

KLP (2009) KLP Skadeforsikring, http://www.klp.no/web/klpno.nsf/pages/aboutklp.html, http://www.klp.no/web/klpmm.nsf/lupgraphics/Q1_2009_engelsk.pdf/$file/Q1_2009_engelsk.pdf

KommuneForsikring (2009) http://www.kommuneforsikring.dk/files/uploads/FF_Aarsrap_Resume_2008_UK_web.pdf

LAML (2007a) The Establishment of LAML, http://www.londonauthoritiesmutual.co.uk/view/finance-and-cover/20070420171217 (accessed 16 April 2008).

LAML (2007b) LAML Takes on Challenge, http://www.londonauthoritiesmutual.co.uk/view/archive/20070807164110 (accessed 16 April 2008).

LAML (2009) *Press Release*, http://www.londonauthoritiesmutual.co.uk/view/archive/20090610163716/ (accessed 11 June 2009).

LASAAC (2005) *Accounting for Insurance in Local Authorities in Scotland,* Local Authority (Scotland) Accounts Advisory Committee. Edinburgh: CIPFA.

London Centre of Excellence (2007) *London Insurance Company Set for Go-Ahead,* www.lcpe.gov.uk/latestnews (accessed 8 March 2008).

Municipal Journal (2008) *Of Mutual Benefit?,* http://www.localgov.co.uk/index.cfm?method=news.detail&ID=64979&&keywords=of%20mutual%20benefit (accessed 18 March 2008).

Nawaz, S. and Stein, W. (1998) Risk Financing 'ART' and the Future, *Journal of the Society of Fellows: The Chartered Insurance Institute,* 13 (1): 68–81.

Punter, A. (2000) New Solutions for the Financing of risk, *Insurance Research & Practice,* 15 (2): 28–39. [Authorquery: Please provide in-text citation or delete this reference.]

Punter, A. (2002) Reinventing Re/insurance for the Twenty-First Century, *The Geneva Papers on Risk and Insurance Theory,* 27: 102–112

Punter, A. (2007) *Risk Financing and Management.* (2nd edition). London: IFS School of Finance.

Royal Courts of Justice (2009) The Supreme Court of Judicature Court of Appeal (Civil Division), Royal Courts Of Justice, Strand, London, 9th July, 2009. Before: Lord Justice Pill, Lord Justice Moore-Bick, And Lord Justice Hughes. Brent London Borough Council (Appellants) Risk Management Partners Limited (Respondents) and London Authorities Mutual Limited & Harrow London Borough Council (Interested Parties).

Scottish Executive (2006) *EGF – Stage 1 – 006 Scottish Local Authority Insurance – Bid,* www.scotland.gov.uk/Publications/2006/02/23134928/0 (accessed 12 March 2008).

Standard and Poor's (2000) Public Finance. Publication date: 06 November 2000. Reprinted from *Ratings Direct.* Oslo (City of). Analyst: Kersti Talving and Anders Sars.

Stewart, J. (1984) The Role of Accounting in Public Accountability. In A. Hopwood and C. Tomkins (eds) *Issues in Public Sector Accounting.* London: Philip Alan, 13–34.

Svenska Kommunförbundet (1997) Skadefinansiering i kommunal verksamhet: Försäkringar och alternativ. Stockholm.

Winter, R. (1989) *The Dynamics of Competitive Insurance Markets,* Working Paper, Toronto: University of Toronto.

Young, P. (1989) Local Government Risk Financing and Risk Control Pools: Understanding their Forms, Functions and Purposes, *Public Budgeting & Finance*, 9 (4): 40–54.

Young, P., Sugimoto, Y. and Yamazaki, H. (1999) Pooling in Japan, *Public Risk*, 13 (5): 18–21.

8
Innovations in Financing Higher Education in Slovakia

Miroslav Beblavý, Peter Mederly and Emília Sičáková-Beblavá

Introduction

In the developed countries, higher education has been in continuous flux for decades, and the speed of change has accelerated in recent years. Increases in student numbers, observed in many developed countries in the 1990s and 2000s have created unprecedented demand for higher education, but also unprecedented pressures on the institutions themselves and the public purse that traditionally financed most of the cost in all but few OECD countries. As higher education and its costs grew, so too did concerns about its efficiency and outcomes. The general tend-ency in post-industrial societies to emphasise individual needs and client orientation in public services also contributed to the changing environment of higher education financing and organisation.

Governments all over the world responded to these developments through a plethora of initiatives, which tended to include introduction or strengthening of private resources including student fees. In 2002, the Slovak government also introduced a major reform of higher education but, for political reasons, fees were not an important element. Rather, the government decided to pursue changes in how the public subsidy is spent by creating a strong set of incentives for universities to pursue government objectives and by changing the rules so as to allow the universities to utilise both their tangible and intangible assets flexibly in response to the new conditions. The nature of the reform and its impact are discussed in this chapter.

The chapter is organised in the following manner. We start with a brief review of existing literature on innovations in financing public services in general and higher education in particular, with focus on so-called

160

quasi-markets. The following section contains relevant background information on the Slovak higher education reform of 2002, especially changes in financial areas. The third section examines how the new funding formula, which is at the core of the paper, had an impact on the behaviour of higher educations institutions (HEIs) as a group. We then try to prise open the 'black box' of university decision-making and look at how the reform influenced their internal formula for distributing funding to internal units. The chapter ends with conclusion summarising our findings.

Innovations in financing public services, including higher education

There are many definitions of public services. For example Grout and Stevens (2003, 2) see public services as 'any service provided for a large numbers of citizens, in which there is a potential significant market failure (broadly interpreted to include equity as well as efficiency) justifying government involvement – whether in production, finance, or regulation'. Le Grand (2007, 4) refers 'specifically to services that are of fundamental importance to public...And it usually implies services for which there is some form of state or government intervention, whether in its finance, provision, regulation or all three.'

Higher education is one of the important public services. Barr (2004, 1) writes: 'No longer only a consumption good enjoyed by an elite, it is an important element in national economic performance. So it is no accident that the numbers in higher education have increased in all advanced countries. However, a mass, high-quality university system is expensive and competes for public funds with other imperatives.'

For developed economies, the OECD documents rapid growth during 1990s and 2000s, with the only difference between countries having to do with the rate of growth. Dealing with the rapidly surging capacity needs in what has traditionally been a tax-funded public service required a number of organisational and financial innovations. Barr (2005) indicates that problems in financing higher education appear all over the world without exception.

Le Grand (2007, 14–37) distinguishes four potential routes towards improvements in public services:

- Trust – letting professionals do the job;
- Voice – giving feedback mechanisms to clients;

- Command and control – hierarchy and targets;
- Choice and competition – giving the client the ability to choose a service provided.

Innovations in organisation and financing of public services generally tend to fall into either voice or, even more frequently, into the choice and competition category as opposed to traditional (i.e. trust, command and control) approaches. In higher education, recent innovations in financing frequently involve either a graduate tax or differentiated fees/income-contingent loans (Greenaway and Haynes 2000, 60–98; Barr 2003, 150–165). Both assume that those who benefit from higher education should contribute more to the costs. The graduate tax is an additional tax provided from graduates' salaries. The second idea is to allow universities greater freedom in setting fees, because universities can have different cost structures (subject mix, research, wage structure) and the costs of education are higher than in the past. This is complemented by scholarships and income-contingent loans so as to minimise potential barriers to accessing universities faced by poorer students.

On the other hand, innovations are also possible in how public funding is distributed. Good examples are vouchers and voucher-like mechanisms through which a grant follows the student (Barr 1993, 722). The government can create quasi-markets, with students and governments as consumers. Such mechanisms can also be integrated into traditional funding formulae for universities.

Genua (2001, 610) describes three channels for direct financing of higher education by the state:

- *Incremental funding* – 'funds are allocated on the basis of past expenditure levels with incremental resources made available for the development of new activities';
- *Formula funding* – 'the budget of the institution is determined by some form of assessment of the actual institutional expenditure per student enrolled or expected to be enrolled. ... Research funds can also be determined by a formula system that allows the distribution of the funds in a selective way on the basis of research record';
- *Contractual funding* – 'is applied via tender schemes. Public funding agencies issue targets in terms of student numbers or research and the various institutions apply for the funds to carry out specified tasks'.

He finds that 'although there is a high level of diversity in the mix of the different funding systems in the EU, recent years have seen an increasing reliance upon formula and contract funding' (ibid).

Jongbloed (2008, 13) suggests that funding on the basis of outputs has better economic results than on the basis of inputs. Output funding 'is believed to contain more incentives for efficient behaviour than input funding. If budgets depend on performance measures, there is reason to believe that those who receive the budgets will pay increased attention to their performance.'

Innovations in funding and financial management in 2002

Innovations in the financing of Slovak higher education analysed in this paper span a decade and three governments. They were started in 2000 by a government White Paper called 'Concept of Further Development of Slovak Higher Education in the 21st Century'. The paper called for a radical change in the legal framework of higher education and accompanying changes in governance and financing. While some of these changes were then piloted during the 2000–2001 period, it was the new Act on Higher Education approved in 2002 that set the stage for the new system.

Until 2002, the funding and financial management system of the Slovak public higher education institutions (HEIs)[1] can be characterised by the following five features:

- HEIs had to transfer all revenue to the central budget;
- The budgeting for individual HEIs was primarily incremental and generally did not take into account outputs (students, graduates, publications, etc.) although it did take into account actual expenditure from the previous year (underspending);
- HEIs were given an internally structured subsidy by the government and could not modify it (e.g. shift funding from goods and services to wages);
- HEIs did not own any property, but instead held all their assets as publicly owned property in trust and the government provided discretionary and targeted subsidies for investment to individual HEIs, thereby controlling HEIs' capital budgets;
- HEIs (in line with the rest of the Slovak public sector at the time) used cash-based rather than accrual accounting.

It is worth noting that, from 1990, the Slovak public HEIs already had extensive autonomy in non-financial matters. The chief executives were elected by, and accountable to, academic senates, composed solely of staff and students' representatives. HEIs were free to set their own admissions procedures and largely ran their own examinations as they saw fit. As a result, the HEIs were free to respond to whatever incentives government policy, especially funding policy, presented.

The key problems with the pre-2002 funding mechanism were as follows:

- Distorted incentives with regard to student numbers. The system did not provide motivation for growth in full-time student numbers since they did not translate into higher subsidies. However, due to lack of clarity with regard to payment of fees by part-time students, universities had an incentive to grow their numbers and charge fees;
- No incentives for improvements in research since the funding formula did not take the research outputs or outcomes into account;
- No incentives for savings/efficient asset management since any savings (e.g. in energy use) would be immediately cut from the next year's budget;
- Lack of a sustainable approach to financial/asset management and an absence of long-term planning, coupled with political interference and client-responsive practices in investment subsidies.

The new system, in place from 2002 onwards, can be characterised by the following main features, which have not changed in principle although their application and weight varies. Probably the most important change has been that the government subsidy has shifted to a mixture of input- and output-based budgeting. Individual HEIs receive their subsidy based on a publicly known (and publicly consulted) formula, which primarily reflects the following factors:[2]

- Number of students (weighted by standardised cost coefficients for individual areas of study – e.g. natural sciences versus social sciences);
- Number of graduates (weighted in a similar manner);
- Number of Ph.D. students and graduates (not weighted);
- Professional and education structure of the teaching staff (number of full professors, associate professors and other teachers with Ph.D.s);
- Research publications weighted by the category, which should reflect their importance and quality;
- Volume of research grants from domestic and foreign sources.

The second important group of changes was related to incentives for HEIs to generate their own revenue and to use their tangible and intangible assets more efficiently and effectively. According to the new law, HEIs:

- Could keep all their own revenue regardless of its source;
- Received into their ownership the assets they had previously held in trust and could utilise these freely to generate additional revenue;
- Received the government subsidy in an unstructured grant, which they were free to utilise as they saw fit;
- Any unspent funds could be carried over into the following years.

Lastly, the new rules aimed to introduce a more long-term and strategic perspective and sustainability into the HEI management by, in addition to the measures already mentioned:

- Switching to accrual accounting, thus forcing the HEIs to switch from a cash-based way of looking at their operations to one where they also look at non-cash costs of their activities (primarily depreciation of assets);
- Capital grants previously distributed by the central government on a discretionary basis were, to a large extent, converted into the regular subsidies although the government kept a portion for 'development projects' of HEIs.

Analysis of the main features and their impact at the system level

From an economic point of view, the main impact of the new system is that it created, for the first time, a clear set of 'prices' for various educational and research outputs. Therefore, this section will look at how the prices for individual outputs developed and whether there is any evidence of their impact on the behaviour of the HEIs.

In higher education and research, the ability of the system as a whole, and of individual institutions, to respond rapidly to changing incentives is limited. There are several factors that point to lengthy adjustment periods. One reason is the sheer length of the relevant processes. Even if new students are accepted immediately, or papers submitted to journals or grant applications written, it takes anywhere between one and three years before those students graduate, papers are actually published and the bulk of the grant money starts to flow. The second reason is that the capacity of the higher education system to respond to the incentives takes many years to build. This is true for the tangible assets (buildings and equipment), as well as for human resources. Obviously, it takes at least several years to produce a new member of the teaching and/or research staff. Of course, individual institutions can recruit academics from other schools (poaching), but to increase the overall capacity of the system rapidly would require either inflow of talent from outside the higher education sector and/or its importation from other countries.

Despite rising finance, the Slovak system is not generous in terms of pay compared either to private sector employment in Slovakia or to other, neighbouring markets (particularly the Czech Republic with its cultural and linguistic affinity). Thus, there is a limited ability to import talent from other sectors and countries.

At the same time, there is a range of instruments available to managers of HEIs to allow them to respond to these incentives, even if there are short- to medium-term supply constraints. These are, for example:

- An increase in the student-teacher ratio;
- An increase in the number of research outputs without changes in the underlying research production.

These measures have one thing in common: increasing productivity, potentially at the expense of intangibles such as quality. They have also been observed in other countries. (Butler 2001; Genua 2001). Therefore, we will examine to what extent the data allow us to observe their occurrence in the Slovak higher education system.

Starting with the payments per student, Figures 8.1 and 8.2 show developments in unit prices (thousands of Slovak crowns, Sk) for various fields of study at the undergraduate and graduate levels. We can observe significant nominal decrease in the unit price for undergraduate students of all types. This is despite the fact that the ratio of the overall government subsidy to number of students did NOT decrease over time. Therefore, the steep price decrease is due to the internal reallocation of the funding formula away from undergraduate student numbers. The prices paid for graduate students on the other hand have been fairly stable in nominal terms. This shift away from payments for undergraduate students is due to growing concern about increasing quantity at the expense of quality and gradual shift of resources towards research outputs (including Ph.D. students).

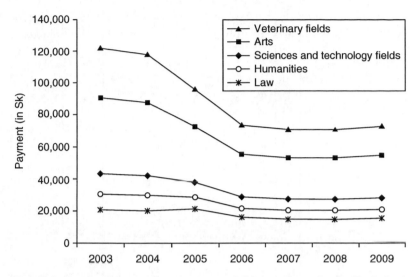

Figure 8.1 Payments per student in various fields – undergraduates (Bachelors)
Source: Authors.

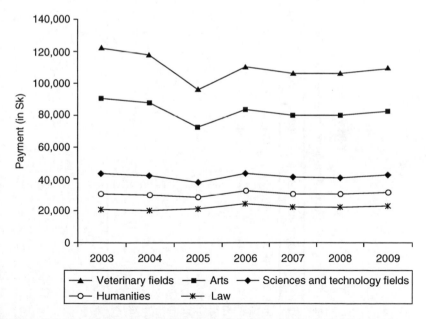

Figure 8.2 Payments per student in various fields – postgraduates (Masters)
Source: Authors.

Table 8.1 Developments in student numbers in Slovakia, 2000–2009

	2000	2001	2002	2003	2004	2005	2006	2007	2008	2009
Full-time students	88,192	90,446	92,140	97,932	97,759	106,194	113,197	121,058	126,325	131,048
Part-time students	29,240	33,060	38,948	38,990	44,494	50,367	56,309	60,576	56,944	51,307
Annual growth rate in full-time students (%)	–	2.6	1.9	6.3	–0.2	8.6	6.6	6.9	4.4	3.7
Annual growth in part-time students (%)	–	13.1	17.8	0.1	14.1	13.2	11.8	7.6	–6.0	–9.9

Source: Authors.

Table 8.1 shows developments in the numbers of full- and part-time students in public universities in Slovakia between 2000 and 2009. The table shows the following:

- After the introduction of the new system, we can observe acceleration in the growth of full-time student numbers that has only begun to taper off in 2008 and 2009 (but still growing relatively strongly). The only exception is the year 2004 for unrelated reasons.[3] In this sense, the new system produced results;
- The number of part-time students continued to grow even more strongly until 2007 so the goal of the reform – to shift students from the illegal fee-paying part-time system to the official full-time system largely failed. The part-time system began to shrink only in 2008 and 2009, when the new private institutions became significant players in the market.

The pricing for Ph.D. students is somewhat more complicated. It consists of three payments:

- Payments for Ph.D. students based on the expected cost of their field of study. Ph.D. students were divided into three categories (medicine; natural, agricultural and technical sciences; others) and the formula provided differentiated subsidies, substantially higher than a similar subsidy per student at the undergraduate or postgraduate level;
- Additional bonus payments for Ph.D. students, which were not differentiated;
- Bonus payments per Ph.D. graduate, which were also not differentiated.

To give an example, the payment for a mathematics student at the Masters level in 2007 was Sk37,858. For a Ph.D. student in the same field, the HEI received Sk93,134 in the first category (costs of teaching) and Sk107,754 in the second category (research excellence), which together is Sk200,888, or nearly six times the price per a postgraduate Masters student.

We can observe considerable fluctuation in prices over years, but what remains is the significant premium paid for Ph.D. students compared to undergraduate and graduate students. The premium was quite intentional and its objective was to increase the number of Ph.D. students and graduates significantly. In this respect, it succeeded without reservation. As Table 8.2 shows, the number of full-time Ph.D.

Table 8.2   Number of full-time Ph.D. students in Slovakia, 2002–2008

	2002	2003	2004	2005	2006	2007	2008
Number of full-time Ph.D. students	2008	2236	2751	3370	3368	3718	4321
Annual growth rate (%)	n.a.	11.4	23.0	22.5	−0.1	10.4	16.2

Note: The number of Ph.D. students refers to the number on October 31 of a given year.
Source: Authors.

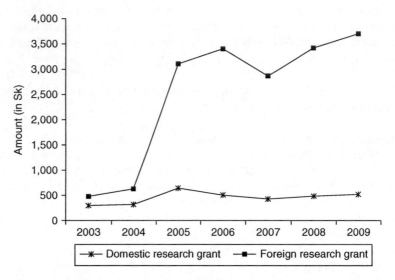

Figure 8.3   Subsidy received based on domestic and foreign research grants (per Sk1000)
Source: Authors.

students in Slovakia grew in double digits between 2002 and 2008 (with the exception of 2006), more than doubling overall during the period.

The next set of prices was attached to research grants received from sources in Slovakia and abroad. Due to limitations on the type of grants eligible, the only grants effectively counted in were:

- In the case of Slovak grants, support from official government grant agencies (no private sources);

- In the case of international grants, grants awarded on a competitive basis (primarily the EU Framework Research Programme, European Science Foundation, National Institutes of Health in the US).

The price setting is an ex-post matching, where the public subsidy is based on the volume of a grant in the previous year. As we can see in Figure 8.3, the ratio started at around 0.4–0.5 in 2003 (i.e. €400 per €1000 of grant) and, in the case of foreign grants, grew dramatically to the range of 3–4:1 between 2005 and 2009. For the domestic grants, the price stagnated at a ratio of around 0.5. The reward for foreign grants is enormous when one realises that they imply the provision of an additional untied 300–400 per cent premium over the resources already received, which are likely to be quite generous themselves, given the higher funding standards of the funding agencies in Western Europe/US. It is difficult to imagine any stronger incentive for application for foreign grant resources.[4]

However, the success of such applications is conditional on a significant degree of integration into international networks of researchers and research institutions – one of the Achilles' heels of the Slovak higher education establishments. Such integration cannot be produced by fiat and internal production or recruitment of research of such calibre requires internal institutional conditions (salaries, equipment, processes, etc) that are not amenable to simple or quick fixes.

Reaction of the Slovak HEIs is therefore likely to illustrate the success (or limits) of the financial innovation itself in bringing rapid and deep changes in the way HEIs operate. Table 8.3 shows developments in the volume of eligible foreign grants between 2001 and 2008. As we can see, there is an upwards trend after 2005, but there is a caveat – a structural break in the data. The ministry relaxed eligibility conditions, and this is associated with the massive jump between 2005 and 2007.

In sharp contrast, for domestic grants (where there is no international competition) the higher education sector reacted much more dynamically,

Table 8.3 Eligible research grants documents by HEIs between 2001 and 2008 (Sk1000)[5]

Year	2001/2	2002/3	2003/4	2004/5	2005/6	2007	2008
Domestic grants	267,634	433,217	881,843	1,299,987	1,605,668	1,956,405	2,160,313
Foreign grants	167,057	225,383	185,417	193,241	243,535	279,248	307,241

Source: Authors.

increasing outputs by nearly 800 per cent, ten times more than in the case of foreign grants. This is despite much weaker incentives.

The next group of prices concerns research outputs – publications. They were introduced into the pricing formula in 2006 to reward research outputs. The funding formula uses a system that converts all outputs into a single indicator using weights that should take into account quality/research intensity of the output. Between 2006 and 2009, we can observe a marked increase in the total standardised volume of publications from 154,554 to 564,528.[6] Some of the increase can be attributed to a statistical illusion – an increase in average weights in 2008 and 2009. This factor, however, is unlikely to explain most of the improvement. Therefore, it seems that the research output reacted to incentives and grew rapidly.

Unfortunately, that does not mean that the actual research conducted in HEIs improved. If there is no effective quality control, there are two potential strategies that can increase production without any improvement:

- Dilution of the same amount research into a higher number of outputs (or repeated publication of the same research via its repackaging);
- Increase in research quantity at the expense of quality/relevance.

To compensate for these problems, the funding formula gradually introduced a more discriminating pricing mechanism to reward outputs of higher quality. However, the higher quality output category contains both outputs that have sufficient external quality control mechanisms and ones that do not. To give an example, the category contains both papers in journals listed in the ISI Current Contents database (with particular reward for foreign journals) and research monographs published domestically or abroad (category A1). Monographs command significantly higher prices since they are supposed to be more labour intensive. The gate-keeping function for the journal papers is provided by their peer reviewers, which is difficult to game, particularly for foreign journals (only one humanities journal and two social science journals in Slovakia are in the ISI database). On the other hand, all one needs to have a formally recognised monograph is 60 pages of text with an ISBN number and two names of academic peer reviewers. This makes it much easier to game. Therefore, the increasing rewards for both types of output provide a strong incentive to increase the A1 and A2 categories rather than publications in journals, as made clear in Figure 8.4.

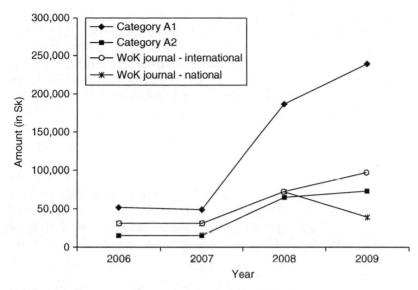

Figure 8.4 Unit prices for various research publications
Source: Authors.

The last set of prices that we analyse here is concerned with the seniority/qualifications structure of the HEI staff. Slovakia has a standard career ladder – progressing from lecturer to senior lecturer, then associate professor to professor. For associate and full professors, there is a special appointment process conducted by the institution itself, but based on nationally determined criteria (the criteria were fairly loose until 2008, when they became quite rigidly regulated by the ministry). Therefore, the qualification structure of the staff is largely, but not completely under the control of the institution itself.

The government policy was to improve the staff qualifications, particularly by decreasing the numbers of academic staff without a Ph.D. Therefore, the qualifications structure was priced into the formula. The prices have been fairly stable in nominal terms since 2005 and this has been accompanied by a gradual improvement in the qualifications structure. The number of teachers overall grew by only 1 per cent from 9481 in 2003 to 9581 in 2009, but the number of teachers without a Ph.D. fell by 27.5 per cent from 3873 in 2003 to 2806 in 2009.

The pressure for better qualifications, together with lack of direct incentives for hiring, meant that growth in student numbers and research outputs translated into better pay, but not higher numbers.

Average academic pay grew by 102 per cent between 2001 and 2008 (from Sk15,441 monthly to Sk31,224), which was faster than over-all wage growth in the economy over the same period (76 per cent), increasing the relative wage of academics from 124.9 per cent of the average wage in 2001 to 143.3 per cent in 2008. The numbers on the other hand remained nearly unchanged (see above).

So far, we have analysed prices per outputs introduced by the fund-ing formula, but we did not comment on what is missing. Based on the discussion so far, there are two outputs omitted from the system despite the fact that they would be fully in line with the formula philosophy.

The first one is the lack of any incentive to attract private sector research and development (R&D) funding. There is ample evidence that all governments had this as a goal, particularly given the low level of private sector R&D expenditure in Slovakia. Based on interviews and personal experience of the authors, the explanation of the absence seems a combination of:

- Lack of belief that private sector funding could be significant enough to warrant inclusion into the formula;
- Worry about gaming/fraud of the criterion.

The second major omission is the lack of use of citations as a measure of weighting the quality of research. This is largely explained by the unresolved technical complexity of the criterion both in terms of what citations should be used and what periods should be counted.

There are two additional items for discussion at the level of the sys-tem as a whole. The first one is the overall instability of the funding formula. We have already discussed the lags in how both the overall system and individual institutions can react to changes in the formula. Genuine improvements and innovations (new degree programmes, new research topics and researchers) require long-term investment. In such an environment, the predictability and stability of the formula is of paramount importance. If participants face even moderate uncertainty about whether the rules of the game might change, they will be reluct-ant to invest, or they might pursue a diversification strategy under which they produce a great variety of types of outputs to ensure success under any variation of the formula. Such a diversification is likely to be a negative phenomenon as teaching and research excellence are more likely to require specialisation and different internal strategies.

We are discussing the issue at length because the previous pages have shown that, in many areas, higher education has witnessed dramatic fluctuation of prices even though the types of outputs that are rewarded have not changed much over time. In other words, what HEIs can derive from such an environment is that while the goods for which the 'market' pays stay the same, there is an unpredictable pricing environment. At the same time, it should be said that the fluctuations in prices occurred more in the early years of the system between 2002 and 2005, and were much more stable thereafter. Fluctuations in the prices for publications have occurred ever since 2006, the year this criterion was introduced. This indicates that after a set of prices is introduced, it takes three to four years before an 'optimal' level is found, from which it then does not diverge radically.

Analysis of the impact at the HEI level

HEIs are generally large, internally highly differentiated and decentralised bodies. Decisions about what degree programmes to offer, how many students to enrol and what research projects to pursue are generally made at a much lower level than that of university leadership, although the top management usually has power of veto. Is it therefore very interesting and revealing to see how the innovations in higher education financing worked their way through the system into incentives systems for individual departments or other parts of universities.

In Slovakia, universities are internally divided into faculties, relatively large bodies with a long tradition and legally prescribed governance structures mimicking those of the universities themselves (with the dean as the chief executive and the faculty academic senate as the 'legislature'). Faculties are then free to organise themselves internally as they see fit. The dominant model is the division of faculties into departments (*'katedry'*, *'ústavy'*), relatively small bodies whose size can range anywhere from five staff members to 20.

The 2002 reform treated HEIs as black boxes and made no prescriptions about how they should distribute the funding internally. This section looks, from both theoretical and empirical perspectives, at what we can expect inside the 'black box'.

In this respect, it is important to note that, by law, the budget of an HEI is proposed by the rector, but has to be approved by the academic senate. The budget of a faculty is proposed by the dean but has to be approved by the faculty senate.

The university academic senate has an explicit apportioning of seats by faculties, that is, both student and staff representatives are elected in, and as representatives of, 'their' faculties. The faculty senate is elected by the faculty as a whole although students and staff elect their representatives separately. In both cases, out of all candidates, those receiving the highest number of votes are elected.

From a theoretical point of view, there are at least three relevant issues that any funding formula within a Slovak university has to deal with as a part of the decision-making process on distributing public subsidies. They also apply to the internal decision-making of the faculties vis-à-vis departments.

First of all, there is the issue of balance between incentives for high production on one hand and redistribution to achieve equality on other. It is a question familiar from general economic and social policy debates on the trade-off between growth and equity. From the university point of view, there is a clear set of exogenously determined prices, so passing along those prices to constituent units in the internal budget formula (after shaving off a percentage for central services) is most likely to produce maximum production in the future because it entails the smallest marginal taxation of the faculty production. On the other hand, the budget has to be approved by the academic senate, which is composed of elected representatives of the constituent units (faculties) in partial proportion to their size, but not to their budget/production. The production-maximising long-term view thus inevitably clashes with the redistributive interests of the less productive majority.

The second consideration is about dealing with long-term investment and strategic management or, to be more precise, at what level should decisions of this kind take place. Again, the fiscal analogy is appropriate. Development of new products (degrees, researchers, etc.) usually requires upfront investment that will only pay back in time and with considerable uncertainty. To pay for the investment, existing producers need to be 'taxed' by getting less for their existing products. The issue is – how much should be taxed and which level should keep the tax, thus effectively gaining control of the strategic management.

The third issue is how to deal with the instability, uncertainty and short-term nature of the funding formula and the resulting fluctuating fiscal position of the constituent units. This is a similar, but distinct problem from the previous one. In smaller constituent units (smaller faculties, departments within faculties), production inevitably fluctuates. For example, it is not possible (or any, in case, desirable) to have smooth production levels of research monographs or papers published in prestigious journals. Student numbers can fluctuate from year to year even in a programme that has stable long-term demand. Since Slovak universities and their constituent units are officially forbidden to borrow, they must have a balanced cash budget on an annual basis. Lack of solidarity between units would potentially lead to the need for redund-ancies and other savings purely on the basis of extremely short-term cash considerations even in cases where the long-term productivity is not threatened. On the other hand, it is not always easy to distinguish between short-term fluctuations and a declining trend in production.

Before examining strategies chosen by individual Slovak universities and some of their faculties, let us also review an additional factor that needs to be taken into account. Hirschmann (1970) formulated, in his seminal book, the two principal options available to anyone dissatisfied with the state of the organisation where she (or he) finds herself: voice or exit. What are the options available in the Slovak higher education establishment to faculties, departments or individuals who, for example, consider themselves to be taxed too highly (i.e. who receive significantly less than the university receives from the government for their products)?

Exit is, technically speaking, feasible only at the individual level. While there is no legal rule against departments or even faculties moving from one university to another, a host of political and technical complications make this extremely unlikely. Of course, there is no way to prevent a coordinated group of individuals from exiting together and setting up shop elsewhere, which has occasionally happened. However, even this strategy is more likely in areas where tangible assets (which cannot be taken) are unimportant, for example, social sciences and humanities. This would seem to favour majoritarian, redistributive strategies since the more highly productive individuals and units would be trapped in their existing institutions. In such a case, the voice of the productive minority is unlikely to produce much impact.

However, there is also a third option, applicable in this case – shirking. Producing less, but bearing only part of the costs of reduced production due to a high level of redistribution is quite possible, particularly as the ability of the university to monitor the working time of the academics/whole units and whether they are engaging in other activities is limited.

We now look at how these issues played out in our sample of HEIs and their faculties in Slovakia. Our sample consists of five universities spread across the country, ranging from general ones covering all the main fields to a more specialised one, where either social sciences and teacher preparation or technical sciences dominate. We also look at internal funding formulas of seven faculties, of which five are from one university. They present a balanced sample of two natural sciences and three social sciences/humanities faculties. The two remaining faculties from other universities specialise either in technical or natural sciences.

We examined the funding formulas from the following angles:

- Are they based on the government funding formula?
- If there are differences, what are they? Are they simply redistributive towards existing interests or in pursuit of other objectives?
- Is there taxation to support centralised decision-making about investments/strategic development?
- What are the mechanisms to compensate for potential short-term instability of revenue for small units?

At the level of HEIs, we find only gradual and uneven adoption of the state funding mechanism over time, but by 2009, seven years after the formula was introduced, there is a wholesale adoption of the state model with some modifications to take into account internal politics/priorities. We have not observed any substantial reversals of the funding mechanisms so far – the shift from the historical to output-based formula seems to go only in one direction over time.

At the level of faculties, the picture is more complicated, with three strategies present:

- Use of the government formula with minor modifications;
- Partial use of the government formula combined with other factors;
- Absence of formula and reliance on historical/hierarchical decision-making.

The key modifications found in the formulae are:

- Both at the university and faculty levels, use of different weights compared to the ministerial formula to support university priorities or take into account major intra-university interests;
- At the faculty level, use of different periods for assessment, with some faculties preferring three or five years as the proper period for assessment;
- At the university level, the existence of internal/transfer prices for courses to stimulate joint teaching and other types of collaboration in this area.

Additionally, all institutions have a centralised fund at the level of university to drive strategic development, but the fund tends to be quite small and the discretion in its use limited. In this respect, HEIs come across as a very loose federation of faculties. At the faculty level, the situation is quite different, with the faculty management wielding substantial discretionary power with regard to non-salary expenditure.

With regard to short-term fluctuations, universities and those faculties that use a formula have made use of a provision (albeit often modified) in the government formula, which effectively insures HEIs against steep drops in the subsidy on a year-to-year basis. This so-called 'guaranteed minimum' is sometimes, although not always, combined with rules limiting expenditures of those departments and faculties that make use of this provision – for example, limiting budgets for goods and services or taking away discretionary elements of salaries. This serves both to limit the degree of solidarity and to create incentives for the loss-making units to ensure that the 'loss' is indeed a temporary fluctuation.

Therefore, we can conclude that the government methodology serves as a focal point in internal decision-making about the budget of all HEIs and a major percentage of faculties, thus gradually seeping through the system without major reversals. The universities have tried to deal with the dilemmas posed by the system in a way that does not impede future production through high taxation, and are thus production-oriented. Central redistribution and taxation are relatively limited. The strategic management is thus left largely in the hands of faculties. This is, to a lesser degree, also true for faculties although a greater variety of approaches can be observed. It should be kept in mind though that this might also change over time as even those faculties without output-oriented budgeting might shift to a more production-driven formula as the developments so far seem to be only in this direction rather than accompanied by reversals.

Conclusions

This chapter dealt with Slovak innovations in higher education financing following the Higher Education Act of 2002. Unlike in some other countries, the emphasis in higher education financing innovation was not on using fees, but rather on making a strategic shift in the way public subsidy is distributed. This was a part of a major reform that also allowed HEIs to react to incentives by increasing their flexibility in the allocation and utilisation of resources.

Before the reform, the Slovak system already contained a generous portion of trust and voice mechanisms. HEIs were self-governed although the government imposed considerable limitations in the area of financial management. Students participated directly in the management by electing a significant minority of the supreme university decision-making body. The reform greatly relaxed constraints faced by the HEIs in how they use money and preserved the voice of students. To this layer of trust and voice, it added an emphasis on choice and competition by strengthening incentives for HEIs to compete for students. The Slovak mechanisms are therefore an interesting combination of both voice and choice instruments, coupled with a high level of autonomy of HEIs.

This massive change, which assigned a clear set of prices to various products that the government deemed desirable – students, graduates, research outputs, teacher qualifications, etc – appears to have influenced the behaviour of the HEIs as a group considerably. This can be observed in cases where the universities can react more easily and where the incentives were stronger.

For example, the number of full-time students increased by 40 per cent during the six-year period after the reform and the number of Ph.D. students more than doubled. This can be explained both by the fact that the absolute numbers of Ph.D. students are small compared to regular students so recruitment does not pose the same investment challenges and the fact that the government decided to pay significant premiums for Ph.D. students over and above any reasonable cost differentials compared to regular students, whereas the nominal prices for undergraduates declined steeply over the period.

Another example of limitations to the ability of HEIs to react to the government incentives is the price put on domestic and foreign research grants. Despite the fact that the price paid for foreign grants was, in the end, seven to eight times higher than that for domestic grants, domestic grants increased tenfold, whereas foreign grants less than doubled despite the fact that the government relaxed eligibility rules. This demonstrates that, to compete in the international research community, more than strong incentives are needed (at least in the short to medium term).

Therefore, the lesson of the Slovak case is that incentives matter much more where the institutions do not face supply-side constraints and where their long-term sustainability is credible. To be able to break through onto the European (global) research scene also requires supply-side interventions to build capacity. The Slovak government has recently (since 2008) been trying to complement its strategy with such steps, funded by the Structural Funds (e.g. the Centres of Excellence programme).

The Slovak reform is a typical example of a quasi-market, where the public sector mimics the market signals through the public subsidy formula. Our research showed some success in the case of higher education, but there are also serious limitations. The quasi-market, unlike a real market, is always susceptible to gaming by the participants and to under-pricing of outputs that are difficult to observe, such as quality. This has also been the case in Slovakia.

Another weakness of the Slovak model is the limited nature of the competition due to barriers for private/foreign institutions. The 2002 reform significantly liberalised their entry, as evidenced by entry of 11 private/foreign universities since then. However, it excludes them from public financing, which is *not* a consequence of the funding mechanism chosen, but a deliberate political decision.

However, we would argue that once these political decisions (and others such as that not to limit the number of student places funded by the government) have been made, the formula is the technically most efficient manner of distributing the funding (rather than competitive tendering or other mechanisms). Within the public HEI sector, it is a de facto voucher (see Chapter 11) but takes into account differentiated costs of specialised areas of study.

Our research also tried to look into the 'black box' and examine how universities reacted to the new formula in their internal financial decisions. We identified three considerations that need to be taken into account in any internal formula:

- Stimulating production versus equality and redistribution;
- Which level should make strategic development/investment choices;
- How to deal with short-term uncertainty.

Most universities and their constituent units tried, in their internal formulae, to have a highly incentivised pro-production system that is also highly decentralised in the sense that the ability of the centre to conduct strategic steering through finances is limited. On the other hand, there has been a strong emphasis on making sure that this does not lead to capacity destruction due to short-term fluctuations in production at the level of smaller units (e.g. departments) by providing an effective insurance against downside risks. In practical terms, this meant that the government formula has not only been the tool used by the government to distribute funding between universities, but has also seeped into the HEIs themselves and dominated their internal budgeting, even at lower levels (how faculties distribute money to departments). At the same time, as one progresses lower, one encounters more and more modifications and caveats to the utilisation of the formula.

The Slovak experience shows that financial innovations at the system level can and do lead to further complementary changes at the level of individual HEIs, where the rules at the system level serve as the focal point on which various factions within the institution can more easily agree than if they were devising a financing formula from scratch.

The agenda for further research is to understand in detail how organisational innovations of this type seep through individual, large institutions. This would be invaluable in answering the more general question of how and why institutional change happens in reaction to external stimuli.

Notes

1. Private higher education in Slovakia grew significantly during the 2000s, but generally without recourse to public funding. Therefore, this chapter will address only public institutions. However, Chapter 10 considers private finance for universities in the form of co-payments.
2. Additionally, there is a separate subsidy related to social welfare of students, primarily aimed at providing needs-based scholarships and subsidising dormitory and meal costs. Since the focus in this chapter is on funding changes related to the education and research process, we will ignore the 'social' subsidy.
3. In 2004, the intake of the universities was much lower than usual because the size of the graduate class in secondary education was artificially small. This was due to a shift from eight to nine years of primary and lower secondary education four years before, which created a very small 'gap' year graduate population
4. It should be kept in mind that the premium was paid to the university and its internal distribution depends on the internal decision-making processes analysed in the following section.
5. Note: the 2007 and 2008 numbers are doubled to allow comparison, since the 2001–2006 numbers were based on the total grant volume over the previous two years, whereas the 2007 and 2008 numbers are based solely on annual figures (which run from November of one year to October of the next).
6. As with some of the other outputs, the 2008 and 2009 numbers are doubled to allow comparison, since the 2005–2007 numbers were based on the total grant volume over the previous two years, whereas the 2008 and 2009 numbers are based solely on annual figures.

References

Barr, N. (1993) Alternative Funding Resources for Higher Education, *The Economic Journal*, 103 (418): 718–728, Blackwell.

Barr, N. (2003) Financing Higher Education: Comparing the Options. London: London School of Economics and Political Science.

Barr, N. A. (2004) Higher Education Funding. London: LSE Research Online.

Barr, N. (2005) Financing Higher Education. Reforms in Britain May Provide a Useful Framework for Other Countries, *Finance and Development*, 42 (2): International Monetary Fund Publication.

Butler, L. (2003) Explaining Australia's Increased Share of ISI Publications – the Effects of a Funding Formula Based on Publication Counts, *Maryland Heights: Research Policy*, 32 (1): 143–155.

Genua, A. (2001) The Changing Rationale for European University Research Funding: Are There Negative Unintended Consequences? *Journal of Economic Issues*, 35 (3).

Greenaway, D. and Haynes, M. (2000) Funding Universities to Meet National and International Challenges. School of Economics Policy Report. Nottingham: University of Nottingham.

Grout, P. A. and Stevens, M. (2003) Financing and Managing Public Services: An Assessment. CMPO Working Paper Series No. 03/076. Bristol: University of Bristol.

Hirschmann, A. (1970) *Exit, Voice and Loyalty*. Cambridge, MA: Harvard University Press.

Jongbloed, B. (2008) Funding Higher Education: A View from Europe. Center for Higher Education Policy Studies.

Le Grand, J. (2007) *The Other Invisible Hand. Delivering Public Services through Choice and Competition*. Princeton, NJ: Princeton University Press.

9
Innovation in the Turkish Budgetary System: Recent Developments in Public Governance

Hulya Kirmanoglu and Pinar Akkoyunlu

Introduction

From the foundation of the Turkish Republic in 1923, the lack of sufficient entrepreneurs forced the public sector to be active in the economy. Even though the public sector became very important in taking on this facilitative role, Turkey has never adopted strict major state control (*etatism*) of economic activities. Nevertheless, the state's role was crucial, with many state economic enterprises being founded, and it undertook the main infrastructural investments and provided employment possibilities.

The legal framework in which the public sector was managed and audited dates back to 1927. This conventional system, albeit reformed from time to time, was far from meeting recent global trends in making the public sector more efficient and effective. Until 1980, the structure of the economy was inward-oriented. Since 1980, the structure of the economy has changed and market rules have gained importance.

Although, this new system rationalised the production structure of the economy, given the imbalances and governance problems in the public sector, the state of public finances worsened and budget balances deteriorated. As a consequence, high interest payment liabilities and a rising debt burden emerged, seriously impinging upon the economy. The shortage of public funds for social expenditures and public investments was harming long-term social welfare. Combined with economic and financial globalisation creating an environment more open to instabilities, the economy encountered recurrent crises, as did many other emerging economies. Thus, the need to strengthen the governance structure of the economy, in both public and private sectors (including the financial sector), was evident.

The EU became a powerful actor in shaping fundamental economic and political reforms in Turkey as part of the process of its accession to the EU. Some essential parts of these reforms required policy-makers to reorganise the relationships between layers of government and integrate new actors (both domestic and external) into the public provision process, especially for large-scale public investment projects. Furthermore, while defining the rules and objectives of providing the public services society needs in a healthy way, the global shift to new public management necessitated financial and administrative innovations in the public sector.

Following the 2001 crisis, the need for reforms to make the structure of a considerable part of the economy more efficient and sustainable became prominent. This amounts to saying that very substantial reforms were required, including to central government, local governments, state economic enterprises, the banking sector, etc.

In this chapter, we focus on the reforms taking place in the local public sector. After generally introducing the state of public finances from recent decades in Turkey, we will evaluate the administrative and financial positions of Turkish local authorities and make assessments of the innovative character of reforms undertaken in the post-2000 period.

Turkish government budgeting and methods of financing expenditures

In 2001, with the economic measures taken to stabilise the economy, the share of the central government budget reached 36 per cent of GDP. After the crisis, the emphasis on a more liberal economy led to a decline in this share and in 2007 the central budget was approximately 24 per cent of GDP. However, as this amount included a huge amount of interest payments, it is more instructive to look at the expenditures other than interest expenditures (i.e. the primary budget).

Even in 2001, the year with the highest share of the budget, expenditures other than interest were only 18.6 per cent of GDP. In Figure 9.1, the difference between the total expenditure and expenditures other than interest in the central government budget can be seen. This difference is equivalent to the expenditure on interest. As can be seen, the proportion of central government budget expenditure to GDP fell

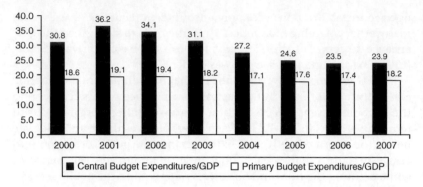

Figure 9.1 The proportion of central budget expenditures and primary budget expenditures to GDP (%)

Source: Budget 2009, 23.

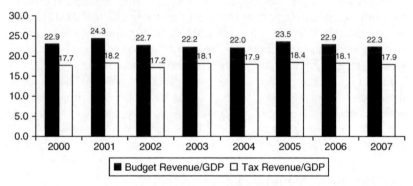

Figure 9.2 The proportion of central government budget revenue and tax revenue to GDP (%)

Source: Budget 2009, 24.

from over a third of GDP in 2001 to just below a quarter in 2005 and subsequent years.

Figure 9.2 shows the proportion of central government budget revenue and tax revenue to GDP. The difference is non-tax receipts – mainly privatisation revenues. As can be seen, the proportion of central government budget revenue to GDP has been more stable than expenditure at just below a quarter of GDP between 2000 and 2007 The same stability applies to tax revenues (the major part of revenue) at approximately 18 per cent of GDP. Neither the tax nor the total revenues are sufficient to finance all budgetary expenses, albeit that the budget came close to balance from 2005 onwards following the reduction in central budget expenditures. In particular, the primary budget came very close to balance against tax revenues.

The distribution of revenues raised by taxes is distorted, with indirect taxes constituting the greater share. Value added tax, the special consumption tax, special communications tax and taxes on international trade and transactions make up approximately 52 per cent of total tax revenue in central government budget revenue. Taxes on property have only a small share in total tax revenue in the budget. The property tax on real-estate ownership is left to local governments and so is not classified in the tax revenue of the central budget (Budget 2009, 39, Table 19).

As already noted, budget revenue has been less than budget expenditure, giving rise to budget deficits. In 2001, the budget deficit was approximately 12 per cent of GDP. Before the year 2000, the primary balance, which is an indicator of the balance between total budget revenue and expenses other than interest payments, was also negative. After the fiscal crisis that Turkey endured, the necessary precautions were taken to stabilise the economy and to create a primary surplus.

In Figure 9.3, both the budgetary deficit and primary surplus can be seen. The primary surplus can be created in two ways: by increasing budgetary revenue (either by increasing taxes or finding new revenue sources) or by reducing budgetary expenditures (other than fixed interest payments).

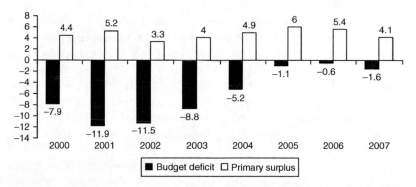

Figure 9.3 The proportion of the budget deficit and primary surplus to GDP (%)
Source: Budget 2009, p.22.

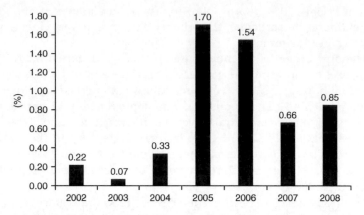

Figure 9.4   The proportion of privatisation revenue to GDP (%)

Source: GDP figures from the Turkish Statistical Institute (www.turkstat.gov.tr). Privatisation figures from Budget 2009, 17.

However, having a high birth-rate, Turkey needs more education and health services. Education and health are major non-interest expenditures and the creation of the primary surplus led to restrictions on social expenditures. Hence, new financing methods had to be found and, with the ruling party's liberal economic policy, privatisation is now used as an important financing option for public expenditure (see Figure 9.4).

The acceleration in privatisations after 2005 yielded very substantial revenues. In the original privatisation law (Law 4046, dated 1994) the proceeds of privatisation, collected in the privatisation fund, were not allowed to be used in budget expenditures. Amendments introduced in 2001 meant that privatisation revenues could now be used in the budget and so they became an important component of budget revenues.

As privatisation revenues increased, the need for income raised by borrowing decreased. Turkey could not rely on borrowing as a source of revenue as it had created large burden of interest payments, which became an obstacle to the realisation of social expenditures. Along with the privatisation policy, the programmes followed in accordance with IMF requirements led non-interest expenditures to decline and created a primary surplus.

The associated decrease in the stock of debt is shown in Figure 9.5. In 2002 the rate of public sector debt to GDP was 61.4 per cent. Thereafter, it fell steadily to less than half of that level by 2007, in which year it was

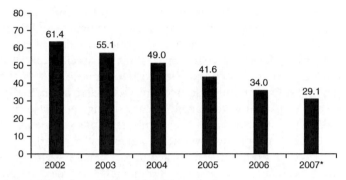

Figure 9.5 Public sector debt to GDP (%)
Source: Budget 2009, 10.
Note: *indicates estimate.

estimated to be only 29.1 per cent of GDP. There has been a particularly sharp decline in foreign borrowing and, in recent years, this became negative in net terms as repayments exceeded new borrowing. Domestic borrowing is now used more than foreign borrowing for financing the overall budget deficit (BBF 2009).

Innovations brought about by the Public Financial Management and Control Law

After having two consecutive crises in 2000 and 2001, the Turkish public management system adopted a series of legislative reforms throughout the 2000s, including the Public Financial Management and Control Law (2003), the Basic Principles and Reconstruction of Public Management Act (2004), the Law of Municipalities (2005), and the Law on Budgetary Revenues Accruing to Municipalities and Special Provincial Administrations (2008).

The most significant of these reforms for our purposes is the Public Financial Management and Control Law (Law 5018), which redefines the public sector and alters all the conventional budgetary procedures. In the context of the new legal framework, the aim of this law was to design a more efficient public management system and rebuild fiscal discipline, which had been deteriorating since the economic crisis of 2001. In this system, strategic planning and performance-based budgeting are accepted as the primary budgetary principles. Internal and external auditing concepts are broadened so as to include performance auditing.

The purpose of Law 5018, as stated, is to regulate both the structure and functioning of the public financial management. The law aims to bring financial control in line with the politics and objectives included in development plans and programmes. With the application of this law, accountability, transparency and effective, economic and efficient collection and utilisation of public resources are expected to be realised (Article 1). Its scope is general government, encompassing central government, social security institutions and local administrations (Article 2).

Law 5018 defines public revenue as 'taxes, levies, charges, holding funds, shares or similar revenues acquired pursuant to their respective laws, revenues from interests, surcharges and fines, all types of revenues acquired from movable and immovables, revenues obtained from services rendered, revenues from premium-sold borrowing instruments, deductions from social security premiums, donations and grants received, and other revenues' (Article 3).

Of all these revenue types, as indicated in Figure 9.2 above, tax revenue is the major source. Fiscal transparency is emphasised, as in many countries,[1] and the acquisition and utilisation of all types of public resources have to be supervised. It is therefore compulsory to establish public accounts in line with a standard accounting system and accounting order in accordance with generally accepted accounting principles (Article 7).

Performance indicators play an important role; public administrations prepare their budgets in accordance with the strategic plans based on these indicators. Those in charge of the use of public resources are held accountable for the use of effective, economic and efficient procedures, this being a measure introduced to prevent the abuse of public resources (Articles 8 and 9).

These articles on the new budgeting system match OECD principles about performance indicators. The OECD underlines the importance of these indicators for citizens to be able to evaluate the effort and work of public administrators and to rank the local governments in their ability to use their capacity effectively (OECD 2006, 5–13).

The Higher Council of Planning designated eight different public organisations as pilot areas for performance-based budgeting. Among them were Kayseri Metropolitan Municipality and the Special Provincial Administration of Denizli.[2] They used indicators concerning fire fighting, irrigation and improvement of rural areas and the level of use of sports facilities. The expectation of the performance-based budgeting system is that with well defined key performance indicators and a reward/penalty scheme, the efficiency of public administrations will be more easily monitored.

Public administrations within the scope of the general budget have to prepare their detailed expenditure programmes in order to achieve effectiveness, economy and efficiency in their expenditures. These programmes have to be submitted to the Ministry of Finance. Budget appropriations have to be utilised according to their specified release rates and detailed expenditure programmes. Public administrations are not allowed to spend in excess of their appropriations. 'The appropriations provided with the budget shall be used in line with the purposes they are allocated for to cover the works done, goods and services purchased and other expenditures made in the pertaining year. Appropriations that could not be used during the current year shall be cancelled at the end of the year' (Article 20). People who have the authority to impose taxes and collect public revenue are also responsible for the proper performance of the different phases of revenue collection (Article 38).

Analysis of Turkish local governments in the new legal framework

The rise of the neo-liberal market economy across the globe during the 1980s and 1990s led to waves of privatisation and decentralisation in many developed and developing countries. The new global approach to governance considers decentralisation among the factors that make public sectors more efficient and more innovative. Strong local fiscal and administrative capacities increasingly became seen as necessary to promote fiscal discipline and efficiency in the public sector. 'Decentralisation is used as a strategy to reduce the monopoly power of the central level over political and economic space by distributing power and resources between different government levels' (Boex 2009, 5).

Within this global policy context, the public sector in Turkey was influenced by two significant policy changes: downsizing and decentralisation. Faced with severe fiscal discipline and inefficiency problems, successive governments intended to implement policies to constrain budgetary expenditures. Since the issue of government failure was coming to prominence, a consensus grew about the need to clear out, and otherwise constrain the scope of, corrupt politicians and bureaucrats by limiting and decentralizing their power.[3]

In Turkey, governments have sought ways to increase the administrative and financial powers of local governments since the 1980s. The ratification in 1993 of the European Charter of Local Self-Government, which underlined devolution of public responsibilities to the authorities closest to the citizens (the principle of subsidiarity), was a sign of the new political priorities. The countries that signed the European Charter of Local Self Government are engaged in decentralisation procedures that are both innovative in themselves and also have the potential to embody the means of stimulating further innovation. This idea faced some resistance in Turkey, however, where the central government's power is predominant both economically and politically.

It was not until the 2000s that decentralisation began to be accomplished. Even though there is strong support for decentralisation reforms at the political level, the media and public have not always been pro-reform and the Supreme Court intervened occasionally by cancelling some aspects of relevant laws. Paradoxically, as is the case in many countries, the reforms were being driven by a central government body – the General Directorate of Local Governments, a sub-unit of the Ministry of Interior.

Throughout the 2000s, the whole body of laws regulating local public finance and management in Turkey was reformed under a vision of greater decentralisation and more efficient public management systems, including the Law of Metropolitan Municipality (2005), the Law of Municipalities (2005), the Law of Special Provincial Administrations (2005), the Law regarding Giving Shares to Municipalities and Special Provincial Administrations From General Budget Tax Revenues (2008).

The new legislative framework altered the system in assigning duties, responsibilities and new revenue resources to local administrative bodies. It has the vision of maintaining a democratic, efficient, accountable, transparent and participatory local public administration through decentralisation. The new Law of Municipalities (Law 5393) has undertaken some changes concerning the authority assigned to local bodies. They are regarded as entities having the sole authority in providing local public services so long as these are not forbidden by law or ceded to another authority. The concept of 'the sole authority' accords with the concept of 'competence' in the European Charter of Local Self Government.[4]

Administrative aspects of innovations in decentralisation

Public services in Turkey are provided by both central and local governments.[5] The essential public services, including health and education, are carried out by ministries and their provincial branches. Historically and culturally, the public functions are shifted towards lower local units through deconcentration, a weaker form of decentralisation. Local governments are responsible for the provision of collective services meeting the common requirements of the residents. The constitution gives central government the authority (in the sense of being the trustee) over local governments to ensure the functioning of local services in accordance with the unitary state principles.

Municipal governments have all classical functions that constitute local public service provision. With the growing population of some cities, metropolitan municipalities were introduced into the system in 1984 and a two-tier structure was created in large cities. The main function of metropolitan municipalities is to provide the large-scale local services and investments which require substantial budgetary funds. Metropolitan municipalities comprise a number of districts among which they undertake coordination, with some of the services assigned to metropolitan municipalities overlapping with those of district municipalities.

For some services, greater decentralisation may conflict with the benefits of large jurisdictions reducing costs through economies of scale (Bailey 2004, 228). Metropolitan municipalities may offer a convenient geographical area to benefit from economies of scale, and their growing number (from three in 1984 to 16 recently) proves their convenience for large-scale local services and investments. However, this two-tier structure may cause problems due to a lack of coordination between district mayors and metropolitan mayors. The district mayors in metropolitan areas have less control over municipal affairs than the mayors in non-metropolitan areas. The authorities of metropolitan municipalities were given more power, especially in implementing land parcel plans and master development plans, in 2005. This approach is not in accordance with new local management principles aiming at taking and implementing decisions regarding public services at the level closest to the people at district level (Kerimoglu and Yilmaz 2005, 7).

Another type of governmental body providing many local services is the 'special provincial administrations'. The territory where they provide public services also covers rural areas, as opposed to municipalities that are responsible only for urban areas. Special provincial administrations are headed by governors appointed by central government and by city councils whose members are elected. They have been given duties in almost all major sectors such as health, education, the environment, industry and trade, culture and tourism, land development and housing at the local level. The special provincial administrations have a vision of sharing some of the developmental roles undertaken by central government, especially in rural areas.[6] As a developing country, it is a necessity for Turkey to institute these developmental institutions to stimulate local potentials; with their mixed structure, partly central and partly local, special provincial administrations are appropriate for this role, but they need to be reformed.

One of the innovations inherent in the new public management system is the obligation to prepare strategic plans. Strategic plans and performance-based budgeting techniques are widely used in efficient and effective public management approaches. The application of this type of approach for local governments strengthens the emphasis of the reforms on efficiency as well as participation and accountability. Municipalities with populations of more than 50,000 are obliged to prepare a strategic plan which constitutes the basis of the budget. Strategic plans are innovative in the sense that fiscal discipline and the accountability of public officials are made possible through performance evaluation. As an example, the performance indicators and the outcomes indicating the realised performances of Kayseri Metropolitan Municipality are given in Table 9.1 and 9.2.

The new governance approach integrates all stakeholders into the governance process, and emphasises partnerships among central and/or local government, non-governmental organisations and other related institutions. In Turkey, decentralisation reforms are enacted by broader reforms aimed at improving participatory governance and ensuring accountability.

Law 5393 regulates activities performed by participating universities, competent groups in organisations with the status of public institutions, trade unions, non-governmental organisations and experts. Although the reforms are claimed to bring about participatory governance and thus to improve the administrative dimension, authority as regards employing personnel and determining wages (which are crucial aspects of administrative authority) is still subject to some central government limitations. The innovative character of the reform is evident in stating that, with some restrictions, the executive committees may

Table 9.1   Performance indicators of Kayseri Metropolitan Municipality

Number of fires attended per fire engine
Rate of deterioration of asphalted motorways over five years
Square metres of paved motorway
Number of persons using sports facilities in the youth centres
Number of persons using the swimming pool and synthetic grass field
   (astroturf)

Source: Nangir (2007), 119.

Table 9.2 Kayseri metropolitan municipality: Construction and maintenance of motorways

	2005	2006	2007
Square metres of motorways made ready for covering with asphalt	911,700	504,800	1,077,600
Square metres of paved motorway	957,817	834,791	1,428,392
Rate of deterioration of asphalted motorways over five years (%)	5	5	5

Source: KMM (2009).

decide to increase the pay of local officials based on their performance (Law 5216).

Local governments do not necessarily make direct provision of local services themselves but they can make contracts with private companies. The municipalities may transfer some services (water supply, disposal of waste water, removal and storage of solid wastes, public transport activities, construction of tunnels and railway systems, etc.) for a period not exceeding 49 years by granting franchises subject to the approval of the Ministry of Interior (Article 15).

Another disclosure of this tendency was the establishment of municipal enterprises. In accordance with the spirit of the liberal market economy, municipal enterprises that were likely to be privatised were re-formed as commercial institutions, especially in the water, gas, electricity distribution and public transport sectors. Since some public services have the character of essential infrastructures, competition has to be created through strong and effective public procurement laws in order that individuals have better quality local services.

Fiscal aspects of innovations in decentralisation

Compared with most EU countries, the size of Turkish local governments is quite small, as indicated by the ratio of local government spending to general government spending. As shown in Table 9.3, local governments have spent little more than 10 per cent of the general government budget in recent years. The slight increase after 2005 can be attributed to the reforms undertaken in that period.

Nevertheless, the figures do not show significant decentralisation on the spending side. Since Turkey is a country where public administration has historically and culturally had a centralised structure, some

Table 9.3   Local government spending as a share of GDP and general government spending

	2004	2005	2006	2007	2008 (provisional)
Share of GDP (%)	2.8	3.2	3.8	3.9	3.6
Share of government spending (%)	7.7	9.6	11.5	11.6	11.1

Source: Compiled from tables at http://www.bumko.gov.tr and www.dpt.gov.tr.

innovations initiated in the reforms (such as devolving some functions to local governments) cannot easily be put into practice. A centralised and hierarchical decision-making system may not be easily reformed and will certainly be vigorously defended (Scott 1996).

Although both municipalities and special provincial administrations have their own sources of revenue, a significant part of those revenues is comprised of tax shared from the central budget and state aids and grants. As the discrepancy between regions in raising their own income is larger in Turkey than in developed countries, the fiscal equalisation role of central government is more crucial.

On the revenue side, fiscal decentralisation means the devolution of fiscal resources to local authorities. In order to achieve an effective fiscal decentralisation reform, the local level of government should be assigned taxes and their rates and bases should be determined by local authorities themselves. In few countries in the world, especially among the developing ones, is revenue autonomy implemented in this way. The reasons for this can be found in the following quotation: 'Central governments may not want to devolve taxing powers for fear of competing with local governments for the same taxing base and at the same time sub-national governments do not want to take on the responsibility of making politically unpopular taxing decisions to meet their budget needs' (Martinez-Vazquez 2008, 31).

The reason why Turkey is not an exception to this rule is because real revenue autonomy is not desirable where large fiscal disparities exist across regions, as is the case in Turkey. Furthermore, such autonomy may lead to greater accountability problems. As an alternative, tax sharing can be made applicable but this requires efficient design of tax-sharing mechanisms.

Law 5779, enacted in 2008, changed the structure of vertical tax sharing between central government and municipalities as well as between tiers of local administrations. It aimed to help to increase tax autonomy but, instead of creating new local revenue sources, the government chose to increase the shares allocated to municipalities from general budget revenues.[7] This compromise casts a large shadow over the innovative character of decentralisation by weakening the financial (and thus administrative) powers of local governments. Real revenue autonomy requires innovation in terms of generating resources and managing them effectively.

However, Law 5779 also introduced new criteria regarding the allocation of general tax revenues across municipalities and special provincial administrations. Accordingly, out of the central budget tax revenues, 2.85 per cent is transferred to non-metropolitan municipalities, 2.5 per cent to metropolitan area district municipalities[8] (30 per cent of this amount being reserved for the relevant metropolitan municipality) and 1.5 per cent to special provincial administrations. Additionally, 5 per cent of taxes collected within the borders of a metropolitan municipality are assigned to that metropolitan municipality. According to the law, for the share of tax accrued to special provincial administrations, the population size determines 50 per cent of the tax allocation, with the remaining 50 per cent being based on socioeconomic indicators such as the number of villages, percentage of rural population, development index and surface area. For the tax shares accruing to municipalities, 80 per cent is distributed according to province.

In Turkey, prior to the enactment of Law 5779, the tax-sharing mechanism did not help solve horizontal equity problems. With the enactment of this law, the sharing of general government revenues by municipalities and special provincial administrations according to their development-related indicators as well as their population makes it possible for less advantaged regions to receive more public funds.

As is shown in Tables 9.4 and 9.5, the rate of own-source shares in total revenues is higher for municipalities. This is because the real-estate tax was assigned municipalities in 1986. Special provincial administrations are much more dependent on central government funds compared to municipalities.

Insufficient self-sourced funds of local governments continue to make them dependent on central government tutelage and control. The relationship between dependency and the lack of innovation may be two-sided. On the one hand, dependence on funds coming from the higher tiers indicates lack of higher-level financial innovation and, on the other, this dependency may cause less innovation by decreasing motivation for it.

Table 9.4   Composition of the revenues of municipalities (%)

	2006	2007	2008
Total revenues	100	100	100
Taxes and fees	16	16	16
Income from enterprises and property ownership	15	16	15
Grants and aids	2	2	2
Other non-tax revenues (interest, fines, capital revenues and others)	20	21	18
Tax shares from central government	47	45	49

Source: www.muhasebat.gov.tr/mbulten/belediye.php.

Table 9.5   Composition of the revenues of special provincial administrations (%)

	2006	2007	2008
Total revenues	100	100	100
Taxes and fees	1	0	2
Income from enterprises and property ownership	2	6	3
Grants and aids	67	62	65
Other non-tax revenues (interest, fines, capital revenues and others)	10	13	9
Tax shares from central government	20	20	22

Note: Shares may not total 100% due to rounding.

Source: www.muhasebat.gov.tr/mbulten/ilozel.php.

Initiatives for cooperating with other actors, both domestic and external, are proving more innovative in the sense of finding new financing methods. The influence of international organisations (the IMF, World Bank and Council of Europe) is crucial in this respect. Domestic legislation was linked with world trends and formed the rules of financing and providing local investments.

In the process of accession to the EU, regional development policies/ programmes and rural development projects financed by EU funds are implemented by many candidate countries in order to reduce the large disparities across regions. The main purposes of these policies are to mobilise local resources, to enhance the role of local actors (such as municipalities, civil societies and enterprises) and to implement partnership principles among those actors for financing and monitoring the programmes devoted to regional development.

To the same ends, the legal framework of Regional Development Agencies was established in Turkey in 2006 in accordance with EU regional policies. These agencies have been established to work on the implementation and coordination of programmes and projects aimed at driving the economic potential and competitiveness of the regions. The Regional Development Agencies are organs established and monitored under the administrative structure of central government. Municipalities are among the actors in this structure but their role is not a major one.

Taking into account the legal amendments enabling local authorities to build partnerships with the private sector, it can be claimed that Turkey has adopted the main body of the local development financing principles of the OECD. Among these, the principles of 'promoting active private sector leadership in local development finance and investment' and 'flexibility in public funding to enable private co-investment in local development' refer directly to the role of the private sector in local development (OECD 2007).

Apart from these projects referring to Public-Private Partnerships, BELDES is another project designed for the development of municipalities deprived of mains water and appropriate road conditions. BELDES is entirely public and earmarks funds from the general budget for municipalities with populations of fewer than 10,000. These funds are to be used for water distribution networks and road construction within the municipal area.

Conclusion

The public sector in Turkey was subject to severe fiscal discipline and inefficiency problems during the 1980s and 1990s. Both the financial and administrative structures of the public sector were weak and negatively affecting other sectors of the economy. After the crisis of 2001, the reform process supported by the IMF maintained recovery to some extent but the need for higher-level reforms (especially restructuring the public sector) continued. Among these, privatisation and decentralisation measures gained importance as a reflection of the market-based policies dominating the global scene. Both measures were supported by international organisations (the IMF, World Bank, Council of Europe, etc.). Consequently, the need for innovations for reforming the public sector was apparent.

The first crucial reform was about regulating both the structure and functioning of public financial management. Afterwards, a series of legal arrangements were put into practice in both fiscal and administrative areas to put the tiers of the governmental system in harmony with the subsidiarity principles of the EU. The new public management approach dominant in the world argued for delegation and devolution of central power and resources to local or non-governmental units. However, some difficulties arose in realising this agenda due to the centralising traditions of the political culture of Turkey. Nevertheless, the legal framework regulating the functions, duties and responsibilities of government units began to be reformed in order to ameliorate public sector imbalances and institute a solid public governance system. The purpose of the reforms was to design a new legal framework by integrating both the financial and administrative dimensions.

In the administrative dimension, the new public management system introduced a variety of innovations such as strategic plans and performance programmes to enforce accountability among public managers, and rules enabling participation of domestic and external stakeholders in financing public services and investments.

The success of reforms in instituting a solid public governance system and in ameliorating public sector imbalances depends on many factors. Among them, the willingness of both political and private actors to be transparent and accountable is crucial.

Decentralisation has remained limited in the fiscal dimension. An important requirement of fiscal decentralisation is revenue autonomy but in Turkey local governments still rely heavily on central government funding. Furthermore, the fiscal equalisation role of government widened with a new law setting different criteria for budgetary revenues accruing to local governments. This seems inevitable when we consider the financial and economic discrepancies across regions in Turkey but it does tend to curb the innovative potential of decentralisation.

Notes

1. A survey by the International Budget Partnership in 2008 reveals that 80 per cent of the countries surveyed (68 out of 85) are not transparent enough to provide the public with the sufficient information on the use of public funds (OBI 2008).
2. The other six pilot areas were the Ministry of Agriculture and Rural Affairs, Hacettepe University, the Turkish Statistical Institute, the General Directorate

of Health for Borders and Coasts, the General Directorate of Highways and Bank of Provinces.

3. In the literature, there are conflicting research results regarding the impact of decentralisation on corruption. While Arikan (2004) and Fisman and Gatti (2002) find a negative relationship between decentralisation and the level of corruption by using several alternative decentralisation measures, Triesman (2002) does not.

4. 'Local authorities shall, within the limits of the law, have full discretion to exercise their initiative with regard to any matter which is not excluded from their competence nor assigned to any other authority', Article 4/2 (CoE 1985).

5. Local administrative bodies in Turkey are organised as municipalities, metropolitan municipalities, special provincial administrations, local government unions and villages. There are 16 metropolitan municipalities, 3225 municipalities and 81 special provincial administrations. Each one of the 81 provinces of Turkey has a special provincial administration.

6. The law that envisaged assigning a greater role to special provincial administrations was vetoed by the former President of the Republic in 2004.

7. As Martinez-Vasquez writes (2008, 35) 'The more generally accepted view is that tax-sharing is not a form of revenue assignment because sub-national governments do not have a direct role in the structure and administration of the tax and, in this view, revenue sharing should be considered just another form of transfers.'

8. District municipalities located in a metropolitan area.

References

Arikan, G. G. (2004) Fiscal Decentralization: A Remedy for Corruption? *International Tax and Public Finance*, 11, 175–195.

Bailey, S. J. (2004) *Strategic Public Finance*. Basingstoke: Palgrave Macmillan.

BBF (2009) *Budget Balance and Financing Tables*, http://www.treasury.gov.tr

Boex, J. (2009) *Fiscal Decentralization and Intergovernmental Finance Reform as an International Development Strategy*. Urban Institute Center on International Development and Governance, IDG Working Paper No. 2009-6, http://www.urban.org/uploadedpdf/411919_fiscal_decentralization.pdf

Budget (2009) *Turkish Republic Ministry of Finance*. Ankara, Turkey, December 2008, http://www.bumko.gov.tr/TR/Genel/BelgeGoster.

CoE (1985) *European Charter of Local Self-Government*. Council of Europe, European Treaty Series – No. 122, Strasbourg, 15.X.1985.

Fisman, R. and Gatti, R. (2002) Decentralization and Corruption: Evidence Across Countries, *Journal of Public Economics*, 83, 325–345.

Kayseri Metropolitan Municipality (2009) *Performance Program*. Kayseri, Turkey, 2008, http://www.kayseri-bld.gov.tr/menu/kbb-perfs2009.pdf

Kerimoğlu, B. and Yılmaz, H. H. (2005) Expenditure Structures in Local Authorities in Terms of the Roles and Responsibilities in Turkey. In *Fiscal Decentralization: A New Approach to Alleviate Poverty and Regional Disparities*, Istanbul, Turkey: TESEV.

KMM (2009) *Performance Program of Kayseri Metropolitan Municipality*, 64, table 32, http://www.kayseri-bld.gov.tr/menu/kbb-perfs2009.pdf

Law 4046, *Law Concerning Arrangements for the Implementation of Privatisation, 1994.* Published in Official Gazette No. 22124, 27 December 1994, http://www.oib.gov.tr/baskanlik/yasa.htm

Law 5018, Public Financial Management and Control Law, 2003. Published in Official Gazette No. 25326, 24 December 2003, Ankara, Turkey, http://www.muhasebat.gov.tr/mevzuat/kanun/docs/5018.doc

Law 5216, *Law of Metropolitan Municipalities, 2004.* Published in Official Gazette No. 25531, 23 July 2004, Ankara, Turkey, http://rega.basbakanlik.gov.tr/main.aspx?home=http://rega.basbakanlik.gov.tr/eskiler/2004/07/20040723.htm&main=http://rega.basbakanlik.gov.tr/eskiler/2004/07/20040723.htm

Law 5393, *Law of Municipalities, 2005.* Published in Official Gazette No. 25874, 13 July 2005, Ankara, Turkey, http://rega.basbakanlik.gov.tr/main.aspx?home=http://rega.basbakanlik.gov.tr/eskiler/2005/07/20050713.htm&main=http://rega.basbakanlik.gov.tr/eskiler/2005/07/20050713.htm

Law 5779, *The Law on Budgetary Revenues Accruing to Municipalities and Special Provincial Administrations, 2008.* Published in Official Gazette No. 26937, 15 July 2008, Ankara, Turkey, http://rega.basbakanlik.gov.tr/main.aspx?home=http://rega.basbakanlik.gov.tr/eskiler/2008/07/20080715.htm&main=http://rega.basbakanlik.gov.tr/eskiler/2008/07/20080715.htm

Martinez-Vazquez, J. (2008) Revenue Assignments in the Practice of Fiscal Decentralization. In N. Bosch and J. M. Duran (eds) *Fiscal Federalism and Political Decentralization Lessons from Spain, Germany and Canada.* Edward-Elgar, Cheltenham, UK and Northampton, MA: 27–55.

Nangir, E. (2007) *Butce Dunyasi*, 2 (24), Ankara, Spring, http://www.debud.org/Html/dergi/25/enangir.pdf

OBI (2008) *Open Budget Index 2008.* International Budget Partnership.

OECD (2006) *Workshop Proceedings: The Efficiency of Sub-Central Spending.* Public Governance and Territorial Development Directorate, Territorial Development Policy Committee, November, http://www.oecd.org/dataoecd/57/60/38270199.pdf

OECD (2007) *Policy Brief,* December, http://www.oecd.org/dataoecd/9/34/39772471.pdf

Republic of Turkey, *Prime Ministry*, Undersecretariat of the Treasury, www.treasury.gov.tr/irj/portal/anonymous/BudgetFinancing/

Republic of Turkey, *Ministry of Finance*, General Directorate of Public Accounts, www.muhasebat.gov.tr/mbulten/belediye.php

Republic of Turkey, *Ministry of Finance*, General Directorate of Budget and Fiscal Control, www.bumko.gov.tr

Scott, I. (1996) Changing Concepts of Decentralization: Old Public Administration and New Public Management in the Asian Context, *Asian Journal of Public Administration*, 18 (1), June: 3–21.

Treisman, D. (2002) The Causes of Corruption: A Cross-National Study, *Journal of Public Economics*, 76 (3): 399–457.

10
Co-Payments: Innovations in the Balance between Public and Private Finance

Stephen J. Bailey

Introduction

This chapter focuses on how charges to service users that recover less than the full costs of services can be used as an innovative way of part-financing public services. It focuses on the UK and, specifically on local government services. However, it excludes charges for trading services provided by municipal companies, irrespective of whether they are subsidised by the state or not.

Charges set at less than full cost are known as 'co-payments'. The term usually refers to the financing of services by both the state (via taxes) and service users (via user charges). However, a third party may act as an external financier, for example an employer helping to finance a skills-training course provided by a public sector vocational college. In that case the government (i.e. taxpayer) and trainee pay only part of the costs, the employer(s) paying the rest (Rhodri et al. 2007). Such an arrangement of triangulated co-payments has also been proposed to help finance UK higher education (Bewick 2010; HM Government 2009; see also Chapters 8 and 11).

The difference between a tax and a charge is that the former is an unrequited payment whereas the latter is conditional upon receipt of service. In principle, assuming the ability to pay, the balance of co-payments between the state (via taxes) and service user (via 'user charges') should reflect the balance between the wider benefits to society and the personal benefits to the individual (see below).

There has been considerable recent discussion in the UK concerning use of co-payments as a means of funding public services. They are also sometimes known as 'shared contributions'. The term 'user charges' is not necessarily compatible with co-payments or shared contributions, in that user charges could be set to cover costs fully without the need for state finance, or even to make a profit. Full cost recovery and profits are more likely when user charges are based on the benefits, rather than costs, of public services (see below).

This chapter will make clear that co-payments exist in a complex policy environment – one that involves important legal, political, social and financial factors. User charges can be inequitable, constraining access to services by low-income groups more than by higher-income groups. Nevertheless, they are a strategic instrument for the achievement of value for money (VFM) and can be used to promote social justice and choice in facilitating access to services by socially excluded groups. Charges, therefore, are not just a balancing item in government accounts meant to raise revenue to fill the gap between expenditures and income, or simply curb demand.

The willingness of the general public to pay for more services on a variable 'pay-as-you-use' basis depends upon whether the UK changes the nature of its welfare state from cradle-to-grave 'take-it-or-leave-it' state paternalism to mutual responsibility based on a variable combination of collective and individual financing via co-payments. Service users will almost always prefer tax financing since they usually capture the bulk of benefits whilst costs are spread across the generality of taxpayers. Service practitioners may also prefer tax financing because it is more certain than income from charges and free services generally improve social welfare.

Regional devolution has been in place in the UK since 1999 and revenues from fees and charges are not subject to regional resource equalisation (HM Treasury 2002), so providing an apparent financial incentive to use charges to generate additional income. Nevertheless, territorial (i.e. regional) governments have been more prone to abolish high profile charges outside the local government sector. The Scottish parliament abolished university tuition fees, charges for personal care for the elderly, charges for prescribed medicines and pharmaceuticals (being phased out by 2011), charges for eyesight and dental checks, off-peak local bus fares for travel by all elderly and disabled concessionary cardholders, charges for admission to national museums and bridge tolls. The Welsh Assembly and Northern Ireland Assembly have similarly abolished many of these charges, but fewer have been abolished in England (see below).

The abolition of the above health-related charges has been justified by referring to the founding principles of the UK's National Health

Service (NHS), namely that it be provided free at the point of delivery and available to all. Additionally, except for hospitals operated under Private Finance Initiatives (PFIs) and Public-Private Partnerships (PPPs) where parking charges are enshrined in contracts (see Chapter 2), all users in Scotland and Wales are now allowed free parking. Nevertheless, co-payments have been suggested for NHS services, with 'hotel charges' levied on use of hospital beds not being the only option (Smith 2006).

However, like England, these three regional governments may be forced to make greater use of charges as revenue-raising devices because of the considerable overhang in public sector debt following the UK government bailing out the banks during the 2007–2009 global credit crunch. Together with the public finance costs of the associated recession, those bailouts mean that aggregate public expenditures must now rise much more slowly than previously planned (see Chapter 2).

Reasons for charging

User charges are levied for a wide variety of reasons. For example:

- To raise revenues in order to cover costs;
- To assist the local authority in meeting financial targets;
- To avoid the local authority having to undertake additional borrowing;
- To reduce abuse of services;
- To meet statutory requirements.

In addition to these reasons, increased use of service charges has been advocated on other grounds, namely that:

- **Charges serve as a signal of demand.** The payment of a charge provides an indication as to what people who make use of a service are willing to pay in order to receive that service;
- **Charges are 'fair'**, in the sense that people who use the service are paying towards the cost of providing the benefit they receive;
- **Charges serve as a means of reducing net public spending** since people are paying directly for a service which otherwise would be financed through other sources of local authority income;
- **Charges are educative** and thus recommended as a way of informing members of the public as to the cost of public service provision. The idea here is that the best way of 'bringing it home to people' how much a service actually costs to provide is to charge for it;

- **Charges improve efficiency in the provision of services** because they introduce the disciplines of the market into local government;
- **Charges are a means of promoting Best Value**, explicit reference to charges as a means of promoting Best Value being made in the English Green Paper on local government finance (see below).

Notwithstanding these many reasons, there is no uniform national policy for the use of local government charges. The result is that charges developed on an ad hoc service-by-service basis, with there very rarely being local corporate policies on service charges. Instead, financial necessity has traditionally served as the principal rationale for the expansion of charging policy in local government. As such, charges help to 'bridge the gap' between the spending needs of local councils and income they receive from local taxes and government grants. Hence, they are often referred to as 'the bottom line' in local authority accounts.

This often leads councils to manage charges on a service-by-service basis, instead of examining common issues in a corporate manner. Consequently, charging systems currently operating are highly variable, involving a web of flat-rate charges, means-tested charges, concessions and exemptions.

Exemptions from charges and concessions in the form of reduced charges serve as 'a pragmatic political compromise' between pro- and anti-charging views (Walsh 1995, 39). Groups such as the low-paid, elderly or unemployed may be unable to pay a charge or it may be accepted that they should not be expected to pay irrespective of their ability to do so. There are two types of exemption:

- *A means test* – assesses a service user's income (and wealth?) to determine the level of payment, if any;
- *A categoric exemption* – people receive a service free of charge or at a reduced rate by virtue of their belonging to a particular group, such as the elderly or the unemployed.

Means tests involve a complicated claiming process and stigma may be attached to their questioning of personal finances. However, proactive approaches by councils to overcome such obstacles make use of 'passport benefits', whereby eligibility for one or more specified national state welfare payments automatically entitles a service user to benefit from exemptions and concessions, for example 'Leisure Cards' giving entitlement to discounted sports and leisure charges (see Chapters 11 and 12).

Categoric exemptions are relatively easy to administer, with exemption on grounds of age merely requiring a claimant to produce proof of age. People in exempt categories are likely to be stable claimants, whereas a claimant for a means-tested exemption may lose exemption at certain times of the year.

Exemptions and concessions, along with financial necessity and other factors (discussed below), mean that political values do not determine charging practices. While marginal differences in the mean level and number of charges levied by local governments of differing political control can be identified, there are also similar differences between local authorities controlled by the same party (Rose 1990).

Equity considerations were also highlighted by the Organisation for Economic Cooperation and Development in its best practice guidelines for charging for government services (OECD 1998):

- Clear legal authority;
- Consultation with users;
- Clear determination of the full costs of service provision;
- An effective and efficient collection system;
- Improvement and monitoring of organisational performance;
- Transparent treatment of receipts;
- Appropriate pricing strategies;
- Competitive neutrality with the private sector ensured;
- Recognition of equity considerations.

UK legislation stipulates a number of public services for which charges cannot be levied, namely core education services in schools, core library services, fire fighting, core police services, electoral registration and the conduct of elections.

Most recently, the Local Government Act 2003 (applicable in England and Wales) and the Local Government in Scotland Act provide a general power for local authorities to charge for discretionary services and for additions or enhancements to mandatory services above the level or standard that an authority has a duty to provide. The UK Labour government's aim is to encourage authorities to provide more wide-ranging, new and innovative services that they otherwise could not afford to provide for free (ODPM 2003) and there are now three distinct categories of services for which charges can be made:

- *Statutory services delivered and charged for locally but for which charges are set centrally.* Examples include charges for planning applications and various licence fees. By their very nature, centrally determined charges do not necessarily achieve full cost recovery for each council;

- *Statutory services delivered locally, charges for which are determined by councils themselves.* Examples include charges for social care and car parking. While locally determined, charges may still be regulated by central government, with social care charges being limited to cost recovery only and there being constraints on how surpluses from parking fees can be used;
- *Discretionary services delivered and charged for at councils' discretion but limited to cost recovery when provided.* Examples include leisure services (the whole service being discretionary) and the discretionary levels of statutory services above national minimum standards allowed by 2003 legislation.

Use of charging powers

In sharp contrast with the decision not to consider increasing charges for municipal services in Scotland (Burt 2006), in England the Lyons Report (2007, paragraph 7.85) noted: 'there is room for a debate about the balance between taxes and user charges in paying for local public services... [in order] to spread the costs of services in a way that is perceived as fair'. The report noted that money raised from sales, fees and charges has grown steadily at the same rate as spending across the whole of English local government. It concluded that the substantial variations between councils of the same type in the proportionate and per capita amounts of revenue raised by charges:

> partly reflects the level of councils' willingness to engage with charging and take a strategic approach to its use... a move towards service users meeting some costs directly, rather than allowing the costs to fall on council tax, might itself be a policy aim, and one which councils could legitimately open up for public debate. User charges have a valid place alongside local taxation, and in some contexts may be perceived as fairer. As a minimum, when local authorities face a choice between increasing charges or council tax, or reducing service provision, that trade-off should be made transparent to citizens, with charging presented as one of the options where available. I would encourage all local authorities to take a strategic approach to the use of charges, including as part of the range of levers available for

managing pressures on budgets and on council tax. (Lyons 2007, paragraphs 7.283 and 7.286)

The Local Government Association (LGA) concluded that the slow take-up of the new powers was due to:

- Lack of clear guidance on their use;
- Significant legal barriers created by the proliferation of separate pieces of legislation including powers to charge.

Both external and internal barriers to charging were identified by the Audit Commission (2008), only the first four of the 22 bullet points listed below being external, the rest internal:

- Prohibited use of charges for core services;
- Nationally uniform charges set by central government;
- Restriction of permitted charges to cost recovery;
- Public acceptance of charges is difficult to secure;
- Absence of political willingness to consider charging schemes;
- Failure to distinguish between discretionary and other services when considering charging schemes;
- Insufficient time to develop opportunities to generate income;
- Lack of a corporate policy for charges;
- Lack of financial data;
- Lack of comparative data about charges elsewhere;
- Lack of user data;
- Lack of public opinion data;
- Lack of understanding about sources of finance;
- Poorly managed charges;
- Local politicians' negative views;
- Lack of delegation of operational decisions leads councillors to neglect strategic and corporate considerations;
- Continuation of past practice;
- Lack of a principles-based approach;
- Lack of understanding of the impact of changes in charging levels on service take-up;
- Lack of a communicated strategy for charges;
- Unnecessarily high collection costs;
- Lack of charging audits.

Past audits of economy, efficiency and effectiveness paid little if any attention to use of charges. In order to help them prepare for these audits, the commission (2008, 48–49) poses a series of questions that councils could reasonably be expected to address in order to maximise the benefits resulting from use of charges. These questions relate to:

- The objectives of charging (income generated, extent of subsidy, changing behaviour, value for money, equity and access);
- The extent to which those objectives are being met;
- The structure of charges;
- The cost-effectiveness of charging mechanisms;
- Comparability with other councils and service providers;
- Consultation with and understanding by local people;
- Evaluation of and consideration of the need for further changes to charging practice.

To help authorities develop charging practices, the commission provides a *charging directory* (providing practical examples of the use of charges to achieve objectives), a *household charges calculator* (to calculate the cumulative impact of charges on different types of household) and a *charging income comparison tool* (to compare a council's charging income with that of other councils). These are available at www.audit-commission.gov.uk/charging.

Current scope of charges in local government

Despite prohibitive legislation, in the vast majority of cases legislation allows local authorities wide discretion in levying charges for services. There are around 600 individual local government services for which charges are levied. In about 500 of these, the decision on the setting of a charge and its level is the responsibility of individual local authorities.

In 2007/08 income from sales, fees and charges accounted for only 9.1 per cent of total expenditure. However, there are distinct variations between the service areas as Table 10.1 demonstrates.

Local authorities' own income from sales fees and charges means income from:

- Sales of products or materials, data technology or surplus products;
- Fees and charges for services, use of facilities, admissions and lettings;

- Rents exclusive of Housing Revenue Account (HRA) rents, tithes, acknowledgements, way leaves and other land- and property-based charges of a non-casual user;
- 'Other income' from interest and recharges exclusive of grants.

School meals account for the bulk of charges for education services, as do residential care for social services, leisure and recreation for cultural and related services and parking for highways. Housing services refers only to the General Fund Revenue Account and so excludes rents for council housing. The table also excludes charges for trading services such as airports and harbours and for infrastructure.

Excluding housing rents, infrastructure and trading services, charges raised only £4 per head of population per week in 2005/06 and 2006/07 (Audit Commission 2008; DCLG 2006; Scottish Executive 2007). Nevertheless, the above table illustrates the endemic nature of charging for services.

Table 10.1   Sales, fees and charges as a percentage of total revenue expenditure and revenue income by local authorities in England 2007/08

	Sales, fees and charges as a percentage of total expenditure	Sales, fees and charges as a percentage of income (excluding grants)
Education services	4.5	39.0
Highways, roads and transport services	25.0	74.8
Social services	10.0	49.4
Housing services (non-Housing Revenue Account)	17.0	53.0
Cultural and related services	19.1	64.6
Environmental services	13.4	58.4
Planning and development services	22.0	61.7
Police services	3.1	40.3
Fire services	1.7	40.8
Court services	2.4	9.0
Central services	8.4	11.2
Other services	22.1	35.7
Total (%)	9.1	38.6

Note: Reproduced under the terms of the Click-Use Licence.

Source: CLG 2009a.

Social services, education and transport accounted for 58 per cent of councils' income from charging in England and Wales in 2006/07. Social services raised £2.3 billion, education £2.0 billion, with £1.5 billion coming from highways, roads (including congestion charges) and transport services (including parking and public transport). However, the above table makes clear that only highways and planning finance more than a fifth of their expenditures with revenue from sales, fees and charges. Nevertheless, even where the proportion of expenditure covered is small, charges account for (sometimes very) substantial proportions of income exclusive of government grants, as shown in the table above for education and the fire and police services.

While some services are capable of fully covering costs, even making an accounting surplus, it seems that educational, cultural and protective services are incapable of achieving high rates of cost recovery through charging their users, with only parking and property enquiries making accounting profits (Accounts Commission 1998).[1]

Trends since 2001

Notwithstanding the strengthened charging powers under the Local Government Act 2003 (see above), Table 10.2 makes it clear that the falling share of fees and charges as a percentage of income excluding grants continues apace. Overall, that share fell from 44.7 per cent in 2001/02 to 38.6 in 2007/08. Education services, social services, non-HRA housing services, cultural and related services and police services each saw a substantial fall of more than ten percentage points in share over those seven years. The only services for which that share rose over the period as a whole were highways, roads and transport services, fire services and central services. The remaining services experienced only moderate percentage point falls either side of fairly considerable fluctuations.

The biggest fall was for education services (by over 20 percentage points). The denominator for that ratio excludes grants and so the falling share cannot be attributed to increased central government funding of school education. The fall must therefore have been largely due to the falling take-up of school meals.

The falling ratios for social services, non-HRA housing services, cultural and related services and police services suggest that internal barriers to charging have become more binding since 2003. This emphasises the need for local authorities to adhere to the recommendations (and to make use of the charging resources provided) by the Audit Commission

Table 10.2 Sales, fees and charges as a percentage of income (excluding grants) by local authorities in England, 2001/02–2007/08

	2001/02	2002/03	2003/04	2004/05	2005/06	2006/07	2007/08
Education services	62.9	57.3	50.8	47.1	44.9	40.6	39.0
Highways, roads and transport services	69.7	73.0	76.9	77.3	75.8	72.0	74.8
Social services	66.9	65.4	58.4	54.4	50.2	51.7	49.4
Housing services (non-HRA)	67.6	63.0	61.0	54.7	57.5	55.6	53.0
Cultural and related services	75.2	70.6	69.7	68.5	65.6	62.6	64.6
Environmental services	65.7	64.2	64.3	62.5	58.4	52.9	58.4
Planning and development services	–	–	66.6	59.6	61.8	62.5	61.7
Police services	52.9	35.4	51.8	53.8	53.0	44.6	40.3
Fire services	17.4	17.0	24.2	17.0	32.2	43.1	40.8
Court services	12.4	21.8	25.0	14.1	30.4	5.1	9.0
Central services	7.7	7.1	11.4	10.5	14.2	12.6	11.2
Other services	35.9	43.2	33.2	28.6	30.0	25.6	35.7
Total	44.7	44.2	43.5	40.8	41.3	39.1	38.6

Note: Reproduced under the terms of the Click-Use Licence.

Source: CLG 2009b.

(see above). If they do not, those ratios can be expected to fall further in future years.

In general, revenue streams and the associated proportions for individual services are affected not just by changing levels of charges but also by changing rates of use of chargeable services.

The considerable variation between councils in the proportion of service expenditures covered by revenue from charges cannot be fully explained by the fact that different types of council provide different services to different populations, both of which, in turn, differ in the scope they provide for charges. In its 2008 report, the Audit Commission concluded that these variations are apparently unrelated to levels of council tax, to council performance (as measured by Comprehensive Performance Assessments, etc.) or to the extent of local levels of deprivation and other such factors influencing councils' approaches to charging.

Figure 10.1 indicates those factors affecting local authority charging policy, as identified by the Accounts Commission (1998, 12).

Given that charges are both highly visible and often politically sensitive as policy options for local government, the political environment is

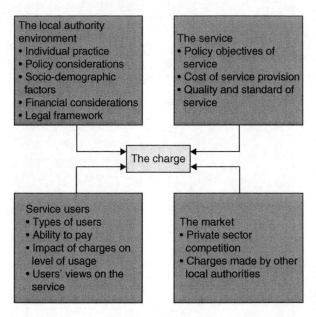

Figure 10.1   Factors affecting local authority charges

Note: Reproduced by permission of the Accounts Commission which holds the copyright.

Source: Accounts Commission, *The Challenge of Charging: A Managed Response* (1998)

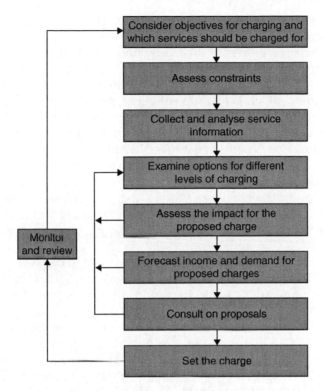

Figure 10.2 Managing charges: A staged process

Note: Reproduced by permission of the Accounts Commission which holds the copyright.

Source: Accounts Commission, *The Challenge of Charging: A Managed Response* (1998)

crucially important. Consequently, any charging regime must involve, as a central element, the participation of councillors. The central involvement of councillors in the development of charging policy has, according to the Accounts Commission (1998, 13), a number of clear advantages:

- Officers are allowed to discuss the overall impact of charges and inform the political judgements necessary on ability to pay;
- Councillors are able to develop their understanding of the reasons for charges, and can be in a position to justify their imposition to their constituents;
- Discussion of proposed charges should take place in committee;
- Potential public relations problems can be minimised.

For the Accounts Commission, local authorities must develop both a *structured* and a *corporate* approach to charging policy. A staged implementation process of the management of charging policy is recommended, as indicated in Figure 10.2.

In terms of achieving VFM, the Audit Commission (1999) noted that the extent to which people are willing to pay for a service can be an accurate indicator of how they value the service. The report emphasised the link between charging and achievement of 'Best Value' in the provision of services. The set of questions in the Audit Commission's 2008 report are much more detailed and challenging than the much shorter list in the 1999 report. Both sets of questions relate to the principles underpinning charging, what drives charging decisions, how much is raised, whether exemptions and concessions are well structured, whether the resulting pattern of subsidy matches council priorities and whether VFM is being achieved.

The 2008 report goes much further in addressing the ways in which internal barriers (listed above) can be overcome. In this respect, the 1999 set of questions is too inward-looking, regarding charges as a politico/technocratic issue to be resolved by councillors and offices, largely isolated from service users, the local community and other stakeholders. In sharp contrast, the 2008 set of questions is more outward-looking, seeking to change not just the internal culture of councillors and officers that imbues charging policy and practice, but also the external culture of a wider range of stakeholders. The latter relates to changing their views on the acceptability of charges, not just as one of the various means by which to finance local public services but also as a means of achieving greater VFM in encouraging positive changes in the behaviour of service users (and providers?) and in more effectively targeting subsidies on prioritised groups of stakeholders. The question then becomes one of balance between taxes and charges.

Setting the right charge

The Audit Commission's 1999 report found that in most local authorities in England and Wales charges were isolated from objectives and knowledge about the impact on service users. This was because the charges were budget driven, with little monitoring or evaluation being undertaken. In other words, charges were not 'joined up' within a corporate charging cycle designed to deliver Best Value.

In its 2008 report, the Audit Commission notes that setting the level and structure of charges involves politically charged decisions regarding balancing the divergent needs of their communities and determining whether the burden of costs should fall most heavily on council taxpayers or service users. Figure 10.3 shows the various considerations.

Figure 10.3 differs from the previous figure reproduced from the Accounts Commission's 1998 report in making explicit the need to consider both strategic and service-specific objectives and to consider the impact on both the levels of use and the expenditures of the various community groups. This demonstrates the point made in the introduction that it is necessary to appreciate that co-payments exist in a complex policy environment involving important legal, political, social and financial factors.

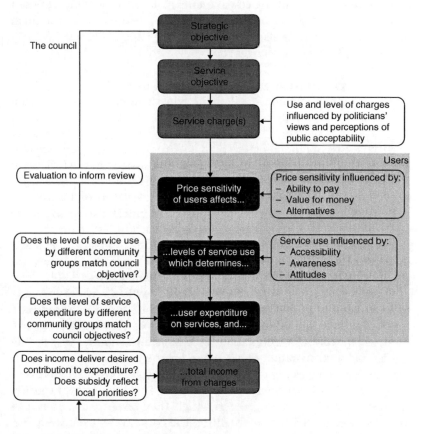

Figure 10.3   The charging system

Note: Reproduced by permission of the Audit Commission which holds the copyright.

Source: Audit Commission (2008).

The two commissions' increasingly sophisticated approach to charges in successive reports demonstrates that such an appreciation has developed over time. In particular, the above figures make clear that both commissions recognise the need to monitor and evaluate the results of charging, to consult with local communities and to communicate effectively to them the rationale for charging.

At present, it is still not clear to what extent charges have generally become 'joined up' with service objectives. Ultimately, the 'bottom line' is to determine whether the balance between 'user pays' and taxpayer subsidies is right, using comprehensive data about the costs and benefits of services to decide who should pay for services and who should be subsidised. The resulting co-payments require consideration of both charging methodologies and philosophies; these are considered much more comprehensively elsewhere (Bailey 1999; 2002; 2004).

In conceptual terms, charges could be based on:

- The costs incurred in providing services to users;
- The benefits individuals and/or the wider community receive from them.

Both charging methodologies could incorporate the various exemptions and concessions noted above. However, the benefits of services are much more difficult to measure than their costs and charging according to benefits received by service users could lead to politically and socially unacceptable profits being made. As noted above, the Local Government Act 2003's powers restrict local authorities' charges to cost recovery. The CIPFA Best Value Accounting Code of Practice has a definition of total cost, to which could be added a contribution towards corporate and democratic core and non-distributed costs.

A prior choice has to be made regarding which services (or parts thereof) are chargeable, which should continue to be financed fully from local taxes and intergovernmental transfers, and which should be financed by various combinations of charge and subsidy. Suspending the legislative constraints noted above for the time being, this choice requires a clear charging philosophy. There are various alternatives.

The 'distribution of benefits' approach. This approach categorises services in terms of the degree to which they benefit society as well as the service user. Services benefiting the community exclusively (i.e. pure public goods) are fully funded by subsidy and services benefiting users exclusively (i.e. pure private goods) are fully funded by user charges.

Examples of pure public goods are development plans produced by the planning service (to regulate the uses of land compatible with protecting the local community from the adverse effects of unregulated development) and community safety improvements provided by the fire service. All citizens can benefit from the service without detracting from the benefits enjoyed by other citizens and it would be difficult if not impossible to try to prevent individuals benefiting if they did not pay charges.

Examples of pure private goods are golf facilities and school meals. The benefits of such services are excludable by preventing use if the individual is unwilling to pay a service charge. They are also rivals in use because the service has a finite capacity. To provide them free of charge would result in inefficiency, for example irresponsible or wasteful use.

As a crude rule of thumb, services from which the community benefits more than users could receive 75 per cent subsidy. Similarly, services benefiting users more than the community could receive 25 per cent subsidy and those where the benefits are equal could receive 50 per cent subsidy (but see below).

The 'categorisation of services' approach. Although based more in terms of social policy analysis, this approach is similar to the first alternative in that it defines services as 'need', 'protective', 'amenity' or 'facility' services. The 'need' services (e.g. social care) would be wholly financed from taxation and so free at the point of use while the 'facility' services (e.g. photocopying materials at public libraries) would be wholly financed by charges. In between these extremes, the 'protective' services (e.g. meals-on-wheels for elderly people) and 'amenity' services (e.g. keep-fit classes) would be financed by a combination of taxes and charges, income from subsidies exceeding charges for the former and the reverse for the latter.

Both approaches are over-simplistic as well as essentially arbitrary and subjective in that they are based on practitioners' impressions of the nature of benefits derived from individual services. The examples given reflect the author's own subjective impressions of service benefits.

The 'subsidy-by-default' rationale. Here, the rule is to charge fully for services unless there are good reasons to the contrary. This approach is based on a presumption in favour of charging so that subsidies are only paid by default. It was followed in the UK by the 1976 Layfield Report (Cm 6453) and by a consultative document in 1986 (Cm 9714). Good reasons to the contrary relate to control of access; to the acceptability, incidence and administrative cost of charging; to the nature and extent of benefits; to the ability to pay; to demand and cost factors and, finally, to efficiency and effectiveness.

The minimum standards approach. This approach uses taxation to finance collectively determined minimum service levels, charges thereafter financing discretionary increases in service provision. A variant of this approach was recommended in two notes of reservation to the 1976 Layfield Report (Cm 6453). The minimum standards approach was resurrected in the Local Government Act 2003, which, as noted above, provides a general power to charge for discretionary services provided under well being powers in the Local Government Act 2000. This includes additions or enhancements to mandatory services above the level or standard that an authority has a duty to provide.

The basic and non-basic services approach. Different services and/ or their components could be classified as basic (and therefore provided free) and non-basic (and therefore chargeable at full cost). This approach assumes that there are some service components which are germane to the service and others that are not essential.

This is questionable but was recommended by the then UK Conservative government in respect of public library services (Cm 324). For example, it suggested that book borrowing should be a free basic service while specialist information services and non-print materials (e.g. those emanating from computers) should be chargeable non-basic services.

There are no clear principles upon which such a distinction can be based. The proposed distinction between books and computer printouts is technology-driven and, as information in electronic form increasingly replaces that in book form, user charges would be extended by default.

The customised value-added services approach. Here, charges are levied only where there is substantial real discretion on the part of service users themselves to customise the levels and mix of service outputs. In other words, either local governments have no monopoly power or they do not exercise it by restricting output.

This is distinct from the other approaches in that it does not require definitions of minimum standards or basic and non-basic services, or an assessment of the balance of benefit between the individual user and the community. It is incremental in approach and relates to the development of both new services or variants of existing ones, but only those that are specifically designed to provide customised value-added services at the discretion of the individual user.

Variants of this approach underpin the general power for Best Value authorities to charge for discretionary services under the Local Government Act 2003, as long as those who receive such services have agreed to their provision and to pay for them via a charge (see above). It underpins the current development of personalised services in England (Bailey 2006; Leadbeater 2004; Lent and Arend 2004; National Consumer Council 2004) and legislation in 2004 for both the fire and planning services (see below).

Ultimately, in determining the balance between charges and related subsidies, in combination they must secure the public nature of the service. This principle is most clearly developed in respect of planning fees (see below).

In practical policy terms, it may only be possible to charge for completely new services, for new variants of existing services or for demonstrably improved quality of service. Initial endowments relating to service use have to be recognised. This is the position adopted by the Local Government Act 2003. Such developments generally have to promote rather than restrict service evolution and take-up. They must avoid discrimination against prioritised groups, dilution of service characteristics or displacement of objectives and, at all times, any element of compulsion regarding payment for services.

Examples of use of co-payments in UK local government

Further details of the following examples are available elsewhere, including financial data, service-specific legislation and discussion of developments in both policy and practice (Bailey 2009; Cook 2005).

Rents for municipal housing are being raised in England in accordance with a central government formula to levels charged by housing associations (registered social landlords separate from local government). Housing authorities could also levy new or higher service charges for communal cleaning and concierge services as well as for internal redecoration, home security services, energy advice, etc.

Centrally prescribed planning fees are continuing to rise in order to recover a higher proportion of the costs of processing planning applications. Planning obligations negotiated between local authorities and developers and/or locally determined planning charges are expected to be of greater proportionate importance in the future. This might help to recover councils' infrastructure costs related to physical development, especially in fast-growing suburban municipalities and in south-east England. A 'planning gain supplement' has been actively considered for some time as a form of local betterment tax.

Discretionary charges for city road use are currently restricted to London and Durham, with revenues being less than foreseen because more people than expected changed transport mode or their time of travel (outside the charging period). This behavioural response, however, has been seen as beneficial in environmental terms and in reducing traffic congestion. A referendum in Edinburgh in early 2005 rejected 'congestion charges', perhaps reinforcing the reluctance of other city municipalities actively to pursue them. However, they may be more willing to introduce charges following the introduction of a nationwide scheme of road charging some time in the future. This scheme will be introduced subject to the outcome of trials in various local authority areas of alternative road-pricing technologies, including satellite technology. This could monitor use of particular roads by individual vehicles and charge them accordingly and so allow a direct connection to be made between demand, charge, investment revenues and capital funding.

Variable charges for the collection of household waste based on volume and/or weight could be used as part of a 'polluter pays' philosophy, with the amount paid in charges being reduced if households participate in doorstep recycling schemes. A public education campaign reducing production of waste by increasing recycling would reduce the money raised from direct variable charges. Nonetheless, this is a desirable outcome just as city road charges are successful if they lead to a reduction in traffic congestion and so raise less money than expected. Indeed, very substantial revenues raised from direct charges for the collection of household waste would indicate failure to meet environmental, social and economic objectives and failure to change the UK's waste-making culture. In the meantime, new or higher charges could be levied for the collection of bulk waste, removal of abandoned vehicles, etc.

Charges for use of sports and leisure facilities are already very well developed but they could be increased to be more comparable with levels in the private sector and new charges could be developed, for example for provision of personal trainers. Culture and related services could charge for access to historical records and to special exhibitions at museums and galleries, while maintaining free admission to their main collections. This is already the case for the UK national museums and galleries.

Fire and rescue services could increase their use of charges for non-fire fighting (special) services, especially for discretionary services provided to commercial organisations seeking to profit from them. These include charging insurance companies for the costs of dealing with non-fire related emergencies (e.g. road traffic accidents, releasing jammed lifts or lift rescues from silos and sewers), non-emergency calls (e.g. effecting entry to premises, pumping water out of flooded buildings, dealing with chemical spillages and other hazardous materials and for the use of high-reach vehicles), fire safety training (provided to commercial companies, including North Sea oil companies), and humanitarian incidents (e.g. rescuing horses and cows from ditches, slurry pits and bogs, extraction from which requires use of heavy lifting equipment).

Police services could make more use of charges for crowd control at football matches and festivals in public parks or for late-night policing of 'alcohol disorder zones' in city centres with many pubs and clubs. Those organisations could pay the charges related to number of officers required to provide the extra level of policing they require (i.e. over and above the normal level without such events). Charges could also be levied on companies receiving training in security and crime prevention and charges could achieve higher cost-recovery ratios in providing improved services in respect of community safety, much like the fire service.

Non-core education user charges may increasingly be levied in the form of 'voluntary' contributions by parents to schools, for example, for special equipment. School meals services might have to raise meals charges (which cover little more than half of costs) if they are to meet the government's nutritional guidelines. Low-income parents whose children already receive free school meals would be protected from higher charges. Charges could also be levied for non-statutory home-to-school transport.

It was noted in the introduction that personal care of elderly people (e.g. help with washing and dressing) is provided free of charge in Scotland. However, there are charges for accommodation in residential institutions and for meals whether provided in those institutions or in elderly people's own houses in Scotland. Charges are levied for all three of these social care services in the rest of the UK, where it seems to be generally accepted that social care of elderly people should not operate on the same principle as the NHS: meaning that it should not be free of charge. Instead, there seems to be a growing political and social consensus that social care should be financed by a fair, stable, adequate and easy-to-understand mix of funding from individuals, families and the state. The seemingly intractable problem is how to determine that sustainable mix in an increasingly aged demographic profile.

The UK's municipal libraries are not allowed to charge for the borrowing of books and other written materials. Ignoring prohibitive UK legislation, potential library charges could include those for access to the use of services (library cards and entrance or a 'turnstile' charge), lending of materials (including books, periodicals, DVDs and CDs), lending of audio-visual equipment (overhead, slide and data projectors and CD and DVD players), access to information, material and search services (inter-library loans, computer-based reference services and internet facilities), copying, scanning and desk-top publishing services, programming and use of buildings (for meetings and events) and lost and damaged items.

Conclusion

Clearly, co-payments exist in an increasingly complex policy environment, involving legal, political and financial factors and the ability and willingness of service users to pay the charge. The two commissions' increasingly sophisticated approach to charges in successive reports demonstrates that such an appreciation has developed over time. In particular, the above figures make clear that both commissions recognise the need to monitor and evaluate the results of charging, to consult with local communities and to communicate effectively to them the rationale for charging.

Determining willingness to pay charges and/or higher taxes is methodologically problematic because responses to public opinion surveys are heavily influenced by the wording and context of questions. Nevertheless, it seems that the majority of people are not willing to pay charges if it means paying more. This apparent lack of public willingness to accept greater use of charges may simply reflect the fact that a convincing case has yet to be made for a policy of changing the balance of funding from taxation to charges.

The Institute for Public Policy Research (Robinson 2004) has argued that the future of charges lies in the extent to which they promote attainment of key social, environmental and economic objectives and are recognised as legitimate by electorates. The attainment of these three categories of objectives is an extension of VFM and Best Value, including economy, efficiency and effectiveness as well as equity. Charges are not likely to be acceptable to electorates if their sole or primary aim is simply to raise revenue. To be acceptable, they must, at the very least, be offset by reductions in taxation or, alternatively, used to finance improvements in service standards.

There is a limit to the extent to which charges can be increased, not least because of equity issues. Nonetheless, service take-up is often proportionately greatest among affluent groups and constrained tax finances limit wider service availability to disadvantaged groups. Moreover, it is unethical to adopt patterns of irresponsible behaviour leading to unwelcome environmental and social degradation and economic waste simply because services are free at the point of use. The generation of household waste simply because of the failure to participate in recycling schemes and heavily congested roads due to unwillingness to use public transport are cases in point. There is evidence that charging for the collection of household waste and for the use of roads makes people use these services more responsibly.

As long ago as 1976, the Layfield Committee on local government finance considered a substantially increased role for charges but recognised the profound implications for the welfare state. Today, the focus of the welfare state is increasingly on the relationship between the citizen and the state being one of mutual responsibility, not one of paternalism. Charging for services is increasingly being seen as a means of promoting Best Value. Taxes are being used to spend more on pre-school and school education (as well as the NHS) while charges are being used to increase spending on universities and roads, etc.

It is clear that the 'bottom line' (of the accounts) financial necessity approach to charging is much too narrow a view of the potential of charges. In the recast welfare state charges have the potential to be a key instrument for delivering VFM and Best Value by distinguishing between the private and public characteristics of services. They can also help to deliver social justice by helping target subsidies on those judged to be most in need of a service and yet least able to pay for it. They can also facilitate increasing choice within the public sector by helping to make available the finance to provide discretionary services under the 2003 legislation.

Even though increased charging powers have been made available to local government, for which councils lobbied strongly, very little use has been made of them so far. As was demonstrated above, many of the barriers to increased use of charges are internal to local authorities and so their tendency to blame central government constraints is both misplaced and largely unwarranted.

Devolution clearly has the potential to lead to significant differences in the use of charges, although seemingly largely arbitrary differences already exist. Ongoing reforms of charging policy and of charging structures for services are also being driven by supranational policies regarding the protection of the environment and sustainable development (e.g. the European Union Directives dealing with municipal waste management).

As already noted, the main argument against the increased use of charges is that they increase inequality by excluding low-income groups too poor to pay them. This is only the case if charges are not means tested. However, administration of means testing may be so expensive that charges cost more to introduce than the money they raise and means testing is often so demeaning and intrusive of personal circumstances that it deters service take-up amongst the poor. In neither case does it create VFM. Nevertheless, to oppose all charges on equity grounds or because they might raise little revenue is simply not tenable and there is clearly considerable scope for charging strategies to be much more fully developed than is presently the case. Moreover, these objections will generally not apply to charges paid by organisations rather than by individuals.

Note

1. The Accounts Commission for Scotland is separate from the Audit Commission for England and Wales.

References

Accounts Commission (1998) *The Challenge of Charging: A Managed Response.* Edinburgh: Accounts Commission for Scotland.
Audit Commission (1999) *The Price is Right? Charges for Council Services.* London: HMSO.
Audit Commission (2008) *Positively Charged: Maximising the Benefits of Local public Service Charges,* www.audit-commission.gov.uk
Bailey, S. J. (1999) *Local Government Economics: Principles and Practice.* Basingstoke: Palgrave Macmillan.
Bailey, S. J. (2002) *Public Sector Economics: Theory, Policy and Practice.* (2nd edition) Basingstoke: Palgrave Macmillan.
Bailey, S. J. (2004) *Strategic Public Finance.* Basingstoke: Palgrave Macmillan.
Bailey, S. J. (2006) Facilitating Choice in English Local Government, *Economic Affairs,* 26 (1), March.
Bailey, S. J. (2009) *Local Government Charges,* CIPFA Technical Information Services. London: Chartered Institute of Public Finance and Accountancy, www.tisonline.net.
Bewick, T. (2010) Premium Investment, *The Guardian,* 5 January, 6 (Education Guardian Section), http://www.guardian.co.uk/theguardian
Burt (2006) A Fairer Way: Report by the Local Government Finance Review Committee (The Burt Report).
CLG (2009a) *Local Authority Revenue Expenditure and Financing England, 2007/08 Final Outturn.* Department of Communities and Local Government.
CLG (2009b) CLG Local Authority Revenue Expenditure and Financing England Statistics.
Cm 324 (1988) *Financing Our Public Library Service: Four Subjects For Debate.* London: HMSO.

Cm 6453 (1976) *Local Government Finance: Report of the Committee of Enquiry* (The Layfield Report). London: HMSO.

Cm 9714 (1986) *Paying for Local Government.* London: HMSO.

Cook, P. (2005) *A Practical Guide for Local Authorities on Discretionary Income Generation.* London: Chartered Institute of Public Finance and Accountancy, www.cipfa.org.uk

DCLG (2006) *Local Authority Revenue Expenditure and Financing England 2005–06 Outturn.* Department for Communities and Local Government.

HM Government (2009) *Higher Ambitions – The Future of Universities in a Knowledge Economy.* London: Department for Business, Innovation and Skills, http://www.bis.gov.uk/wp-content/uploads/publications/Higher-Ambitions.pdf

HM Treasury (2002) Funding the Scottish Parliament, National Assembly for Wales and Northern Ireland Assembly, (3rd edition) London: HM Treasury.

Leadbeater, C. (2004) *Personalisation through Participation: A New Script for Public Services.* London: Demos.

Lent, A. and Arend, N. (2004) *Making Choices: How Can Choice Improve Local Public Services.* London: New Local Government Network.

Local Government Act 2000.

Local Government Act 2003.

Local Government in Scotland Act 2003.

Lyons, M. (2007) Lyons Inquiry into Local Government: Place-Shaping: A Shared Ambition for the Future of Local Government. Department of Communities and Local Government, London.

National Consumer Council (2004) *Making Public Services Personal: A New Compact for Public Services.* London: National Consumer Council.

ODPM (2003) General Power for Best Value Authorities to Charge for Discretionary Services – Guidance on the Power in the Local Government Act 2003. London: Office of the Deputy Prime Minister.

OECD (1998) *Best Practice Guidelines for User Charging for Government Services,* Puma Policy Brief No. 3. Public Management Service: Organisation for Economic Cooperation and Development, March.

Rhodri, T., Parsons, D., Barry, J. and Rowe, V. (2007) Employer Co-funded Training in the UK: Current Practice and Policy Considerations, *Education + Training,* 49 (2): 112–125.

Robinson, P. (2004) *How Do We Pay? Funding Public Services in Europe.* London: Institute for Public Policy Research, www.ippr.org

Rose, R. (1990) *Charging for Public Services,* Public Administration, 68 (2): 297–313.

Scottish Executive (2007) Scottish Local Government Financial Statistics 2005–06, Scottish Executive.

Smith, P. C. (2006) User Charges for Health Care: History and Prospects. In J. Asato (ed.) *Charging Ahead? Spreading the Costs of Modern Public Services.* London: Social Market Foundation.

Walsh, K. (1995) *Public Services and Market Mechanisms.* Basingstoke: Macmillan.

11
Vouchers as Innovative Funding of Public Services

Pekka Valkama, Stephen J. Bailey and Ian C. Elliott

Introduction: Defining public service vouchers

A voucher is an instrument issued by a principal that can be redeemed by the holder for a service, commodity or other such benefit provided by an agent. The principal is the organisation that finances and issues the voucher. The holder is the person receiving the voucher and, thereby, the service, commodity or other such benefit. The agent provides the service, commodity or other such benefit in exchange for the redeemable voucher.

This generic definition incorporates *choice, benefit and payment* and so is much more comprehensive than other partial definitions of vouchers (Colin 2005; Collin et al. 1990; Glennerster 1992; Greve 2002; Lamming and Bessant 1988; Nisberg 1988; OECD 1998), discussed elsewhere (Valkama and Bailey 2001). Derived from it, a *public service voucher* is simultaneously *publicly directed consumption with individualised choice of production and payment*:

- *Publicly directed consumption* because it is given to those in need of a service; is limited in its value, purpose and manner of use; enables the use of public and/or private services and transfers both rights and responsibilities to its holder and to the service producer (see below);
- *Individualised choice of production* because, within a competitive system of plural provision, vouchers enable choice of eligible service producer in any or all of the public sector, the non-profit sector and the private sector;
- *Individualised choice of payment* because choice of service producer determines which of the eligible suppliers receives payment and payment can be withdrawn via exit.

Therefore, consumption is publicly directed because the voucher leads to increased consumption of a particular service of regulated quantity and quality, while holders of vouchers are allowed to choose their preferred production outlet and to make payment via the voucher.

Vouchers can be used to distribute all goods and services except those which are purely collective. Non-collective or 'private' goods (and services) are excludable and rival in use (e.g. a municipal tennis court). Collective or 'public' goods (and services) are non-excludable and non-rival in use, the service benefits everyone simultaneously and no-one can be prevented from benefiting (e.g. municipal environmental health services). The financing of collective goods (pure public goods) can be based only on tax income, because nobody can be excluded from using them and so payment (by money and/or voucher) cannot be enforced. Hence, private goods are the most suitable goods for distribution through vouchers because payment can be enforced at the point of use of service.

Only a small number of local government services are pure public goods. Such services as schooling, personal social services and culture and leisure services are private goods, because a person can be prevented from consuming them and rivalry in use is present (Bailey 1999). Hence, they are suited to use of vouchers.

Main types of vouchers

The main types of vouchers are depicted in Figure 11.1, which makes it clear that vouchers can be used in the public, enterprise (private) and third (voluntary) sectors. In all of these sectors, vouchers can be separated into internal and external vouchers. Use of internal vouchers is restricted to services or facilities provided by the organisation giving the voucher. External vouchers can be used to access services or facilities provided by other organisations as well as the one issuing the voucher.

Focusing on public sector vouchers, Figure 11.1 shows three categories:

- Privatisation vouchers given to the public free of charge or for a registration fee (in many East European countries). With these vouchers, citizens have been able to buy stocks in the privatised companies. Alternatively, they have been able to entrust their vouchers to unit trusts (Uvalic and Vaughan-Whitehead 1997; see also Chapter 5, footnote 6 and Chapter 12).
- Employment vouchers help to get people into work by subsidising work or training.

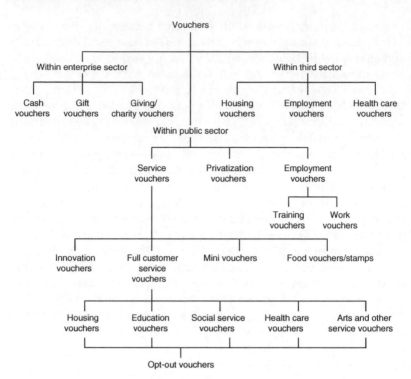

Figure 11.1   External vouchers in the enterprise, third and public sectors

- *Job vouchers.* When a job seeker qualifying for a voucher finds a job, the state pays the employer financial support that covers part of the salary costs (perhaps for a maximum of one year). The objectives are to familiarise those entering the labour market with working life, to help the unemployed maintain their professional skills and their ability to work and to make households more independent of state income support by subsidising the salary of the previously unemployed head of household. The payment for work consists of two elements: the work voucher paid to the employee by the state and the so-called 'excess share' for which the employers are themselves responsible (Rönkkö 1999).
- *Training vouchers.* These vouchers are used to cover all or a share of the fixed and variable costs of training. For example, they could be used to enable university and college students look for a trainee position in private sector companies, either as part of their studies or after graduating (Becker and Becker 1997). Likewise they can

finance training of the unemployed to improve their chances of finding jobs. For example, both Germany, where public policy represents a conservative welfare regime, and the USA, where public services are based more on a liberal welfare regime, have recently introduced training vouchers for the unemployed (Bruttel 2005; Hipp and Warner 2008).

- Service Vouchers: given to those eligible to use or otherwise benefit from services and provide discounts on charges and/or additional service availability.
  - *Food vouchers* or stamps are given to poor and underprivileged people (sometimes including refugees) by social welfare workers. The holder buys food in participating grocery shops. In order to encourage full use of the voucher, change may not be given if the purchased food items do not fully exhaust the monetary value of the voucher. After the purchase, the shop exchanges the coupon for money through the social welfare office. These food vouchers differ from meals vouchers in that they are meant for buying unprepared food rather than for catering services (Roson 2000; Savas 1987).
  - *Innovation vouchers* are given to small and medium enterprises (SMEs) and voluntary organisations. Innovation vouchers for SMEs are used as a form of industrial policy state grant because they can be used to acquire external R&D and consultancy services. Innovation vouchers for voluntary and non-profit organisations are used in cases when national or regional funding bodies do not want to give direct funding to voluntary organisations. These organisations can use innovation vouchers for knowledge transfer services and purchases for academic advice and support.
  - *Mini vouchers* afford holders additional levels of service. For example, all pupils could be offered the basic level of schooling but for further studies, such as supplementary courses and ancillary educational services, pupils could, with their mini vouchers, select courses from the private or public sectors according to their individual preferences (Levin 1997).

Full customer service vouchers differ from mini vouchers in that they entitle the holder to the full public service. They include:

- *Housing vouchers:* used in the USA in particular, the policy goal being to support those facing the worst housing conditions and the greatest rent burden (Kingsley 1991; OECD 1993).

- *Education vouchers:* used for free choice of school or of higher education institutions (universities and colleges). School vouchers are used where parents have free choice of school for their children and schools receive state support in proportion to the number of pupils they educate. With these vouchers, parents 'purchase' education for their children in any approved institution run by either profit-making or non-profit bodies. Education vouchers were proposed several centuries ago by Adam Smith in *The Wealth of Nations* (1776), by Thomas Paine in *The Rights of Man* (1791) and, more recently, by Friedman (1962), Maynard (1975), Blaug (1984), Ahonen (1994) and Cohn (1997). School vouchers schemes and experiments are most common in the USA. Many interest groups and lobbying organisations have actively campaigned for and against them (Sawhill and Smith 2000). According to Hauptman (2000), education vouchers in higher education have been much more acceptable than in primary education in the USA. The notion of applying vouchers to financing both public and private higher education institutions has been politically and legally acceptable. There is a competitive higher education market as universities compete with each other to recruit students, and paying charges is well established in higher education (Hess 2007; Seldon 1986; 1991).
- *Social service vouchers:* increasingly common in several European countries, including nursery, meals on wheels, taxi service and home help and nursing vouchers. The last are used in old people's home-help services and in home nursing. Elderly people can usually choose between private and public services. The old person is usually him/herself the voucher, because there are no actual coupons but the municipality pays the care costs. Elderly people can usually buy additional services at their own expense. Capacity in the public sector to respond to emerging social needs is often heavily constrained and the use of vouchers for social care services has not caused as much political tension and argument as school vouchers.
- *Health service vouchers:* used for operations, rehabilitation services and to provide medical aid equipment. The degree to which both Medicare (for the elderly and disabled) and Medicaid (for the poor) in the US represent a public service voucher is debatable (Bradford and Shaviro 2000; Reischauer 2000). Particularly with Medicare such an association is problematic as it traditionally covers all medical expenses without limit. In contrast vouchers always have a fixed monetary value. Yet in terms of their effects both these schemes do correspond closely to the nature of a public service voucher and thus are 'voucher-like' (Bradford and Shaviro 2000).

- *Arts vouchers*: given to low-income groups and children to try to stimulate their attendance at museums and galleries (Pommerehne and Frey 1997; West 1986). This assumes they are easily deterred by an admission charge.

Any or all of the full service vouchers listed above may allow (or indeed require) holders to use their own financial resources to supplement (top up) the value of the voucher in order to purchase services (Heikkilä et al. 1997; Suomen Kuntaliitto 1994). This is particularly the case for *opt-out vouchers*, which allow service users to choose private services instead of public ones (e.g. for home helps, nursing or medical services). Private health care services are generally more expensive, but the queues are usually shorter. If a patient does not want to be on a long waiting list, he/she could ask the public health care authority for a voucher, the value of which would be equal to the expense of treatment in public health care. The patient could then supplement the voucher's value with his/her own money in order to get faster treatment in the private sector.

Opt-out health service vouchers allow service users greater choice in terms of speed of service, and their top-up payments could be used to increase health service capacity in the private sector – but not in the public sector (which must still pay its 'share' of costs). The possibility of 'queue jumping' by those with greater ability to pay (as distinct from greater medical need) arises because the top-up payments pre-empt public funds. Here, people of equal or greater medical need but unable to pay a top-up charge are made to wait longer for the public service (possibly leading to a deterioration in their medical condition) than those with higher incomes. However, by enabling those who can provide a 'top-up' to exit the public sector, queues may be reduced and thus the public sector can focus on those with the greatest welfare need. Moreover, the greater the use of the opt-out facility, the more individualised choice overrides central planning of health services.

A conceptual typology of vouchers

A conceptual typology of vouchers is depicted in Figure 11.2.
The foundations of public sector voucher schemes are based on three models:

- *Vouchers defined in law.* Such vouchers are nationally important and politically challenging to introduce but also inflexible.

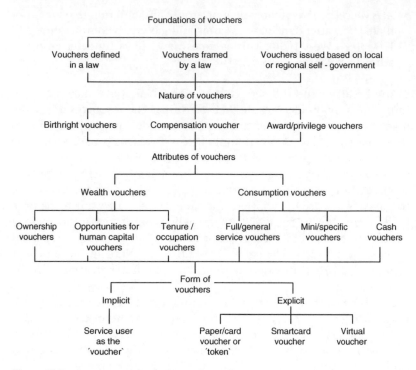

Figure 11.2   A conceptual typology of vouchers

- *Vouchers framed in law.* Only the broad framework of a voucher scheme is defined by a parliament, which makes it possible for public authorities to make modifications and introduce local variations.
- *Vouchers issued based on local or regional self-government.* In countries where regional and local governments have strong self-govern-ance and general competence powers (as in the Nordic countries – see Chapter 12), local and regional councils may have enough legal powers and sufficient local resources to introduce vouchers independently.

The nature of vouchers has three basic forms:

- *Birthright vouchers.* Such vouchers are distributed to those who are registered citizens but not to temporary residents or immigrants (at least those not yet granted nationality), for example privatisation vouchers.

- *Compensation vouchers.* These vouchers are distributed to those judged to be in need of a public service (e.g. hospital treatment) but to whom access to that service is denied because of a shortage of supply or other such capacity constraint. Such vouchers can be used to access comparable (e.g. medical) services in the private and/or voluntary sectors and so compensate the holder for lack (or poor quality) of public supply. Opt-out vouchers may effectively act as compensation vouchers. Internal service vouchers, luncheon and meals vouchers may be intended (at least in part) to compensate employees for relatively low wages and salaries.
- *Award/privilege vouchers.* This category of voucher is allocated neither as compensation nor as a birthright. Instead, such vouchers confer privileges on their holders, examples being higher education vouchers (perhaps means tested) and employment vouchers (perhaps based on length of unemployment or lack of skills). Private sector gift vouchers fall into this category.

The attributes of vouchers can be divided into two distinct categories:

- *Consumption vouchers.* This type of voucher increases the recipient's consumption possibilities, either generally (i.e. cash vouchers) or specifically in respect of a particular good (e.g. gift and luncheon/food vouchers) or service (i.e. service vouchers).
- *Wealth vouchers.* Wealth vouchers lead to direct or indirect increases in the wealth (rather than consumption) of the recipient. Privatisation vouchers increase the recipient's wealth directly in terms of giving the holder ownership of a share of the value of a capital asset or business. Vouchers may also give holders rights of tenure, occupation or other such use of capital assets without conferring ownership. Examples are vouchers for use of land or property. In this case they confer only limited (not full) property rights. Employment and training vouchers increase the recipient's wealth indirectly by allowing the holder to accumulate 'human capital' in terms of acquired skills and work experience.

Vouchers can be explicit or implicit. *Explicit vouchers* have physical form, such as plastic cards carrying information about the holder and his or her eligibility for subsidy on a magnetic strip. 'Smart' cards incorporate an electronic chip, which allows more information to be input and also processed, for example about the frequency, location and type of use of services. *Implicit vouchers* use the beneficiary as the voucher.

This is the case for consumption vouchers conferring a right of access to public services (e.g. school education or health care) where 'the money follows the user' without an explicit voucher being used. Wealth vouchers are likewise implicit where trainees are sent on training schemes by a public sector agency without using physical vouchers.

Voucher schemes may have both explicit and implicit characteristics. For example, a specified (or maximum) number of children may be able to use a service even without a voucher if they are accompanied by an adult who does possess a voucher. Such vouchers are used for access to museums and to public transport services. It is clear that many vouchers are, in effect, multi-attribute vouchers.

A general model of vouchers

The three basic features of vouchers are:

- The user of the service is given a voucher worth a certain cash value;
- A voucher can only be used by the holder and only to purchase a specified commodity (good or service) for him- or herself. If the good or service is not defined, the voucher is no longer a voucher but, instead, an income transfer, such as a child benefit;
- The value of a voucher, in the form of a good or service, can only be redeemed from an approved supplier(s).

The first feature means the state is not necessarily committing itself to cover all the expenses involved in the use of a particular service. The second feature excludes the possibility of the voucher being transferred to another person (Ahonen 1994; Lacasse 1992). The third feature enables the voucher supplier to retain some degree of quality assurance and control over the transaction.

Figure 11.3 illustrates a voucher model. The solid lines denote financial flows (thick lines vouchers, thin line money) whilst the dashed line denotes non-financial flows (i.e. service provision). The arrows indicate the direction of flow.

The government supports the service user's (consumer's) purchasing power by giving him/her a voucher (thick line), allowing him/her to select the service producer. The service producer can be a private firm, a non-profit organisation or a public sector service unit. The service producer delivers the service to the consumer (dashed line) and

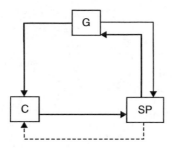

Figure 11.3 A simplified voucher model

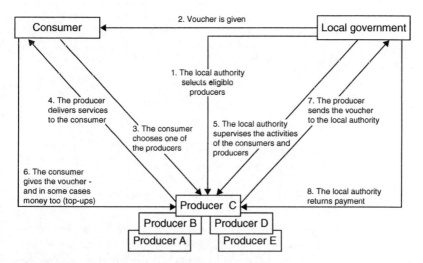

Figure 11.4 A local government voucher model

the consumer 'pays' the producer using the voucher (thick line). The service producer hands the voucher to the government, exchanging the voucher for money (thin line).

A more detailed model of vouchers within local government is outlined in Figure 11.4, which demonstrates the technicalities in delivering a public service funded through vouchers. Furthermore, in illustrating the separation of public funding from service provision, it highlights the extent to which the voucher concept represents a significant challenge to the *traditional* model of public service delivery. As such the voucher concept demonstrates the distinctive elements of an innovation (Osborne and Brown 2005).

LEVEL OF INTEREST

		Low	High
POWER	Low	Non-users Private sector	Users NGOs and interest groups Trade Unions
	High	Voters	Regional Government Local Government Central Government

Figure 11.5   A stakeholder analysis of opt-out vouchers
Source: Adapted from Elliott (2007) and Johnson et al. (2005).

The rather restricted basic voucher model can be relaxed as follows:

- The voucher can be either of a fixed monetary value or be income-related (i.e. means tested – see Chapter 10);
- The voucher can be given to a representative of the service user, instead of to the user him/herself;
- Vouchers can be defined in service rather than cash terms (e.g. entitling the holder to one hour of domestic help or to a specified amount of dental treatment);
- The voucher may directly benefit both the holder and someone else (e.g. school education vouchers held by parents benefit both them and their children).

Figure 11.5 provides an analysis of many other key stakeholder groups that would necessarily be involved in the design and *implementation* of an opt-out voucher scheme. This figure provides a wider illustration of the potential complexities behind the introduction of such an innovative scheme. The degree to which implementation of vouchers represents a significant change also raises issues surrounding the complexities associated with change in a public service context (Macleod and By 2009).

The way in which interest groups and lobbying organisations may hinder the implementation of public service vouchers can be seen in the difficulties surrounding implementation of the first education voucher scheme at Alum Rock (Sawhill and Smith 2000). Yet these barriers to implementation are not insurmountable as, since the late 1990s, education voucher schemes have flourished across the USA (Peterson and Campbell 2001). Furthermore, as noted by Greene, 'the findings of school choice studies, at least on some questions, have been uniformly positive' (2001, 84).

Perspectives for analysing arguments for and against vouchers

Table 11.1 lists ideological, theoretical, populist and pragmatic perspectives for and against vouchers. Right-wing 'think-tanks' advocate 'rolling back the frontiers of the state' to enhance individual liberty and so are ideologically predisposed in favour of vouchers as one means of achieving their objectives. Left-wing groups are typically ideologically predisposed against vouchers, instead preferring a greater direct role for the state in society and economy. However, Walsh (1995) claims vouchers that gained support among leftist parties because they can be used to limit the power of technocrats.

Free-market economists are theoretically predisposed in favour of vouchers as a means of strengthening market mechanisms via competition, leading to improved efficiency in both production and consumption of services. However, institutional economists argue that these beneficial effects will not be achieved because the free-market theoretical case fails to take account of institutional, behavioural and cultural barriers to competition. Populists are not concerned with ideology or theory, instead focusing on the experiences of those using vouchers, in particular whether voucher schemes provide a better standard of service for users. Pragmatists are concerned with whether voucher schemes actually work, not just in terms of acceptability to service users but also in reducing costs, increasing choice and meeting other objectives such as targeting subsidies more accurately and improving service quality.

The arguments presented in the literature (whether in favour of or against vouchers) are considered in detail elsewhere (Valkama and Bailey 2001). Suffice it to say that they are mostly unsubstantiated, being based mainly on conventional wisdom and presuppositions instead of on research data or practical experiences. The arguments are predominantly a priori and anecdotal. Literature that does draw on empirical research is often from the USA and based on local or federal

Table 11.1 Perspectives for analysing vouchers

Perspective	Objective	Rationale	Response
Ideological	To promote individual liberty, freedom of choice, privatisation and markets. To defend public services, public employees and democracy and to increase participation and collective control.	People know their own needs best and can fulfil them using vouchers to choose the supplier, location and time of service use. Vouchers threaten public sector service providers and it is for political decision-makers to bear responsibility for democratic decisions.	Service professionals are the best judges of need for service and market forces are not suitable for public services because clients are vulnerable. The rationale for local government is not to protect in-house service providers; vouchers deny neither democratic decision-making nor collective control of subsidy; they increase participation in service use.
Theoretical	To abolish public sector monopolies by introducing competition which, in turn, stimulates internal and external entrepreneurship and cost control.	Vouchers promote pluralism in service supply and so encourage customer orientation through competition for clients. This renews patterns of resource allocation, improves availability and use of information and avoids wasteful public spending.	Vouchers would not be successful because of excessive transaction costs and significant barriers to entry against potential new suppliers. More suppliers of a given output would result in lost economies of scale and so higher costs. In theory, the market optimum is unobtainable.
Populist	To support the interests of ordinary people by making living easier.	Vouchers decrease dependence on bureaucratic decision-making and so living becomes more care free.	Having to handle vouchers would increase the amount of work for service users and actually increase bureaucracy in allocating vouchers.
Pragmatic	To improve the supply of publicly and privately financed and produced services and to make more effective use of resources.	Vouchers encourage rational behaviour, which, in turn, improves the allocation and utilisation of resources through better targeting of subsidies and careful use of vouchers by their holders.	For vouchers to be functional, alternative competing producers are required. They usually do not exist, nor would they develop quickly enough. Hence vouchers would not bring any significant gains and the risk of failure is too great in practice.

schemes. The preponderance of pragmatic arguments against vouchers simply emphasises the need for further evaluation of voucher schemes, particularly across Europe, to see which arguments are substantiated and which refuted by empirical evidence. Those empirical outcomes will, in turn, be crucially dependent upon the dimensions and characteristics of vouchers and on the rights and responsibilities they entail.

Again, the complexity of the voucher concept impedes any simplistic analysis. Table 11.2 demonstrates that vouchers may be opposed by right-wing libertarians (who believe in a minimal state) and left-wing social democrats (who believe in extensive state intervention). Neo-liberals can be expected to support use of vouchers to complement (rather than replace) private sector market provision of services whose provision is thought socially and economically desirable.

Ultimately, any voucher scheme will only be viable if it is consistent with the dominant ideology of the policy-making body or organisation, attracts the support of those who finance and those who use the scheme and is both theoretically and empirically validated in terms of the expected and actual outcomes satisfying the scheme's objectives. More specifically, an effective voucher system must satisfy the following conditions (Savas 1987):

- There have to be widespread differences in people's preferences for the service, and these differences are recognised and accepted as legitimate;
- Individuals must have incentives to shop aggressively for the service (i.e. to find the best supplier);
- Individuals have to be well informed about market conditions;
- An optimal market situation needs many competing service suppliers, or else start-up costs need to be so low that the market is fully contestable – even if there are only very few producers;
- Service users can easily assess and determine the quality of the service;
- The service has to be relatively inexpensive and purchased frequently, so the users learn by experience.

Put concisely, heterogeneous preferences and low transaction costs have to exist simultaneously if a voucher system is to work effectively, namely to enable public policy-making and yet maximise consumer choice (Kogan 1988). These strict conditions limit the feasibility of voucher schemes where:

- Some preferences are not legitimised by the policy-making body (e.g. opting out of public sector health care services into the private sector);

Table 11.2 Political economy of public service vouchers

	Libertarian	Social democratic	Neo-liberal
Perceived role of government	Regulatory	Distributive and stabilisation	Allocative
Arguments	1. Vouchers would enhance dependency on public finance and (if not opt-out) on public sector 2. Government intervention stifles private sector growth 3. Injection of public funds would take resources away from protection of negative rights and private resources from production of wealth	1. Vouchers are a form of privatisation that would threaten public sector jobs 2. Public sector professionals are the best judges of the need for services 3. Private sector would fail to cooperate due to the administration involved and lack of financial incentives	1. Vouchers enable consumers to choose their preferred suppliers of services 2. Government can, through targeting, influence the market to meet public objectives 3. Private companies may prosper due to increasing use by those with vouchers
Key terms	Laissez-faire; negative rights	Professionalism; welfare; positive rights; human capital	Government failure; market failure; competition; efficacy; accountability
Key authors	Smith, Ricardo, Malthus	Keynes, Marshall	Friedman

Sources: Adapted from Elliott (2007) and Bailey (2002).

- Individuals have either have limited ability to shop aggressively for the service or are unwilling to do so;
- There is a lack of information about alternative suppliers or an inability to comprehend information that may be highly complex and/or subject to frequent change and revision;
- The private sector either lacks the organisational capacity to provide the service or newly established providers simply cannot cover their costs;
- Individuals are unable to distinguish between good and poor quality of service, for example health services or personal social services;
- The service is used infrequently, for example one-off medical treatments such as a hip replacement.

However, these constraints may be relaxed by carefully designed voucher schemes, the operation of which is monitored and modified as necessary after an initial pilot scheme or over time for full-blown schemes. The particular dimensions, characteristics, rights and responsibilities of voucher schemes are considered in detail below but, clearly, opt-out vouchers would not be used where the issuing authority wants to prevent voucher holders using private sector providers. Individuals can be expected to become more discriminating between alternative service providers as information and experience is accumulated over time – aided by public disclosure of information regarding the success rates of hospitals in treating medical conditions, the examination performances of schools, etc. Private sector capacity usually takes time to grow. Almost certainly, a transitional period will be required if voucher schemes are to be adopted as a long-term approach towards improving delivery of service.

Dimensions and characteristics of vouchers

There is no single voucher type or voucher system, Figure 11.6 illustrates the decisions that must be made when designing a voucher scheme. However, voucher schemes have three generic dimensions into which any scheme's criteria can be grouped (Ahonen 1994; Harisalo 1993; Levin 1997):

- The finance dimension:
  - The measurement unit used to determine the voucher's value;
  - The value of the voucher;
  - Whether the service producer can charge the holder more than the value of the voucher;

- Whether the service user can purchase additional services (top-ups);
- Whether any unused part of a voucher can be given as cash to the service user.
- The regulation dimension:
  - To whom the voucher is given;
  - What goods or services it can be used for;
  - The voucher's geographic area of validity;
  - The service producers from whom the voucher will be redeemed;
  - The conditions and criteria of the service producers' operations.
- The information dimension:
  - Eligibility criteria for receipt of the voucher;
  - Information on the service available to the holder of the voucher;
  - From which suppliers the consumer can obtain services;
  - What to do in the event of unsatisfactory service provision.

The last two bullet points refer to 'exit' and 'voice' respectively. *Exit* means the consumer is able to choose from alternative service producers and this is the most common argument for vouchers. If one is dissatisfied with the supply, one may use the exit option and choose another producer. Procedures, such as general liberalisation, competitive tendering, quasi-markets and privatisation, can be used to reinforce the exit option. *Voice* is used to express one's opinion, for example by complaining and participating in a pressure group to improve service quality. The use of voice is potentially useful when there is little or no competition.

A voucher valid in a free or quasi-market increases the scope for exit because a choice can be made between service units in the public, private and non-profit sectors. In theory, this stimulates competition that, in turn, stimulates greater productive efficiency and cost savings. This is especially the case for a free market extending beyond local boundaries (i.e. at the regional, national or even European Union level). The savings potential depends on the relative effectiveness of the public sector's service providers (Appleton 1997; Blaug 1984).

It is generally assumed that it is more appropriate to express one's preferences about services provided by local governments by using voice rather than exit, with the latter being considered more appropriate within the private sector. Customers are considered selfish, whereas municipal residents are regarded as people who consider the community, even though customers and residents are often the same individuals. However, if voice is not reinforced by the exit option, local governments and service providers may not have adequate incentives

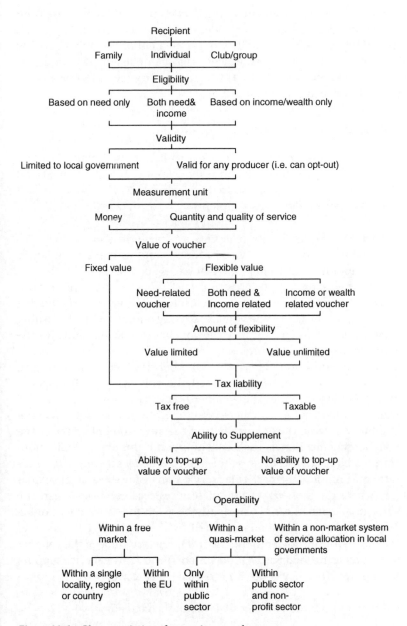

Figure 11.6 Characteristics of a service voucher

to meet residents' requirements. Vouchers reinforce voice because their use directly affects a service provider's finances when exit is possible (Bailey 1999). Likewise, the ability to supplement or top up a voucher's value reinforces the use of voice. Voice is also enhanced if the measurement unit is in terms of the quantity and quality (i.e. level) of service, defined after consulting service users.

Rights and responsibilities of vouchers

A voucher is not just an allocation instrument: it is also a control instrument, transferring both rights and responsibilities to the recipient and to the service producer, as illustrated by Figure 11.7.

A voucher gives *rights* to its recipient:

- *Consumption rights*: rights to access a service, to receive appropriate treatment from the service producer, and to make complaints. Consumption rights therefore reinforce use of voice;
- *Property rights*: exclusive rights to use the voucher. No other person has a right to use the voucher, so reinforcing the voice of the holder. However, ownership of the voucher usually remains with the issuing organisation. This ensures that the voucher can be used only for the purposes for which it is intended;
- *Transfer rights*: these determine whether the recipient can give (as a gift, bequest or pledge) or sell the voucher to a third party. Transferability increases the voucher holder's exit options. However, transfer could lead to vouchers being used by people not satisfying eligibility criteria, thus contradicting the aims and objectives of the voucher scheme. Hence, their consumption rights are normally nontransferable. Likewise, because the aim of voucher schemes is to facilitate consumption of a particular service, any unused value or surplus (i.e. where the monetary value of services received is less than the value of a voucher) cannot normally be given to the voucher holder. Any such surplus is usually retained by the supplier. This provides incentives for the holder to use the full monetary value of the voucher (e.g. purchasing food with a food voucher) and for the service supplier to improve efficiency (since any cost savings are retained).

A voucher also bestows *responsibilities* on its recipient:

- *Consumption responsibilities*: a person receiving a voucher is obliged to consume (a specified level of) the service. Consumption

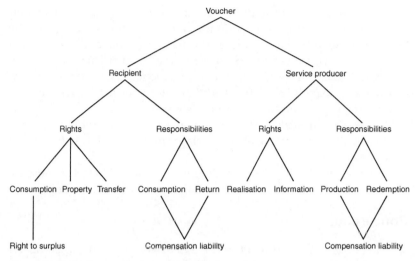

Figure 11.7 Rights and responsibilities of vouchers

responsibilities may oblige the recipient to acquire offers from several service producers and to use the least expensive producer;
- *Responsibility to return the voucher*: if the recipient has given the issuer false information regarding his or her eligibility or is no longer eligible, or if it is not used within a given period of time. This means that the voucher cannot be stored and added to other vouchers received later;
- *Compensation liability*: recipients can be made liable to pay compensation for any misuse of vouchers, including fraud or a similar offence.

The service producer also has *rights*:

- *Realisation right*: the service producer is entitled to exchange vouchers for money paid by the issuer of the voucher;
- *Information rights*: a competitive supply scenario requires that potential/alternative service producers receive information about voucher schemes.

The service producer also has *responsibilities*:

- *Production responsibilities*: the service producer must have suitable premises in which to provide the service(s); the staff hired by the

service producer must meet certain formal requirements regarding skills, expertise or experience; and the services must meet the
required quality. Furthermore, the service producer must not dis-
criminate against customers on grounds of their ethnic background,
sex, age, etc. A monitoring system may be necessary to ensure that
these responsibilities are fulfilled. This may require the authorities to
make regular or random supervisory visits;

- *Redemption responsibilities*: these oblige the service producer to have
the voucher redeemed within a certain time limit, after which it will
be invalidated;
- *Compensation liability*: as for recipients, service producers can also be
made liable to pay compensation for any misuse of vouchers.

Conclusions

Vouchers could be used much more extensively than at present as an
alternative, innovative public service delivery system, especially for
local government services. They could be used to promote greater economic and social equality by basing both their allocation and their
value on ability to pay and on medical and/or social need. They are
a means to an end, not an end in themselves, but the end in mind
will not necessarily be achieved by an ill-prepared voucher scheme. The
example of opt-out vouchers for health services demonstrates just how
easily the use of vouchers to pursue multiple objectives could be coun-
terproductive.

Vouchers designed to give greater freedom of choice may conflict with
more equal access to services by all social groups. Freedom of choice of
service level through willingness to pay additional amounts (on top
of the voucher's value) may deny services for those equally in need of
service yet unable to pay top-ups because of low incomes. Hence, the
details of individual voucher schemes have to be constructed carefully
if objectives are to be met and unethical or otherwise undesirable outcomes avoided.

Given its wide service responsibilities, experimentation with and
introduction of public service vouchers has usually depended on local
government initiatives. National voucher systems typically relate to
employment and training. Changes brought about by vouchers are primarily linked to the change in the role and status of the recipient as
customer.

The strengthening of exit and voice through voucher systems is potentially their greatest value in public policy terms because they guide the

financing of services. These two key attributes of vouchers are encompassed within the generic definition of public service vouchers used in this chapter, namely *publicly directed consumption with individualised choice of production and payment*. Earlier definitions of vouchers were incomplete because they did not incorporate exit and voice.

Voucher systems must be carefully designed and regularly evaluated against objectives if increased potential for exit and voice is to benefit prioritised groups. They have enormous potential as an alternative system by which to deliver and finance efficient, effective and equitable public sector services.

Whether that potential can be achieved in practice is open to question. Individual voucher schemes differ radically in terms of the type of voucher, their characteristics, the rights and responsibilities of holders and service producers, the feasibility of monitoring and influencing their use, the potential for use of exit and voice, etc. Hence, it would be methodologically invalid to judge all public service voucher schemes on the basis of a few (possibly idiosyncratic) schemes. Learning from the success or failure of individual voucher schemes has to pay attention to the schema outlined in Figures 11.1 to 11.7 above. This schema should be borne in mind when reading Chapter 12, which provides details of voucher schemes in Finland and the UK.

References

Ahonen Esa (1994) Koulutussetelit korkeakoulussa. Opiskelijan asema korkeakoulujen rahoituksessa. Opetusministeriö. Koulutus- ja tiedepolitiikan linjan julkaisusarja, 17. Helsinki.

Appleton Simon (1997) User Fees, Expenditure Restructuring and Voucher Systems in Education. The United Nations University: World Institute for Development Economics Research (WIDER). Working Papers No. 134, May.

Bailey, Stephen J. (1999) *Local Government Economics: Principles and Practice*. Basingstoke: Macmillan Press.

Bailey, Stephen J. (2002) *Strategic Public Finance: Theory, Policy and Practice*. (2nd edition) Basingstoke: Macmillan Press.

Blaug Mark (1984) Education Vouchers – It All Depends on What You Mean. In Julian Le Grand and Ray Robinson (eds) *Privatisation and the Welfare State*. George Allen & Unwin.

Bradford, D. F. and Shaviro, D. N. (2000) The Economics of Vouchers. In C. Eugene Steuerle, Van Doorn Ooms, George Peterson and Robert D. Reischauser (eds), *Vouchers and the Provision of Public Services*. Washington, DC: Brookings Institution Press.

Bruttel, Oliver (2005) Delivering Active Labour Market Policy through Vouchers: Experiences With Training Vouchers in Germany, *International Review of Administrative Sciences*, 71 (3): 391–404.

Becker, Gary S. and Becker, Guity Nashat (1997) *The Economics of Life: From Baseball to Affirmative Action in Immigration, How Real World Issues Affect Our Everyday Life.* Blacklick, OH: The McGraw-Hill Companies.

Cohn Elchanan (1997) Public and Private School Choices: Theoretical Considerations and Empirical Evidence. In Elchanan Cohn (ed.) *Market Approaches to Education. Vouchers and School Choice.* Oxford: Elsevier Science.

Colin, Frédéric (2005) Public Service Vouchers, *International Review of Administrative Sciences,* 71 (1): 19–34.

Collin, P. H., Carol, Weiland and John, Derek S. (1990) *American Business Dictionary.* Teddington, Middlesex: Peter Collin Publishing.

Elliott, Ian C. (2007) Barriers to the Implementation of Opt-Out Vouchers For Public Leisure Services (Unpublished PhD Thesis). Glasgow: Glasgow Caledonian University.

Friedman Milton (1962) *Capitalism and Freedom.* Chicago, IL: The University of Chicago Press.

Glennerster Howard (1992) *Paying for Welfare The 1990's.* Hemel Hempstead: Harvester Wheatsheaf.

Greene, J. P. (2001) The Hidden Research Consensus for Choice. In Peterson, P. E. and Campbell, D. E. (eds) *Charters, Vouchers & Public Education.* Washington, DC: Brookings.

Greve Bent (2002) Vouchers – nye styrings- og leveringsmåder I velfærdsstaten. Jurist- og økonomiforbundets forlag.

Harisalo Risto (1993) Julkisten palveluiden tukijärjestelmä kunnallishallinnossa. Kokeiluja, kokemuksia ja ideoita. Suomen Kunnallisliitto. Helsinki.

Hauptman, Arthur M. (2000) Vouchers and American Higher Education. In C. Eugene Steuerle, Van Doorn Ooms, George Peterson and Robert D. Reischauer (eds) *Vouchers and the Provision of Public Services.* Washington, DC: Brookings Institution Press, 336–367.

Heikkilä Matti, Törmä Sinikka and Mattila Kati (1997) Palveluseteli lasten päivähoidossa. Raportti valtakunnallisesta kokeilusta. Sosiaali- ja terveysalan tutkimus- ja kehittämiskeskus. Sosiaali- ja terveysministeriö. Raportteja, 216. Jyväskylä.

Hess, Frederick M. (2007) A Market for Knowledge? Competition in American Education. In Marc K. Landy, Martin A. Levin and Martin Shapiro (eds) *Creating Competitive Markets: The Politics of Regulatory Reform.* Washington, DC: Brookings Institition Press, 184–212.

Hipp, Lena and Warner, Mildred E. (2008) Market Forces for the Unemployed? Training Vouchers in Germany and the USA, *Social Policy & Administration,* 42 (1), February: 77–101.

Johnson, G., Scholes, K. and Whittington, R. (2005) *Exploring Corporate Strategy: Text and Cases.* (7th Edition) Essex: Pearson Education Limited.

Kingsley, G. T. (1991) Housing Vouchers and America's Changing Housing Problems. In W. T. Jr. Gormley (ed.) *Privatization and Its Alternatives.* Wisconsin: University of Wisconsin Press.

Kogan Maurice (1988) Normative Models of Accountability. In Ron Glatter, Margaret Preedy, Colin Riches and Mary Masterton (eds) *Understanding School Management.* Milton Keynes: Open University Press.

Lacasse, Francois (1992) Vouchers: Issues and Experiences in OECD/PUMA, Market-Type Mechanisms Series No. 4. Paris.

Lamming, Richard and Bessant, John (1988) *Macmillan Dictionary of Business and Management*. Basingstoke: Macmillan Press.

Levin, Henry M. (1997) The Economics of Educational Choice. In Elchanan Cohn (ed.) *Market Approaches to Education: Vouchers and School Choice*. Oxfrod: Elsevier Science.

Macleod, Calum and By, Rune (2009) *Managing Organizational Change in Public Services: International Issues, Challenges and Cases*. London: Routledge.

Maynard, Alan (1975) Experiment with Choice in Education. London: The Institute of Economic Affairs.

Nisberg, Jay N. (1988) Handbook of Business Terms. London: Random House.

OECD (1993) Managing with Market-Type Mechanisms. Puma Public Management Studies. Organisation for Economic Co-operation and Development.

OECD (1998) Voucher Programmes and their Role in Distributing Services. Puma Public Management Committee. Organisation for Economic Co-operation and Development.

Osborne, Stephen P. and Brown, Kerry (2005) *Managing Change and Innovation in Public Service Organisations*. London: Routledge.

Peterson, P. E. and Campbell, D. E. (2001) Introduction. In P. E. Peterson and D. E. Campbell (eds) *Charters, Vouchers & Public Education*. Washington, DC: Brookings.

Pommerehne, Werner W. and Frey, Bruno S. (1997) Public Promotion of the Arts: A Survey of Means. In Ruth Towse (ed.) *Kirjoitus teoksessa Cultural Economics: The Arts, the Heritage and the Media Industries*. Volume II. Cheltenham: Edward Elgar. Also published in *Journal of Cultural Economics* (1990), 14 (2), December: 73–95.

Reischauer, R. D. (2000) Medicare Vouchers. In C. Eugene Steuerle, Van Doorn Ooms, George Peterson and Robert D. Reischauser (eds) *Vouchers and the Provision of Public Services*. Washington, DC: Brookings Institution Press.

Roson, Roberto (2000) Auction in a Two-Sided Network: The Market for Meal Voucher Services, *Network and Spatial Economics*, 5: 339–350.

Rönkkö, Pentti (1999) Kotitaloustyön tukimuotojen arviointi ja kehittäminen. Artikkeli teoksessa Oulasvirta Lasse – Rönkkö Pentti & Yli-Olli Päivi, Pitkäaikaistyöttömyyden rakenne ja siihen haetut ratkaisumallit Tampereella. Tampereen seudun kumppanuusprojekti yhteistyössä Tampereen yliopiston kanssa. 2/99. Tampereen Seudun Kumppanuusprojekti.

Savas, E. S. (1987) *Privatization: The Key to Better Government*. New York: Chatman House Publishers.

Sawhill, Isabel V. and Smith, Shannon L. (2000) Vouchers for Elementary and Secondary Education. In C. Eugene Steuerle, Van Doorn Ooms, George Peterson and Robert D. Reischauser (eds), *Vouchers and the Provision of Public Services*. Washington, DC: Brookings Institution Press, 251–291.

Seldon, Arthur (1986) The Riddle of the Voucher. An Inquiry into the Obstacles to Introducing Choice and Competition in State Schools. Hobart Paperback No. 21. London: Institute of Economic Affairs.

Seldon, Marjorie (1991) Vouchers for Schooling. In David G. Green (ed.) *Empowering the Parents: How to Break the Schools Monopoly*. Choice in Welfare No. 9. IEA Health and Welfare Unit. London: Institute of Economic Affairs, 55–63.

Suomen, Kuntaliitto (1994) *Palveluseteli ja peruspalvelut.* The Association of Finnish Local and Regional Authorities, Helsinki, Finland.

Uvalic, Milica (1997) Vaughan-Whitehead. In Daniel (ed.) *Privatization Surprises in Transition Economies: Employee-Ownership in Central and Eastern Europe.* Cheltanham: Edward Elgar.

Valkama, P. and Bailey, S. J. (2001) Vouchers as an Alternative Public Sector Funding System, *Public Policy and Administration*, 116 (1): 32–58.

Walsh, Kieron (1995) *Public Services and Market Mechanisms. Competition, Contracting and the New Public Management.* London: Macmillan Press.

West, Edwin G. (1997) Arts Vouchers to Replace Grants. In Ruth Towse (ed.) *Cultural Economics: The Arts, the Heritage and the Media Industries.* Volume II. Cheltenham: Edward Elgar. Also published in *Economic Affairs* (1986), 6 (3) February – March: 9–11, 16.

12
Public Service Vouchers in the UK and Finland

Ian C. Elliott, Pekka Valkama and Stephen J. Bailey

Introduction

The aim of this chapter is to map out an overall picture of the use and applications of public service vouchers in the UK and Finland. We will also describe the forms of vouchers in use in the both countries. The analytical framework for this practice-based discussion is provided in Chapter 11.

The UK has significant experience of vouchers, particularly as part of the New Public Management (NPM) and the Best Value regime to encourage both competition and collaboration between the public and private sectors. Various models of public-private collaboration have emerged including the use of vouchers. These driving forces are likely to extend under a framework of New Public Governance associated with increasingly complex, plural and fragmented service delivery (Osborne 2010).

Finland is one of the Nordic welfare states characterised by professionalism, decentralisation and Weberian style bureaucracy. However, in the early 1990s the economic and political context of the country changed due to a severe economic recession following loss of exports to the collapsing eastern European communist regimes. Political decision-makers started to liberalise the institutional framework of both the business and public sectors to promote competition. The introduction of public vouchers is one part of these reforms to promote a more efficient public sector (Cf. Koivuranta 2006; Ministry of Finance 2006, 7–8).

Methodological problems for empirical analysis

It is important to highlight three challenges for empirical analysis of vouchers:

- Their association with NPM;
- Lack of statistics or national evaluations;
- The range of definitions.

First, the association with NPM, and the politically charged nature of this reform agenda, makes any objective analysis of vouchers rather difficult. As noted in Chapter 11, vouchers may be used to achieve both left-wing and right-wing political goals and can have a variety of labels.

Second, a comprehensive account of voucher schemes currently in use is significantly hindered by a general lack of nationwide voucher statistics and extensive policy evaluations. Vouchers are relatively new in Europe as instruments of public service delivery and most of the statistical information is based on the revenues and costs of public authorities. In Finland, local governments can be very flexible in introducing new voucher schemes, making modifications to existing schemes and controlling them closely if necessary.

Third, the various definitions of vouchers remain contested and a plethora of alternative terms have been used to describe arrangements that are voucher schemes in all but name. Blaug (1984) illustrates the myriad of potential voucher scheme designs which Chapter 11 simplified by presenting both a classification and a more comprehensive definition of vouchers. In considering the practice of public service vouchers it is as important to consider the effects (or outcomes) of a scheme as the design of the scheme itself. Voucher-like (or quasi-voucher) schemes may be as valuable for analysis as true vouchers. This is particularly important due to the often emergent nature of public policy and management.

In Chapter 11, public service vouchers are classified as:

- Explicit – where the scheme is specifically labelled as a voucher scheme; and
- Implicit – where the scheme holds the key characteristics of a voucher and has the potential to develop into a fuller, explicit, voucher scheme.

A particular problem, especially with voucher-like or implicit voucher schemes, is that they may limit some of the key features of classical voucher ideas. These limitations may be related to real consumer choices or the 'money follows the user' principle. For example, parents have been able to choose which school to send their children to in England since 1989 (albeit that the most popular schools are over-subscribed). Approximately 75 per cent of school funding is based on a per-pupil formula so, in many respects, this operates as an implicit voucher scheme. Yet only state (i.e. public sector not private sector) schools are eligible under the scheme. Thus school choice operates as an opt-in voucher scheme. In Finland, local education authorities allocate schools for pupils at primary school level. Children and their parents can apply to attend a different primary school and local governments allow the change to take place if there are enough places available, but local government may also prioritise local children over pupils from neighbouring local areas (Hallituksen esitys 86/1997; Etelä-Suomen lääninhallitus).

In response to the methodological challenges noted above, the following empirical analysis is based on a wide range of sources of information. Data have been collected from central and local government documentary sources, from legal provisions and laws and from various research publications.

UK voucher schemes

The term 'voucher' is not widely used within current policy circles in the UK. However, while this term may be rather unpopular within public policy circles, the concept is becoming more prevalent across a wide number of public services. The terms associated with vouchers or voucher-like schemes include the following: card, passport, choice, entitlement, co-production and credit. Vouchers are increasingly being used in a rather hidden way.

The following section will outline some explicit and implicit voucher schemes currently in use in the UK. These will be assessed against three dimensions:

- Perception involves *explicit* (the scheme is deliberately labelled 'voucher'), *implicit* (deliberately not labelled 'voucher') and *tacit* (not known as 'voucher' but not deliberately so);
- Scale involves either national (led by the UK central government or a national agency) or local (local government or local trust, etc.);
- Scope involves access to any or all of the public, third or private sectors.

Explicit UK voucher schemes

Childcare voucher Scheme

The childcare voucher scheme is a so-called salary-sacrifice scheme, in that employees can choose to receive up to £55 per week (or £243 per month) of childcare vouchers from their employer rather than take-home pay. The scheme was set in the legislature in the Finance Act 2004 and the first schemes were established in 2005. As such they enable employers to help their employees with childcare costs. The financial incentive for taking part in the scheme, for both employer and employee, is in the form of tax relief of up to 20 per cent on childcare costs. There is no limit on the amount that employees can choose to receive as childcare vouchers but relief on income tax and National Insurance is limited to amounts under £55 a week.

The income tax and National Insurance (NI) exemptions within the scheme mean that participating employees can benefit by up to £1196 a year per parent. The National Insurance exemptions also mean that employers can benefit by up to £370 a year per participating employee.

In order for an employee to be eligible for vouchers the following conditions must be met:

- Vouchers can only be used for registered or approved childcare;
- The child:
  - Must be a child or stepchild of the voucher holder who must also be, at least in part, financially responsible for the child; or
  - Must reside with the voucher holder who must have parental responsibility for the child;
  - Will qualify up to 1 September after their fifteenth birthday (or 1 September after their sixteenth birthday if they are disabled);
- The employer must offer the scheme to all employees.

This is clearly perceived as an explicit voucher scheme and is national in scale. Nevertheless, it must be managed by individual employers and because of this there is limited uptake of the scheme. Lack of uptake may also be due to a lack of promotion of the scheme.

As regards scope, vouchers can be only redeemed at registered childcare facilities, registration being managed on a regional basis across the UK. Childcare facilities include private sector and third sector nurseries, foster carers, out-of-hours school clubs and nannies or child minders. As such this is an opt-out voucher scheme.[1]

Innovation vouchers

Innovation vouchers were first announced in the Innovation Nation White Paper (DIUS 2008), which set the goal of distributing vouchers (worth approximately £3000 each) to at least 500 small and medium enterprises (SMEs) across the English regions. This number was to increase, dependent upon evidence of their effectiveness, to at least 1000 SMEs by 2011.

This voucher scheme is designed to provide funding to SMEs in order to stimulate knowledge exchange relationships between SMEs and public research institutions. The scheme is coordinated by Regional Development Agencies (RDAs) across the UK. Having originated in the West Midlands (piloted by Aston University), there are now innovation voucher schemes running across most parts of the UK: north-west (NWDA), north-east (One North East), Yorkshire (Yorkshire Forward), East Anglia (EEDA), south-west of England (South-West RDA), south-east (SEEDA) West Midlands (Advantage West Midlands), East Midlands (EMDA), London (London Development Agency), Northern Ireland (Invest NI) and Scotland (Scottish Funding Council, SFC). The Welsh Assembly government has not yet developed such a scheme although it has been recommended (Enterprise and Learning Committee, 2009).

The innovation voucher scheme is a demand-led innovation scheme in that SMEs apply to the scheme with a particular business need, which is then circulated across public research institutions (mainly further and higher education establishments). Where a research institution is in a position to provide relevant support they will submit their case to the coordinating body (usually the Regional Development Agency), which then passes on these details to the SME who has the final choice of which supplier to use.

This is perceived as an explicit voucher scheme operating on a regional scale. Schemes are coordinated by RDAs, except in the West Midlands (where it is coordinated by a university) and in Scotland (where it is coordinated by the SFC).

Most schemes are restricted in scope to further and higher education establishments. As such this represents, for the most part, an opt-in voucher scheme.[2]

Eye-care vouchers

The Optical Voucher scheme was introduced in 1986. It is a national explicit voucher scheme coordinated by the NHS and NHS Scotland. Vouchers are provided to select groups to assist in meeting the costs of spectacles or contact lenses. The groups included within the scheme are all children under 16 years old, anyone under 18 years old who is still in full-time education, all those who require complex lenses, those eligible for certain welfare state benefits and those entitled to an NHS Tax Credit Exception Certificate or on low income (with a completed HC2 certificate).

Vouchers are worth a set amount, depending on the nature of eye care required, above which the holder must pay the difference (top up).

They are eligible for use across commercial and NHS optometrists. As regards the scheme's scope, a wide range of commercial and NHS opticians can be used to redeem the value of the vouchers. As such it is an opt-out voucher scheme.

Food vouchers

The UK Government provides asylum seekers with food vouchers. This scheme was previously scrapped due, in part, to the stigma attached to the vouchers. However, it was been reintroduced in 2005, providing food vouchers worth £35 per week to eligible asylum seekers.

Stop-smoking reward vouchers

'Give It Up For Baby' is a reward scheme run by NHS Tayside, Dundee City Council and a supermarket (Asda), which uses financial incentives in the form of grocery vouchers to encourage pregnant smokers to quit smoking. The vouchers are worth up to £50 a month and are awarded following carbon monoxide breath testing to prove that the pregnant smoker has now stopped smoking. The scheme is linked to the National Entitlement Card, which is discussed separately below.

Implicit and tacit UK vouchers

Training vouchers

'Skills for Jobs' is an initiative of the Learning and Skills Council (LSC). The scheme offers vocationally relevant training and life skills to individuals who are deemed to be far from entering the workforce. These short courses are run by partners within a Local Employment Partnership (LEP), including colleges and specialist training providers. As such the funding follows the individual (the holder is the voucher).

Learning vouchers

'Individual Learning Accounts' (ILAs) worth either £200 (for short courses) or £500 (for higher education or professional courses) are issued by ILA Scotland to people with less than £22,000 income per year or who are on state benefits. The courses must be delivered by a registered provider.

Hospital vouchers

'Patient Choice' is a Department of Health initiative which enables patients to choose a hospital in England to provide treatment and when they receive it after they have been referred by their general practitioner (GP) for a non-urgent specialist procedure. The choice of hospital includes NHS hospitals and registered independent hospitals and other treatment centres. Thus the patient is the voucher as the public finance follows the user without any tangible card being used. Separate arrangements exist in Scotland, Wales and Northern Ireland.

Multi-service vouchers

The National Entitlement Card scheme is a smart card system for a number of public services and is coordinated by the Scottish Government and Scottish local authorities. The card enables the holder to access discounted public transport, through the national concessionary travel scheme, as well as other local services such as library and leisure services.

Savings vouchers for children

Child Trust Fund cash vouchers, also known as Baby Bonds, give every child born after September 2002 at least £250. The voucher must be lodged in an approved bank account or other savings scheme. Up to £1200 can be invested each year on a tax-free basis. At the age of seven the government provides another voucher payment of £250, or £500 for those in lower income families. A tax-exempt £1200 may continue to be paid into the account until the child reaches the age of 18. This policy was introduced under the Child Trust Funds Act (HM Government 2004).

Physical activity health vouchers

GP referral schemes enable family doctors to prescribe physical activity as an alternative (or complement) to pharmaceutical drugs in the treatment of adverse health conditions where appropriate and effective. Within these schemes the prescription acts as a voucher for physical activity within a municipal leisure facility. These schemes are common throughout Britain and are seen by leisure practitioners as contributing to Best Value (Foley et al. 2000). These vouchers do not enable users to choose to opt out of the public sector but through the scheme service users can exit the NHS and use public sector leisure services as an alternative.

Discussion of UK vouchers

While there may be potential for greater use of vouchers than outlined above, it must be recognised that they may be more suitable for certain public services than others. Table 12.1 sets down the necessary conditions for use of vouchers as outlined in Chapter 11 for four public services. It makes clear that the complexity associated with health services leads to greater barriers to the use of vouchers than is the case for other public services, particularly municipal housing and sport services (such as swimming facilities). This is not to downplay the challenge of implementing such an innovative funding mechanism within a public service. Rather it is held that the different contexts of different public services must be taken into account when considering any such change. Indeed the nature of the public sector arguably makes context particularly important in implementing change (Macleod and By 2009). In general however, voucher schemes are conceptually compatible with the nature of many local government services operating in a mixed economy.

As demonstrated in Chapter 11, vouchers can represent a form of public service innovation in that they may hold the characteristics of newness, invention, process and outcome and may lead to 'discontinuity with the prevailing organizational, product/service or market paradigm' (Osborne and Brown 2005, 122). Yet by the same token the degree to which vouchers represent change means that they might represent a significant challenge in implementation (Sawhill and Smith 2000; West 1997). This is seen in the fierce opposition to public service vouchers faced by consecutive UK Conservative and Labour governments since 1979.

Yet crucially this opposition does not appear to extend to the general public. Recent research suggests that nearly two-thirds of people would choose a social enterprise to manage local services such as health care, household waste collection and transport on condition that usage costs remained the same (Mills 2009). Furthermore, with growing political interest in the concept of co-production (Horne and Shirley 2009) the use of vouchers offers one method of extending co-production across

Table 12.1   Viability of opt-out voucher schemes

Necessary conditions	Sport	Housing	Education	Health
Widespread preferences	High	High	High	Low
Legitimate choice	High	High	Medium	Low
Incentives to choose	High	High	High	High
Well-informed citizens	High	High	Low	Medium
Contestable markets	High	High	Medium	Medium
Easy to access and assess	High	Medium	Low	Low
Affordable and regular use	High	Low	Low	Low

Source: Adapted from Elliott (2008).

a range of public services. Indeed it is already the case that the UK is ranked highly within Europe for public involvement in the management of public services (ibid). In order to extend choice further through the use of vouchers, issues around terms of the employment of public sector workers will need to be addressed (Geddes, 2001; Grimshaw et al. 2002).

Despite the applicability of the voucher scheme to many UK public services they remain largely untested in their most comprehensive format, as outlined in Chapter 11. Nonetheless, as discussed above, many voucher-like schemes have been widely tested across a number of public services. Nevertheless, a voucher-like scheme might not provide many of the benefits of a more comprehensive opt-out voucher scheme and possess some significant disadvantages. For example, it might involve additional (or duplication of) administration costs and lack many of the advantages such as greater efficiency and effectiveness.

While table 12.2 makes clear that voucher-like schemes might not realise the full potential benefits of the voucher concept they might represent an important step in the development towards a fuller voucher scheme. As Sawhill and Smith (2000) note, the Alum Rock education voucher scheme (1972–1976) in the USA included many compromises and was not, in the strictest sense, a voucher scheme. But this does not negate the fact that this first trial represented the first of many and led towards the eventual implementation of three publicly funded schemes and 68 privately funded education voucher schemes across the US in 1999–2000 (Peterson and Campbell 2001).

Vouchers in Finland

In Finland, the first explicit public service voucher schemes were introduced in the 1980s by individual local governments. At that time, vouchers were relatively unknown, and there were no national policy guidelines available on how to issue and apply vouchers in a public policy context. These first voucher schemes were very small-scale local programmes with only a limited number of recipients. They were typically used in public transport and meal services. They have since been extended to many areas of personal social care (Volk and Laukkanen 2007, 25).

As noted above, in the early 1990s there was a deep economic recession in Finland and some local governments started to distribute study vouchers to unemployed people in order to encourage them to attend community colleges. Nowadays, the Ministry of Education allocates

Table 12.2 Best value and vouchers

BV Criteria: the 4 Cs	Definition	Achievement through quasi-vouchers	Achievement through full opt-out vouchers
Challenge	'Challenging why and how a service is provided requires a fundamental rethink. Asking basic questions about the needs that each service is intended to address and the method of procurement that is used.' (DETR 1999, 12)	Do not usually challenge public sector provision – tend to be opt-in schemes thereby reinforcing public sector provision.	Challenges traditional public sector delivery by offering choice of private, non-profit or public sector provider. Challenge is reinforced by public finance following demand rather than supply.
Compare	'... need to compare their [local authority] current and prospective performance against other public sector bodies, and those in the private and voluntary sectors.' (DETR 1999, 13)	Do not tend to enable customer choice outside current public sector providers. Thus public sector retains responsibility for setting the terms of comparison.	Extending voice through vouchers would enable customers to compare on their own terms. Analysis of these choices would allow for comparison of success in attracting and retaining customers.
Consult	'... consult a wide range of local and other interest as to the way in which they fulfil their duties to secure best value.' (DETR 1999, 14)	Tend not to enhance exit or voice through use of cards but may give the principal more information upon which to plan and manage resources.	Stakeholders could be consulted in the selection of suitable suppliers. Customers would be empowered to choose their preferred supplier – enhancing exit and voice.
Compete	'[F]air and open competition will be expected to play an essential and enduring role in the Review Programme...the future for public service provision is one where there is real variety in the way services are delivered and genuine plurality amongst service providers.' (DETR 1999, 15)	Competition tends to be restricted to within the public sector. Finance of cards tends to be an additional cost and therefore does not contribute to greater efficiency (though they might improve effectiveness and equity).	Suppliers would be compelled to compete in efficiency, effectiveness, economy and equity in order to attract and retain customers and continue to meet government standards (in order to remain part of the scheme).

Sources: Adapted from Elliott (2008) and DETR (1999).

Table 12.3 Summary of the most important legislative voucher reforms in Finland

Year of reform	2004	2009
Enactment	Vouchers were included in national legislation for the first time.	The first specific voucher law was passed.
Service sectors	Public social and health care and especially home help services.	Public social and health care and services.
Key aims	To legalise vouchers given by municipalities, loosely regulate use of vouchers and ensure state grants for municipal expenses related to voucher schemes.	To create conditions for more extensive use of public service vouchers, to diversify delivery models of municipal services and to support development of cooperation between the private and public sectors.
Main arguments given by the government	1) Vouchers are a tool to make social and health services more effective. 2) Vouchers can support development of service markets. 3) Vouchers can be used to support elderly people living in their own homes as long as possible and facilitate choice of services they prefer.	1) Choices by voucher recipients will increase competition between service providers, reduce municipal costs and increase transparency of public services. 2) A diversified municipal service delivery system will increase accessibility and flexibility of public services and support development of know-how of public services. 3) A use of vouchers will support positive development of entrepreneurship and employment.

Source: Adapted from Hallituksen esitys 74/2003; Hallituksen esitys 20/2009.

annual educational allowances directly to the private and public community colleges, and groups such as the unemployed, immigrants and elderly people can apply for education vouchers from the colleges and select suitable courses (Opintosetelikokeilu, työryhmän loppuraportti 2002, 1–2).

The public service voucher concept was introduced in national legislation in 2004, when the law on the planning and state grant systems of social and health care was changed (See Table 12.3). This was a significant reform in the sense that vouchers were officially authorised for local governments as a lawful alternative public social and health service delivery system.

With the reform of 2004 the government hoped to increase the use of explicit vouchers in social and health care services, but after a few years it had to recognise that the utilisation rate of vouchers schemes was not very high. According to survey data collected from local governments in 2006 and 2007, around 25 per cent of local governments used vouchers in some local public services. Nevertheless, the number of voucher customers was still very modest at only a few thousands (Volk and Laukkanen 2007, 25).

Based on these findings, the government decided that a separate voucher law was needed in order to create a firm and clear regulatory framework for vouchers, and a new voucher law was passed in 2009 (See Table 12.3). The new law harmonises the voucher statutes by concentrating the regulatory norms of vouchers in a single act and clarifying some characteristics of vouchers and the rights of voucher recipients. With this reform, the government is encouraging local governments to make more use of voucher schemes. However, each local government can still decide independently whether or not to introduce voucher schemes.

Figure 12.1 classifies the most important public voucher schemes in use in Finland. Explicit vouchers are usually distributed by local governments. Implicit voucher schemes are run by the central government authorities. Most of the voucher schemes are quite new, but patient choice in National Health Insurance is long established. Most public service vouchers are given for personal social care purposes, for example home help, home cleaning and respite services of people who care for close relatives.

Finnish voucher schemes are innovation as a bottom-up process. Originally, local governments developed and introduced very small voucher schemes for strictly defined local needs. Thereafter, central government became interested in vouchers and launched national voucher scheme experiments in different service sectors. Evaluation of these

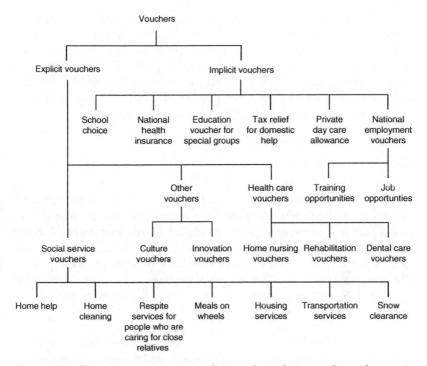

Figure 12.1   The most important explicit and implicit voucher schemes in Finland

Source: Adapted from Volk and Laukkanen (2007, 25); Räty (2004, 10).

experiments showed that the experiences of the various stakeholders of voucher services were positive and so the government introduced formalised voucher schemes (Lapsen maailma 1996, 23).

Although the 2009 reform leaves some space for local governments to fine tune voucher schemes, the law standardised certain characteristics for them and institutionalised them alongside conventional service-delivery systems such as in-house and outsourced services.

This could be characterised as a teleological innovation process (van den Ven and Poole 1995). Some public authorities were dissatisfied with traditional public service delivery systems, because some potential customers could not be reached by traditional means. Public authorities had certain service obligations and functions that had to be fulfilled but also certain local problems. For example, difficulties in recruiting new professional staff members and building new service facilities forced local governments to develop supplementary manage-ment solutions and to work adaptively in a changing environment.

The first pilot schemes were mostly implemented cautiously on a small scale in order to avoid strong opposition from stakeholders and other political parties. By such means, decision-makers successfully built consensus around the moderate use of vouchers and successfully managed to prevent the emergence of strong opposition.

Explicit voucher schemes in Finland

Home help and cleaning vouchers

Home help and cleaning vouchers are possibly the most common types of social service vouchers. The idea of these vouchers is to support peo-ple living in their own homes as long as possible because institution-alised care is a more expensive option for municipalities (Kaskiharju and Seppänen 2004, 51). Like all social care vouchers, home help and cleaning vouchers are delivered by local governments and valid only in the private sector. If a customer is not willing to use a voucher offered by the public authorities, the local government is obliged to provide the service in another way.

Snow clearance vouchers

Some cities have introduced snow clearance vouchers for elderly people living in detached houses. The purpose is to encourage the elderly to live in their own homes as long as possible by letting them hire some-body to clear snow from their front yards in winter.

Health care vouchers

A dental care voucher was introduced by the city of Helsinki in 2007, mainly because there were long queues for municipal dentists. Through dental care vouchers the city government utilises private sector dental care capacity in order to cut patient waiting times. Otherwise, vouchers are not as common in health services as in social services because the Finnish public health care system is relatively well established and has a longer history than the public social care system (Räty et al. 2004, 39).

Culture vouchers

Some cities give culture vouchers to students living in their jurisdic-tion in order to support their access to cultural institutions and artistic performances. Unlike social and health care voucher schemes, cul-ture voucher schemes are not regulated by any specific legal statutes.

Individual local governments can decide whether culture vouchers are valid in either the private or the public sector, or both.

Innovation vouchers

Innovation vouchers are meant for SMEs, and their purpose is similar to that of the UK innovation vouchers. However, innovation voucher schemes are not yet well established, and different applications are still being sought. A new version of the innovation voucher is the knowledge voucher, which is more extensively valid as it can be used for business services in several European countries.

Implicit and tacit vouchers

National Health Insurance (NHI)

People can choose whether to use the services of a private or public sector physician but the NHI scheme gives compensation only for private sector service costs. However, the NHI does not fully cover private doctors' fees and meets only a proportion of the costs of examinations and treatments prescribed by a private doctor. Fees and costs are much higher in the private sector than in municipal health centres but, as a result of this compensation for extra costs only being partial, affluent people are much more likely to use private services than those on low incomes.[3]

Tax relief for domestic help

The national 'tax relief for domestic help' initiative was introduced after pilot schemes in 2001. Households can deduct a proportion of the costs of external household services through their personal taxes. This includes cleaning, home repairs, care of an elderly person or child in the home and installation and maintenance of information technology (IT) equipment. The annual maximum deductible amount is €3000, if the household has purchased services from enterprises worth at least €5200. This initiative does not benefit people with very low incomes, because they do not pay taxes (Uotinen 2009, 65–66).[4]

Private day care allowance

Parents of children of a certain age can choose a private or a municipal childcare provider. If they opt for a private childcare provider, a private day care allowance will be paid to the service provider. Such providers may be individuals or organisations offering fee-based childcare services, or a non-family member contracted to the family for at least one month (Uotinen 2009, 67–68).[5]

Training vouchers

Labour market training is organised by the Ministry of Labour to maintain and develop the vocational skills of unemployed people or those at imminent risk of unemployment. Trainees are entitled to a training allowance or labour market support and also to a maintenance allowance. Adults who want to participate in training need to apply for a suitable course, and the employment authorities procure training services from public or private educational institutions or service providers.[6]

Some higher education institutions issue training vouchers for students who need to have a period of practical training as a part of their studies. A student finds a suitable employer who can hire him or her and pay a part of his or her salary. The training voucher typically covers one or two months' salary.

Job opportunities

Employment authorities create job opportunities by providing employment subsidies for the long-term unemployed, the handicapped, young people under 25 and unemployed people threatened by long-term unemployment or at risk of labour market marginalisation. Central government can support jobs in both the private and public sectors, but the conditions for receiving subsidies differs.[7]

Discussion of Finnish vouchers

Data on the number of users for all explicit voucher schemes are not collected centrally but most schemes are small and local. They involve only a few thousand users because the target groups for the use of vouchers are well defined and rigorously selected.

Most explicit vouchers are delivered for people (or their relatives) who need to be taken care of and have some support services at their homes. Due to the introduction of the separate voucher law there are expectations that the number of both voucher schemes and customers will increase (Lith 2009). There are a couple of national development projects, which produce guidebooks on how to design voucher schemes and guidelines on how to determine values of vouchers.[8]

Explicit vouchers have mainly been used in new or expanding public services. Voucher schemes have not been used to reform existing public service structures or the funding models of institutional public service activities. Ageing demography and changing family structures create growing needs for social care, and it has become imperative for public authorities to find and create new service capacity in order to respond to these needs (Valpola 2002, 20). In this case, vouchers have been seen as a practical solution to support building the capacity of private enterprises and non-profit service organisations.

Political decision-makers have been careful not to create competition between the public and private sectors. Most explicit vouchers are valid only in the private sector. Only in very limited cases for services other than social and health care can vouchers be valid in both sectors. One obvious reason for this policy is that the rules do not apply equally to public and private services providers.

The geographical jurisdictions of the explicit voucher schemes are often somewhat limited, because the schemes are run by individual local governments. However, service areas are not identical with these administrative jurisdictions and, in the future, there will be a growing need to merge schemes and create joint local voucher schemes. Service enterprises prefer larger areas for voucher schemes because they want to maximise potential customer numbers (Lith 2009, 33).

Both fixed- and flexible-value vouchers are used in social and health services: local decision-makers can usually choose which they prefer. If flexible values are used, vouchers are based on needs alone, or on both needs and incomes of recipients. For example, some local governments give more valuable vouchers to those who live in remote districts because the extra distance to be travelled creates additional costs.

The wealth of recipients is not taken into account. Until 2009, regulations were quite strict concerning how much customers could be asked to pay as an excess fee. The 2009 voucher law gave more freedom of action to local public authorities. If customers feel that they cannot pay the excess fee defined in a voucher scheme, they can refuse the voucher and ask for the more traditional service delivery. On the other hand, service users can top up the value of the voucher based on their willingness and ability to pay more.

Public surveys have shown that most people support more extensive use of vouchers and choice for individuals. Representatives of local governments have pointed out that the most important goal of vouchers is to increase the scope for user choice. The next most important goal is to diversify service supply and support entrepreneurship, especially women's opportunities to establish their own enterprises in social services (Lith 2009; Volk and Laukkanen 2007, 15). Studies have shown that vouchers have significantly increased the number of enterprises in social services and social care is one of the fastest-growing service sectors in the country (Heikkilä et al. 1997; Suomen Yrittäjät 2007).

Although the experiences with vouchers are predominantly positive, there is also some cause for criticism. Some very old people have not been eager to make choices, and vouchers are not suitable for very sick people (Kaskiharju and Seppänen 2004, 39; Vaarama et al. 1999; Volk and Laukkanen 2007, 29). Vouchers have increased the administrative burden both in municipalities and service enterprises. Local government officials have had to learn new procedures and enterprises have had to develop extra billing processes (Kaskiharju and Seppänen 2004, 46, 48; Volk and Laukkanen 2007, 61).

Many Finnish vouchers can be seen as falling somewhere between full and mini vouchers. Some customers have complained that home help vouchers are usually defined too strictly and customers themselves should have a right to define more broadly what specific services are required to be delivered in people's homes (Kaskiharju and Seppänen 2004, 41; Volk and Laukkanen 2007, 51).

The future development of Finnish voucher schemes seems to be promising. At least, implicit voucher schemes can be expected to expand in important welfare services. According to the latest suggestions announced by the Ministry of Social Affairs and Health, central government is planning legal reforms in order to introduce new systems of citizen choice for local public day care and health care. One aim is to give rights to the parents of small children and patients to be able to choose a public nursery or a municipal hospital regardless of their home municipalities. (Terveyhdenhuoltolakityöryhmän muistio 2008; Pokki 2009).

Overall conclusions

Successful voucher schemes tend to provide additional government spending. They tend to come up against more significant barriers to implementation where they are intended to shift public finance from a supply-led to a demand-led scheme. This opposition occurs despite the fact that vouchers that offer additional government spending do not in any way question the status quo of established public services and are not nearly as innovative as a voucher scheme that shifts the emphasis of previously established public finance. This raises important questions about the potential for use of fully fledged voucher schemes in established services such as education, health and housing.

Implicit and tacit voucher schemes tend either to replace existing funding or add a greater degree of consumer choice, especially where there is greater competition through opt-out vouchers. By definition, these schemes are not referred to as voucher schemes. However, it is unclear whether they have developed without any conscious consideration of the voucher concept (tacit voucher) or whether the voucher term has been deliberately avoided (implicit voucher).

Consumers seem to like the extra flexibility and choice offered by voucher schemes and they do not seem to have any predisposition towards direct public provision of public services, rather than provision by the private or third sectors. For example a proposal to withdraw tax relief for the UK's Childcare Voucher Scheme led to an online petition[9] which received 92,741 signatures. Subsequently, plans to phase out tax relief for childcare vouchers were revised to limiting tax relief to 20 per cent for all taxpayers.

With growing interest in alternative forms of co-production, it is anticipated that the voucher concept will continue to provide a valuable model of public finance. At the moment, we do not know much about the financial values of services consumed by voucher-holders and the extent to which they top up their values. There is a growing need to develop comprehensive evaluations of voucher schemes and to compile statistics about this relatively hidden part of public finance.

Notes

1. Further information on the Childcare Voucher scheme is available at http://www.hmrc.gov.uk/childcare/
2. Further information is available on the RDAs' (or other appropriate) websites.
3. Further information is available at http://www.kela.fi/in/internet/english.nsf/NET/240708151439HS?OpenDocument
4. Further information is available at http://www.eurofound.europa.eu/areas/labourmarket/tackling/cases/fi004.htm
5. Further information is available at http://www.kela.fi/in/internet/english.nsf/NET/150502155913EH?OpenDocument
6. Further information is available at http://www.mol.fi/mol/en/99_pdf/en/92_brochures/6033eteksti.pdf
7. Further information is available at http://www.expat-finland.com/entrepreneurship/employer_information.html
8. Further information is available at http://www.stm.fi/en/focus/article/view/1421597 and http://www.sitra.fi/en/Programmes/municipal_programme/news/mediarelease20091022_servicevouchers.htm
9. at http://petitions.number10.gov.uk/keepvouchers/

References

Blaug, Mark (1984) Education Vouchers – It All Depends on What You Mean. In J. Le Grand and R. Robinson (ed.) *Privatisation and the Welfare State*. London: Allen & Unwin.

Department of the Environment, Transport and the Regions (DETR) (1999) Implementing Best Value – A Consultation Paper on Draft Guidance. London: HMSO.

Department for Innovation, Universities and Skills (DIUS) (2008) *Innovation Nation* cmnd 7345. London: HMSO.

Enterprise and Learning Committee (2009) The Economic Contribution of Higher Education in Wales. Cardiff: National Assembly for Wales, http://www.assemblywales.org/cr-ld7730 (accessed 3 December 2009).

Elliott, Ian C. (2008) Making Space or Enabling Use: The Case of Opt-Out Vouchers for Public Leisure Services. In T. Gale, N. Curry and J. Hill (eds) *Making Space: Managing Resources for Leisure and Tourism*. Leisure Studies Association, No. 97.

Etelä-Suomen (2009) lääninhallitus, Oppilaaksi ottaminen. Read 11 December, http://www.intermin.fi/lh/etela/siv/home.nsf/pages/CF266FB027652310C22 5700000396902?opendocument

Foley, Malcolm, Frew, Matt, McPherson, Gayle and Reid, Gavin (2000) Healthy Public Policy: A Policy Paradox Within Local Government, *Managing Leisure*, 5: 77–89.

Geddes, Mike (2001) What About the Workers? Best Value, Employment and Work in Local Public Services, *Policy and Politics*, 29 (4): 497–508.

Grimshaw, Damien, Vincent, Steve and Willmott, Hugh (2002) Going Privately: Partnership and Outsourcing in UK Public Services, *Public Administration*, 80 (3): 475–502.

HM Government (2004) Child Trust Funds Act. London: The Stationery Office, http://www.opsi.gov.uk/acts/acts2004/ukpga_20040006_en_1 (accessed 17 December 2009).

Hallituksen, esitys (86/1997) Hallituksen esitys Eduskunnalle koulutusta koskevaksi lainsäädännöksi.

Hallituksen, esitys (74/2003) Hallituksen esitys Eduskunnalle laeiksi sosiaali- ja terveyhdenhuollon suunnittelusta ja valtionosuudesta annetun lain 4 §:n, sosiaalihuoltolain sekä sosiaali- ja terveydenhuollon asiakasmaksuista annetun lain 12 §:n muttamisesta.

Hallituksen, esitys 20/2009, Hallituksen esitys Eduskunnalle laeiksi sosiaali- ja terveydenhuollon palvelusetelistä sekä sosiaali- ja terveydenhuollon asiakasmaksuista annetun lain 12 §:n muuttamisesta.

Heikkilä, Matti, Törmä, Sinikka and Mattila, Kati (1997) Palveluseteli lasten päivähoidossa. Raportti valtakunnallisesta kokeilusta. Raportteja 216. Sosiaali- ja terveysalan tutkimus- ja kehittämiskeskus. Jyväskylä: Sosiaali- ja terveysministeriö.

Horne, M. and Shirley, T. (2009) Co-production in Public Services: A New Partnership with Citizens, http://www.cabinetoffice.gov.uk/media/207033/public_services_co-production.pdf

Kaskiharju, Eija and Seppänen, Marjaana (2004) Vaihtoehtona palveluseteli. Lahden seudun viiden kunnan palvelusetelikokeilu. Sosiaali- ja terveysministeriön selvityksiä 2004: 8. Helsinki: Sosiaali- ja terveysministeriö.

Koivuranta, Hannu (2006) The Structure of the Finnish Public Administration. In *Finnish Public Management. Building Sustainable Quality*. Ministry of Finance. Helsinki: Edita Prima, 3–16.

Lapsen, maailma (1996) Kokemukset päivähoidon palvelusetelikokeilusta myönteisiä. 55: 6–7, 23.

Lith, Pekka (2009) Palvelusetelit lisäävät asiakkaan valintoja kuntapalveluissa. Tieto&trendit, 7: 30–33.

Macleod, Calum and By, Rune T. (2009) Organizational Change Management in Public Services: Key Findings and Emerging Themes. In Rune T. By and Calum Macleod (eds) *Managing Organizational Change in Public Services*. Oxon: Routledge.

Mills, Ray (2009) *Social Private Partnerships – Innovation in Public Service Delivery*. London: PriceWaterhouseCoopers.

Opintosetelikokeilu, työryhmän loppuraportti (2002) Opetusministeriön työryhmien muistioita: 2. Helsinki: Opetusministeriö.

Osborne, Stephen P. and Brown, Kelly (2005) *Managing Change and Innovation in Public Service Organizations*. Oxon: Routledge.

Osborne, Stephen P. (2010) *The New Public Governance? Emerging Perspectives on the Theory and Practice of Public Governance*. Oxon: Routledge.

Peterson, Paul E. and Campbell, David E. (2001) Introduction. In P. E. Peterson and D. E. Campbell (ed.) *Charters, Vouchers & Public Education*. Washington, DC: Brookings.

Pokki, Simo (2009) Päivähoitopalvelun valinnanvapauden lisääminen kuntarajat ylittämällä. Selvityshenkilön raportti. Sosiaali- ja terveysministeriön selvityksiä: 63. Helsinki: Sosiaali- ja terveysministeriö.

Räty, Tarmo (2004) Palvelusetelit sosiaalipalveluissa. VATT-keskustelualoitteita 340. Helsinki: Government Institute for Economic Research.

Räty, Tarmo, Luoma, Kalevi and Aronen, Pasi (2004) Palvelusetelit kuntien sosiaalipalveluissa. VATT-Keskustelualoitteita 325. Helsinki: Government Institute for Economic Research.

Sawhill, Isabel V. and Smith, Shannon L. (2000) Vouchers for Elementary and Secondary Education. In C. Eugene Steuerle, George Peterson, Robert D. Reischauer and Van Doorn Ooms (eds) *Vouchers and the Provision of Public Services*. Washington, DC: The Brookings Institute Press.

Suomen, Yrittäjät (2007) Sosiaalipalveluyritysten liikevaihto kasvanut yli 25 prosentilla, 11 December, http://www.yrittajat.fi/fi-FI/uutisarkisto/tiedote/?groupId=fefe50b4-2878-4e00-a3c3-a040462d6561&announcementI d=f09b3192-43dc-4fa3-a72f-cfebe247d4a6 (accessed 16 December 2009).

Terveyhdenhuoltolakityöryhmän muistio (2008) Uusi terveyhdenhuoltolaki. Sosiaali- ja terveysministeriön selvityksiä: 28. Helsinki: Sosiaali- ja terveysministeriö.

Uotinen, Sami (2009) Sosiaali- ja terveydenhuollon palveluseteli. Helsinki: Lakimiesliiton kustannus.

Vaarama, Marja, Törmä, Sinikka, Laaksonen, Seppo and Voutilainen, Päivi (1999) Omaishoitajien tuen tarve ja palvelusetelillä järjestetty tilapäishoito. Omaishoidon palvelusetelikokeilun loppuraportti. Selvityksiä: 10. Helsinki: Sosiaali- ja terveysministeriö ja Stakes.

Valpola, Olli (2002) Palvelusetelillä lisää vapautta valita. Sosiaalivakuutus 5/2000, 20–21.

van de Ven, A. H. and Poole, M. S. (1995) Explaining Development and Change in Organizations, *Academy of Management Review*, 20 (3), July: 510–540.

Volk, Raija and Laukkanen, Tuula (2007) Palvelusetelin käyttö kunnissa. Sosiaali- ja terveysministeriön selvityksiä: 38. Helsinki: Sosiaali- ja terveysministeriö.

West, Edwin G. (1997) Arts Vouchers to Replace Grants. In R. Towse (ed.) *Cultural Economics: The Arts, the Heritage and Media Industries*, Volume II. Cheltenham: Edward Elgar.

Index